Changing Places?

Flexibility has become a central concept in much policy and academic debate. Individuals, organisations and societies are all required to become more flexible and to learn so that they can participate in the ongoing processes of change.

This book explores how the notion of a learning society has developed over recent years: the changes that have given rise to the requirement for flexibility, and the changed discourses and practices that have emerged in the education and training of adults. With increased interest in adults as learners (primarily to support economic competitiveness), the closed field of adult education has now been displaced by a more open discourse of lifelong learning. This involves not only changing practices such as moving towards open and distance and workplace learning, but also changing identities for workers and learners. Learning settings are therefore changing places in a number of senses: they are places in which people change; they are subject to change; and they are changing to include the home and workplace as well as more formal settings.

This book takes an unusually critical standpoint: it challenges many contemporary trends, explores the uncertainties and ambivalences of the processes of change, and is suggestive of different forms of engagement with them. It will prove an important text for policy makers, workplace trainers and those working in the fields of adult, further and higher education.

Richard Edwards is currently a Senior Lecturer in post compulsory education at the Open University.

Changing Places?

Flexibility, lifelong learning and a learning society

Richard Edwards

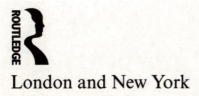

London and New York

First published 1997
by Routledge
11 New Fetter Lane, London EC4P 4EE

Simultaneously published in the USA and Canada
by Routledge
29 West 35th Street, New York, NY 10001

Typeset in Garamond by Routledge
Printed and bound in Great Britain by
Mackays of Chatham PLC, Chatham, Kent

British Library Cataloguing in Publication Data
A catalogue record for this book is available from the British Library

Library of Congress Cataloguing in Publication Data
Edwards, Richard, 1956 July 2–
Changing places: flexibility, lifelong learning, and a learning society /
Richard Edwards.
Includes bibliographical references and index.
1. Continuing education–Social aspects–Great Britain. 2. Adult
education–Social aspects–Great Britain. 3. Postmodernism and
education–Great Britain. 4. Distance education–Great Britain. 5. Open
learning–Great Britain. I. Title.
LC5256.G7E34   1997
373.941–dc21
96-51856
CIP

ISBN 0 415–15339–5 (hbk)
ISBN 0 415–15340–9 (pbk)

In memory of my mother, Joy Edwards (1917–1994)

Contents

Acknowledgements

Debts, I have a few, but then again, too many to mention . . .

A text of this sort is inevitably the outcome of a range of influences, previous work and especially the support of people over a period of time. Charting those is itself a daunting task. However, there are specific factors which have made this particular text possible to which I wish to make reference. Two in particular have had an iterative effect on my work and thinking and encouraged me to engage with the processes of rethinking the present and future for the education and training of adults, to which this text is a further contribution.

The first factor is the work I undertook in 1994 and 1995 in working to prepare written distance education materials for the School of Education at the Open University, United Kingdom. This enabled me to engage with a wide range of literature on the education and training of adults and start to produce the conceptualisations and propositions which are explored here in greater depth and detail. Fundamental to that process were my colleagues on the course team. They both encouraged me in that process and challenged me to clarify my thinking. In the interests of students they also restrained me from developing some of the ideas that I have gone on to develop in this text. My thanks therefore go to Peter Raggatt, Ann Hanson, Nick Small and Sue Parker, all of whom in a variety of ways have been supportive towards me in recent years and who will recognise some of the ideas here as prefigured in Edwards *et al.* (1996) and Raggatt *et al.* (1996). They have demonstrated consistently that, despite difficult times, critical collegiality is still possible. Thanks also need to be extended to John Field, who provided a critical voice at a distance, challenging me to justify the stance I am adopting as preferable to the alternatives. Whether I have done so to his satisfaction is another matter. It is a dialogue to which we will no doubt return.

The second factor is my ongoing collaboration with Robin Usher at the University of Southampton, United Kingdom. Robin and I have spent the last few years examining the ways in which postmodern and poststructuralist perspectives can help to inform and improve our understandings of the education and training of adults in the contemporary period. This collaboration has proved to be one of the most intellectually enriching and challenging experiences of my academic life. It has also provided a legitimate space for me to be able to revive my earlier interests in social and political philosophy. As well as our collaborations, Robin has encouraged me in my own work and the two have fed into and off one another. Thus, in this text there are many perspectives which come from and develop out of some of our joint work, most notably Edwards and Usher (1994a, 1995, 1996, 1997a, 1997b) and Usher and Edwards (1994 and 1995). The personal and inter-textual debt is great, as is the pleasure of it.

Three further debts need to be recognised here too. First, to David Boud and Andrew Gonczi at the School of Adult Education, University of Technology, Sydney, Australia. They invited me to spend my study leave at UTS in 1996. This provided a changed place and space in which to put this text together. In addition, the warmth and engagement of many of the staff and students in the School during my stay cannot be overstated. They both stimulated me to reconsider some of my earlier arguments and made the writing an enjoyable experience. Second, I would like to thank Leonie Jennings, Zbys Klich and the staff and students in the Institute for Workplace Research, Learning and Development at Southern Cross University, Lismore, for providing the time and space to share ideas while on a three-week visit during my time in Australia. Winter temperatures of twenty degrees celsius are indeed an inspiration! Taking study leave seems increasingly like a luxury. So I am indebted also to my colleagues in the School of Education at the Open University for supporting my leave, in particular Bob Glaister and Ron Glatter, but also all those colleagues who filled in for me while I was away.

A text of this sort is not produced fully formed from nothing. As is clear from the above, it is a moment and place in which to bring together many of the strands of my thinking in recent years – where the 'my' is already problematic. Certain of the ideas developed here have seen the light of day in earlier forms which I have drawn upon where relevant (in particular Edwards 1993a, 1995a, 1995b, 1996). Whether this involves a plagiarising of the self or a legitimate rewriting of a text I leave to the reader. While I question the notion of authenticity and originality in the former, I am also conscious of the possibility of repeating myself endlessly!

As well as intellectual and professional factors, there are also the personal ones. Many family members and friends have encouraged me to position myself as an academic and writer, and have put up with my self-doubts and obsessions. The list would be an exceptionally long one and I am fortunate to have that breadth and depth of support.

I may have done it my way, but without the above, to whom I have done insufficient justice, I could well have been left sitting on the dock of the bay. Writing this while in Sydney, there are, of course, worse places to be. Nice work, if you can get it. Small worlds too!

Chapter 1

Introduction
Waiting for the post?

> ... knowing if one can think differently than one thinks, and perceive differently than one sees, is absolutely necessary if one is to go on looking and reflecting at all.
>
> (Foucault 1987: 8)

This text is concerned with thinking differently about some of the changing discourses which have come to govern the education and training of adults in recent years and the consequence for practices. It examines the context for such changes and their contested nature. The focus for the discussion is on differing notions of a learning society and the ways in which that is being constructed in the changing practices and discourses of lifelong learning. The argument will be that to encapsulate those changes new forms of thinking are necessary which involve moving away from the dominant discourses of adult education. While much of the detail will focus on events as they are occurring in the United Kingdom, the suggestion is that many of the general trends have a wider applicability and resonate with much that is going on elsewhere in the world. To support this view a certain amount of literature from beyond the United Kingdom is incorporated into the text. Caution is always necessary in making comparisons between nations and even within nations. However, resonance of certain similarities of influence can be identified, particularly given the greater economic and cultural integration being experienced in contemporary conditions of globalisation.

Like all texts, there is an inevitable locatedness and selectivity which places certain boundaries around what is discussed and how it is presented. And the notion of boundaries will be central to this text. What constitutes the boundaries of a learning society? Who constitutes it as 'a learning society' rather than as 'education' or 'training'? What are the consequences of a learning society being constituted in particular ways? Who are most powerful in defining the directions a learning society should take? How are the boundaries of a learning society maintained, broken down or crossed? These are questions which are central to evaluating the significance of the changes taking place currently and alternative visions for the future. Such issues are not easy ones to evaluate and there is no claim here to a definitive or universal account of a learning society. What is attempted is a contribution to a necessary dialogue if adult educators are to play an engaged role in the processes of change. Otherwise it is suggested they simply will be subjected to change by others.

The work is consciously informed by certain strands of poststructuralist and postmodern analysis. This in itself is controversial. However, such strands of thought signify the need to think differently if the differing conditions of the contemporary period are to be adequately conceptualised and addressed. During the 1980s, this was most noticeable from the Left in the work of the United Kingdom magazine *Marxism Today*, and its attempt to chart 'New Times', a restructuring of the economy and society and a breakdown of the consensual certainties of the post-Second World War period.

> The 'New Times' argument is that the world has changed, not just incrementally but qualitatively, that Britain and other advanced capitalist societies are increasingly characterised by diversity, differentiation and fragmentation, rather than homogeneity, standardisation and the economies and organisations of scale which characterised modern mass society.
>
> (Hall and Jacques 1989: 11)

The 'New Times' thesis, while influential, was not without its critics, and the same is true for poststructuralist and postmodern positions. While not adhering totally to a postmodern analysis, I believe the latter is highly suggestive and to ignore its contemporary power would be misconceived. As Kumar (1995: 195) suggests, 'the contemporary world may not be simply or only post-modern; but post-modernity is now a significant, perhaps central feature of its life, and an important way of thinking about it.'

In this chapter, therefore, I shall provide some background on the approaches underpinning the positions adopted in the text as a whole. First, I shall outline the poststructuralist influence, largely derived from the work of Foucault. In particular, this text will make use of the notions of discourse, power–knowledge and governmentality. Second, I shall outline briefly what is often viewed as constituting postmodernity, the particular perspective of the contemporary world which informs this text. The poststructuralist and postmodern are often deployed as mutually reinforcing, if differing, dimensions of a particular analysis. While this is largely the position adopted here, I also introduce the idea that discourses of postmodernity can themselves be subject to poststructuralist analysis. Finally, I shall outline the various notions of 'changing places' that I am using and lay out the course of the rest of the text.

It may be considered that this is a somewhat abstract and theoretical way to approach the subjects of lifelong learning and a learning society. However, in taking this stance I am attempting to make as clear as possible my own position and to foreground the fact that no text is constructed without assumptions. Readers can question those assumptions, the contradictions, ambiguities and ambivalences within the arguments herein, and foreground assumptions which may be implicit rather than explicit – the 'silences' upon which the text is built. I do not assume a transparency or uniformity in my own writing or in the readings of this text. For me, this is part of the ongoing dialogue necessary in constructing a 'knowledgeable practice' of lifelong learning.

DISCOURSE – POWER–KNOWLEDGE AND GOVERNMENTALITY

The notion of discourse has become increasingly important in academic and public debates in recent years. The roots of the growing influence of discourse analysis are beyond the scope of this text (Macdonell 1991). Primarily, it can be seen as a response to the perceived weaknesses of conventional notions of scientific and social scientific knowledge, in a period when the range and sheer amount of information available to individuals through various media has resulted in greater uncertainty as to what signifies 'knowledge', 'truth' and 'progress'. Language has displaced consciousness as the focus for philosophical and social scientific debate, and science has itself been critiqued as simply another, rather than the privileged, language game.

The notion that scientific method is a neutral avenue for gaining truth about the 'real world' as a condition for knowledge, human emancipation and social progress has been subject to much criticism and, in some quarters, discredited. This criticism has come from both within and outside the scientific community. The validity of scientific method as neutral has been questioned, as has the knowledge gained from science and the consequences of scientific 'progress'. This has been particularly marked in the human sciences. The inevitability of progress to emancipate humanity through the advance of scientific knowledge, what Lyotard (1984) calls the 'grand narratives' of modernity – the justifications for pursuing certain forms of knowledge – has come into question. Stemming from the Enlightenment, Lyotard argues that the grand narratives have provided a teleological rationale for the development of the role of the modern nation state and educational institutions and the narratives which support that development. Modernity is characterised by narratives of the pursuit of truth and emancipation through the application of scientific rationality, of emancipation through learning the world better. Progress is judged by such things as mastery of the physical and social worlds, the growth of scientific knowledge, the spread of a particular kind of rationality and the development of rational, enlightened and autonomous people.

Lyotard argues that the grand narratives of modernity have declined in influence in the contemporary period and no longer have the ability to compel consensus. Emancipation through the application of scientific rationality has been shown to be, at best, ambiguous and, in certain situations, far worse. The application of scientific rationality in Hiroshima and the Holocaust, nuclear tests in the Pacific and China, concerns over environmental degradation and the risks to humanity by the very progress science has brought about, have all led to doubt about the sustainability of the project of modernity. There is now a widespread recognition that there is too much of a gap between the aspirations embedded and promoted in the grand narratives and the constantly reconfigured materiality of want and oppression. Increasingly, the grand narratives are seen as masterful narratives and narratives of mastery, functioning to 'legitimise Western man's self-appointed mission of transforming the entire planet in his own image' (Owens 1985: 66). Their declining influence and power in the contemporary period has also thrown into doubt the subaltern narratives they have helped to shape, including those of adult education and education more generally. Master signifiers are no longer quite as masterful. Universal messages, including those of education's role in fulfilling the project of modernity, are now seen as historically located, cultural constructs, their universality and consequences open to question. Teleological certainty has been replaced by open-ended ambivalence with significant consequences for what constitutes a learning society. In recent years, therefore, the extent and level of doubt over progress have resulted in doubt over the capacity of science to represent the truth of the world.

Beck (1992) suggests that the forms of progress based on science that have been experienced have created what he terms the 'risk society', in which it is the very existence of humanity which is at stake. More specifically, questions have been raised about the interests science supports when its development is embedded in the practices of the state and capitalist institutions. State policy and profit influence science into following particular directions and supporting particular views of progress. While this critique of science has proved very influential in certain quarters, it should not be overstated. Scientific knowledge has maintained credence among many planners and policy-makers and continues to be highly influential in shaping processes of change.

The challenge to traditional science, therefore, has taken a number of forms. The ideological critique of science is that it supports particular interests. However, it masks or mystifies those interests by presenting itself as a neutral and disinterested activity. In other words, the very neutrality suggested is already a specific ideological position, a dimension of ideological hegemony. Ideological hegemony is gained by that grouping in the social formation which can establish its interests and perspectives as 'natural' to the social formation as a whole. While science rests in an assumption of knowledge as universal and generalisable, an ideological critique assumes social formations to be divided and knowledge to be particular to specific groups and interests. This critique is very influential in socialist, marxist and certain branches of feminist and post-colonial analysis. However, scientific method and ideological critique tend to share both the view that the 'truth' can be established and a view of history as progressive, even if its basis is different. More crucially, they share a view that language transparently conveys meaning. It is the critique of the latter which has resulted in the increasing weight being given to forms of discourse analysis within academic study.

The turn to discourse has resulted in part from a similar critique to that offered by an ideological critique. Knowledge is held to be partial and contingent upon the specific factors and contexts within which it is constructed and presented. In questioning the status of scientific method as foundational knowledge, the foundations of discipline-based education are also undermined, to be displaced by a diversity of situated knowledges. There is also an emphasis on the oppressive consequences of assuming knowledge to be universal, that is, true for everyone across time and in all settings. However, discourse analysis differs from ideological critique as it does not assume that language conveys a single transparent meaning. The meaning of language is held to be contingent on the specific contexts in which it is constituted. There are constant processes of constructing different meanings from the same texts. The assumptions within such texts, the issues they exclude and marginalise from legitimate debate and the consequences of the acceptance of what they construct as 'true' become the subject of analysis. Which discourses are most powerful and how they frame practices become significant questions.

In this approach, it is the story-telling capacity of human beings which is held to be fundamental to their being (MacIntyre 1981; Edwards and Usher 1996). Increased attention is given to texts and the ways in which discourses construct certain objects as 'knowable' and 'known' and certain perspectives as 'true' – the ways in which they 'tell a story'. All forms of social reality are textualised in the sense that they are represented and inscribed. The social world is narrated into being through the discursive practices in which we engage and which make our experiences meaningful. Thereby the place and significance of narrative as a 'world-making' practice are foregrounded. Social practices such as the education and training of adults and lifelong learning can be seen as texts, worlds defined, delimited and constituted through narrative processes. A social practice can be multiply 'written' or narrated, it can be 'read' and interpreted with single or multiple meanings and can be 'rewritten' or re-presented with different meanings. In the contemporary conjuncture, it is possible to suggest that there is a rewriting and rereading of adult education taking place.

Through narratives, selves and worlds are simultaneously and interactively made. The narrator is positioned in relation to events and other selves and an identity conferred. Positioning oneself and being positioned in certain discourses becomes therefore the basis for personal self-identity.

Narratives are both unique to individuals, in the sense that each tells their own story, yet at the same time culturally located and therefore transindividual. For instance, an adult educator may tell their own story rooted in their unique autobiographical trajectory, but the narrative is itself sedimented in the narrative practices of adult education and, beyond that, in the wider narratives of the culture and practices in which the adult educator are located. They live these stories; through them they construct others and are interactively constructed by them, as active, meaningful, knowable subjects acting in meaningful and knowable ways.

The result of these trends is a shift from questioning whether or not a discourse gives us a 'true' representation of the 'real world' – a continuation of the modernist scientific approach – to an examination of the ways in which a discourse constructs 'truth' and the consequences of accepting it as true – a form of cultural analysis. In other words, rather than assuming a hierarchy of knowledge with science at the pinnacle giving us 'objective truth' – embedded in the notion of disciplinary knowledge – there is the constant search for the cultural conditions that produce this hierarchy and recognition of the plurality of knowledges. Discourse therefore displaces knowledge as the object of study as problems and inequalities surrounding the universality of knowledge come to the fore. This can be illustrated in the practices of lifelong learning in a shift from a focus on teaching, as the transmission of the (usually) university-generated canon of disciplinary knowledge, to learning, in which greater weight is given to, for instance, the experience of learners and practitioner-generated knowledge. A group of American women adult educators have posed this shift as a question of first,

> who shall be heard and second, what kind of knowledge shall be considered legitimate. The project of formal knowledge construction in our field is characterised by a preference for the knowledge of scholars rather than that of practitioners or the people who are the field's constituencies, and a preference for knowledge born of reason and science rather than emotion and experience. These preferences are woven in complex and subtle ways into an historically and culturally determined web of beliefs, values, and norms that justify the exclusion of some and the inclusion of others in the knowledge-making process.
>
> (Group for Collaborative Inquiry 1993: 44)

The focus on discourse, therefore, has been associated with recognition of the heterogenity of meanings and powerful consequences that are engendered in the use of language and narrative processes.

Macdonell (1991: 1) points out that the emphasis on discourse has 'radical implications not only for the disciplines of the humanities, literary studies and human science, but for all knowledge'. Meaning can no longer be ascribed to human intention or a common language. It is itself a site of contest, to which the trivialising reports over 'political correctness' in parts of the media attest, and can only be elucidated in the exploration of the particular discourses under consideration. The examination of lifelong learning and a learning society, and the changes taking place within them, are themselves subject to these implications, as illustrated by the many different and contested views in which knowledge and truth are constructed through and in a range of discourses.

The use of discourse as a key concept in this text is not uncontroversial. A more conventional text would survey the field and positions within it and attempt to evaluate which visions of lifelong learning and a learning society describe the situation most accurately and/or are normatively more appealing. However, to do so would have been to ignore some of the important debates which have emerged in the wider sphere of intellectual debate and their significance for an understanding of what is occurring in the education and training of adults. It would have required this text to be unreflexive about producing a text which is intended to encourage critical and self-critical reflexivity. For part of the power of academic discourses – of which this is an example – lies in their construction as 'neutral', a universal and privileged position from which 'truth' is established, when they are as partial and as inscribed with power as other discourses. This is particularly significant for a text on education and training, for, as Ball (1990c: 3) suggests, 'educational sites are subject to discourse but are also centrally involved in the propagation and selective dissemination of discourses, the "social appropriation" of discourses. Educational institutions control the access of individuals to various kinds of discourse.'

Discourse analysis is not therefore without its problems and its critics. Nor is it a homogeneous field in itself. However, what it makes possible in the discussion of a learning society and lifelong learning is an examination of who is setting the agendas, how, what those agendas are and where and how they are contested. It takes us beyond the ideological critique, which tends to become reduced to somewhat stale polarities of 'them' or 'us', 'good' or 'bad', 'emancipation' or 'oppression'. Rather it offers an opportunity, through exploiting ambiguities and ambivalences of meaning, to build alliances in specific contexts in which interests may be reconfigured, if not overcome. Here

> discourses are not once and for all subservient to power or raised up against it, any more than silences are. . . . Discourses are tactical elements or blocks operating in the field of force relations; there can exist different and even contradictory discourses within the same strategy; they can, on the contrary, circulate without changing their form from one strategy to another, opposing strategy.
>
> (Foucault 1981: 100–102)

For instance, feminists, the new right and new middle classes may all support experiential learning for differing reasons and use each other's interest to contest and reconfigure opportunities for adults (Edwards 1994b). In this sense, experiential learning does not 'belong' to any of these groups, nor is it inherently emancipatory or part of the interests of particular groups – it has multiple and ambivalent meanings.

The notion of discourse deployed here is derived largely from the work of Foucault (1979a, 1979b, 1980, 1981). His work has become increasingly important to the analysis of education and training, used most extensively in the discussion of initial education (Marshall 1989; Ball 1990a, 1990d; Gore 1993). In opposition to much 'common-sense' thinking that power and knowledge are separate from one another and that the exercise of power invalidates a claim to knowledge, Foucault argues that power and knowledge are inseparable. Knowledge is permeated with power and exercises of power are imbued with knowledge. Further, power is not simply oppressive and distorting, but also has a positive and productive role in making things possible. Foucault examines the development of the human sciences as power–knowledge formations linked to the development of such modern institutions as the prison and the asylum. It is upon these foundations that others, like Ball and Gore, have developed their analysis. Rather than conceptualising issues to be resolved on an either/or basis – either for or against, either in the interests of adult learners or against, either oppressive or emancipatory – this form of analysis results in more contingent, partial and ambivalent readings of situations and possibilities.

The exercise of power through knowledge and the production of knowledge through power in modern social formations is central to a poststructuralist stance. Foucault's work is far from unambiguous on this. However, for the purposes of this text the exercise of power can be analytically separated into the disciplinary and the pastoral. Disciplinary power signifies those processes through which knowledge about the population is gained by the nation state as a condition for the effective management and governance of 'the people'. These processes are embedded in the knowledgeable (expert) discourses of the human sciences, sciences which provide knowledge about madness, deviancy, crime and, of course, education. These discourses constitute the objects of their disciplinary gaze, for example, 'the deviant', 'the prisoner', 'the student', and provide the basis for intervention, for programmatic action. Disciplinary knowledge is therefore associated with certain practices or exercises of power which discipline and position people in certain ways and 'produce' certain forms of experience and subjectivity (Edwards 1991a). To learn a discipline – philosophy – is to learn to be disciplined into a particular identity – a philosopher. For Foucault, certain forms of knowledge, power and subjectivity are integral to one another through which discipline is exercised.

Pastoral power, by contrast, is exercised through 'confession', by which the self is constituted as an object of knowledge, self-regulation, self-improvement and self-development (Foucault 1981). This process has become central in the governance of modern society, displacing externally imposed discipline with the self-discipline of an autonomous subjectivity. In other words, confession actively constitutes a productive and autonomous subject already governed and thereby not requiring externally imposed discipline and regulation. In order to participate 'successfully' in the process of confession, subjects need to have already accepted, or be brought to accept, the legitimacy and 'truth' of confessional practices and the particular meanings that these invoke. For example, as Metcalfe (1991) suggests in relation to careers guidance, the aim is to help align student subjectivity with the various educational and psychological discourses available to help them reach a 'realistic' decision. Confession enables individuals to actively participate in disciplinary regimes by investing their own identity, subjectivity and desires with those ascribed to them through certain knowledgeable discourses.

Pastoral power is a central component of contemporary governmentality, which Foucault (1979b: 20) defines as 'an ensemble formed by the institutions, procedures, analyses and reflections, the calculations and tactics, that allow the exercise of this very specific albeit complex form of power'. For Foucault, the notion of governmentality is a way of thinking power differently. It points to the dispersed 'capillary' nature of power and its embodiment in 'rational' forms of government, administration, management and supervision, what Miller and Rose (1993: 83) term 'government at a distance'. They characterise the modern form of governmentality as a mentality where political rationalities – the aims and purposes of government – are linked with programmes of political action and particular procedures and techniques. Governmentality is discursive, a technology of thought, which constitutes a domain for programmatic action. However, it is not confined simply to the workings or deliberate policies of governments, but exists wherever 'the political programmes and objectives of government have been aligned to the personal and collective conduct of subjects' (Gane and Johnson 1993: 9). In its most contemporary form, governmentality is characterised by 'the entry of the soul of the citizen into the sphere of government' (Rose 1991: 113). Through certain practices and techniques people's 'inner' lives are brought into the domain of power. This, then, is a governmentality where power seeks to govern not only bodies, but also subjectivity and intersubjectivity, and to do so not through force and repression, but through 'educating' people to govern themselves. Governmentality works through bringing people's self-regulating capacities into line with the gaze (and regulation) of 'government', a process where the gaze is interiorised, where 'political power has come to depend upon a web of technologies for fabricating and maintaining self-government' (Miller and Rose 1993: 102). Power is exercised through seduction rather than repression. Lest this seem an inescapable determinism, it is important to note that governmentality is never and can never be complete. Indeed, as du Gay

(1996: 73) argues, the 'very "impossibility" of government justifies and reproduces the attempt to govern'.

The significance of pastoral power for lifelong learning can be illustrated in a wide range of practices to which confession is central, for instance, guidance and counselling, action-planing, the accreditation of prior learning, portfolio-based assessment, learning contracts, records of achievement, continuous assessment, self-evaluation (Usher and Edwards 1995). Nor is this form of governmentality restricted to students. It also operates in relation to staff, where increased importance is given to staff appraisal and human resource development (Ball 1990a; Metcalfe 1991). Thus, people are being encouraged to drive themselves ever harder, to accept even greater individual responsibility for themselves and their contributions to organisations and the social formation. With this responsibility goes increased stress. In this sense, pastoral power becomes self-replicating, creating the conditions for its own proliferation, as the form of 'empowerment' engendered is a basis for the 'problems' it seeks to resolve. Confession is therefore a symptom of the contemporary form of governmentality rather than a cure for its ailments.

Disciplinary and pastoral power are embedded in discourses. Ball argues that discourses are

> about what can be said, and thought, but also about who can speak, when, where and with what authority. Discourses embody meaning and social relationships, they constitute both subjectivity and power relations. . . . Thus, discourses construct certain possibilities for thought. They order and combine words in particular ways and exclude or displace other combinations.
>
> (Ball 1990a: 17)

Rather than taking discourses, or what is said, signed or written for granted, these texts need to be problematised, and their neutrality and the knowledge they purport to provide questioned. In the process, the 'truth' is constructed as a certain discourse becomes powerful in normalising particular strategies and outcomes. Certain 'regimes of truth' are established. For example, Ball argues that the 1988 Education Reform Act in the United Kingdom was made possible through a 'discourse of derision' upon which the new right in and outside government founded their criticism of the ideas and people they held to be responsible for the 'failure' of the education system. This

> discourse of derision acted to debunk and displace not only specific words and meanings – progressivism and comprehensivism, for example – but also the speakers of these words, those 'experts', 'specialists' and 'professionals' referred to as the 'educational establishment'. These privileged speakers have been displaced, their control over meaning lost, their professional preferences replaced by abstract mechanisms and

technologies of 'truth' and 'rationality' – parental choice, the market, efficiency and management.

(Ball 1990a: 18)

While this analysis is of the reform of schooling, the 'discourse of derision' has been deployed against those working elsewhere in the education and training system, including those working with adults. A 'regime of truth' has been established about the failures of the education and training system in relation to the needs of the competitive economy. Nor has this been restricted to the United Kingdom, as Shor (1987) and Kenway (1990) demonstrate for America and Australia respectively. The 'discourse of derision' displaces the views of the education professional and invests authority in those of consumers and employers. This is important insofar as who speaks about lifelong learning and a learning society, how they speak and what they say help to shape the changes to which the provision of learning opportunities are subject. Since the end of the 1970s, this has been most notable in the powerful role of national governments, political parties, employers and trade unions in framing lifelong learning predominantly within a discourse of economic competitiveness, thereby producing a 'need' for the development of occupational competences amongst the labour force.

In examining discourses, therefore, the 'neutrality' of knowledge is undermined, as the latter is suffused with power, which seeks to normalise certain inequalities. As an illustration, we can take the example of discourses about the 'problem' of motivating unemployed adults (McGivney 1992). From a discursive viewpoint, these are not neutral descriptions of 'reality' as is commonly conceived. They construct a view of a reality in which a specific agenda is promoted which places the social and economic 'problems' of unemployment upon the shoulders of those individuals who 'lack' motivation and skills. Knowledge about 'unmotivated unemployed adults', therefore, already assumes a certain exercise of power and has powerful effects in directing greater attention on to the disciplining of the unemployed and driving wedges between the 'deserving' and 'undeserving' unemployed – those who are motivated and those who are not. The lack of employment opportunities, the impoverishment of many unemployed adults and the very fact that emphasising employment as central to people's lives acts as a barrier to participation in training (ACOSS 1996) are thereby marginalised from debate. Meanwhile, changes in policy and practice, in the exercise of power, rely on knowledge being generated about the lack of motivation of unemployed adults. Power–knowledge is embedded in discourses about unemployment and motivation.

The powerful consequences of the impact of discourses can be illustrated also in the discussion of 'access' for adults to learning opportunities. Tight (1993) discusses the ways in which debates and policies over access to higher education for adults in the United Kingdom developed at the end of the

1980s and into the early 1990s. While he does not use an explicit form of discourse analysis, he focuses on the ways in which access to post-school education and training as a whole was narrowed to one of access to higher education. This, in turn, became focused on access courses as the principal route for adults to take into higher education. In other words, access was discursively reshaped and narrowed. Rather than providing a rationale for a broad range of learning opportunities, access became focused on a specific form of provision as a way of establishing a claim to entry to higher education. Implicitly, therefore, Tight highlights some of the different discourses of access and the importance of the meaning of access in terms of the overall effect on the provision of learning opportunities to adults.

Viewing a learning society and lifelong learning as constructed through a range of discourses of unequal power also provides the basis to question whether certain stances and practices are, as is often claimed, inherently more 'empowering' than others. This is brought into question as each set of practices is examined within its particular context. For instance, it is often assumed and asserted that student-centred approaches to teaching and learning result in the discourses of learners being given greater status in relation to those of lecturers or other practitioners. The lecturer is not the disseminator of knowledge and skill, but the facilitator of learning, or, as Bauman (1989) puts it, the educator becomes an interpreter rather than legislator. However, to suggest that this is simply more 'empowering' is problematic. This issue of the learner's 'voice' in education and training settings is one which informs a lot of the debates within critical and feminist pedagogy (Ellsworth 1989; Lather 1991a, 1991b; Whitson 1991; Giroux 1992, 1994; Gore 1993). Certainly, access to learning opportunities for certain groups may provide an opportunity for new discourses to be constructed, as has been the case with the emergence of women's studies as a field of study. This resulted from feminist struggles over and in higher education to create a space to articulate women's knowledge and perspectives which critiqued much that is presented as neutral and universal knowledge as gendered, that is, masculine. However, as Gore (1993) suggests, much critical and feminist pedagogy inscribes fresh forms of exclusion and oppression in their emancipatory practices. Having a 'voice' is certainly important, but it cannot be assumed to be inherently authentic or 'empowering'. Voices are themselves constructed through culturally located discourses.

Different circumstances therefore give rise to certain possibilities for discourse. 'Discourses differ with the kinds of institutions and social practices in which they take shape, and with the positions of those who speak and those whom they address' (Macdonell 1991: 1). Within the provision of lifelong learning this may be even in the very arrangements of learners' seats within a room, for example, in rows, circles, groups, or on a banked or flat surface. Each will affect who speaks and the discourses that learners construct, providing certain possibilities of 'truth'. Gore outlines the ways in which being subject to the gaze of one's peers in a circle may be more intimidating for some learners than sitting in rows, thereby silencing those whom the seating arrangements are meant to encourage to participate. For Gore attempts to produce a more democratic learning setting involve a lot more than a change of seating arrangements.

> The teacher cannot simply attempt to abolish his or her authority by maintaining an experiential realm in which 'shared' narratives are assumed to equalise participants, and which, because the teacher and students learn from each other, is assumed to be a reciprocal enterprise.
>
> (Gore 1993: 125–126)

Obviously, there are a range of discourses on most topics. Within the discussion of lifelong learning and a learning society we have, for instance, the discourses of learners, lecturers, managers, policy-makers, academics, professional bodies, employers, trade unions, awarding bodies, think tanks, journalists and commentators. Each have their own discourses through which the terrain is constructed, contested and challenged, for example, liberal humanist, human resource management, skills training, social action. However, as elsewhere, not all discourses are equal and the power embedded within them also seeks to construct certain discourses as more valid, 'truer' than others. For instance, in a period of financial constraint, the 'truth' of management and efficiency may well take precedence over the 'truth' of learners seeking access to provision. Policy-makers may question the 'success' of letting autonomous professionals determine curriculum. Certain forms of learning are constructed as 'leisure' or 'sport' and therefore not a legitimate case for state support through taxation.

In a sense, therefore, given its challenge to many 'common-sense' views, the approach in this text can itself be seen as an attempt to develop an alternative knowledge and discourse about lifelong learning and a learning society. This is not without its dangers. As Millar (1991: 22) suggests, when discussing a graduate class of adult educators in South Africa, in which analysis of the discursive frameworks that constitute meaningful action was adopted, 'the course seems to favour the more articulate, formally educated and theoretically inclined members of the class'. So, even in constructing this discourse on discourse, power–knowledge and governmentality, I may well be excluding a certain readership. However, in laying out my starting point, possible areas for disagreement and discussion can be foregrounded.

POSTMODERNITY – MADE FUTURE/FUTURE TO BE MADE?

The meaning and significance of postmodernity are subject to much debate (Lyotard 1984; Lash 1990; Giddens 1990; Harvey 1991; Featherstone 1991, 1995, Bauman 1992, Beck 1992; Smart 1992; Lash and Urry 1994; Usher and Edwards 1994). This encompasses many areas traditionally covered by separate academic disciplines and work practices, for example, literature, architecture, the media, advertising, cinema, music. The full range of that debate will not be encompassed here. I intend rather to introduce a broad characterisation of the contemporary period which is argued to be post-modern by some writers. Many of the ideas introduced here will be taken up in later chapters in more detail. In particular, in chapter 2 I shall discuss in a more systematic fashion some of the different dimensions of change which are introduced here.

In economic terms the current conjuncture has often been characterised as a period of revitalised capital accumulation based on globalisation, which has helped bring about and resulted from new forms of production, distribution and consumption. Globalisation involves the integration of the economies of nation states through market mechanisms, accompanied by increased transnational flexibility of capital and labour markets and new forms of information technology. With globalisation comes increased economic competiton and a requirement for flexibility. This has resulted in a shift towards neo- and post-fordist forms of work organisation in fragmented and volatile market for goods and services, where smaller scales of production and customised design for market niches have tended to displace pre-existing forms of mass production for the homogenised consumers of the mass market (Murray 1989). Marketisation and a culture of consumption become central to the economy as a whole. Changes in products, services and working practices reconstruct the workplace and the social definition of skills.

Harvey (1991) argues that the contemporary reconfiguration of capital, which he terms flexible accumulation, depends on new ways of representing space and time, a space–time reorganisation which both produces and is produced by globalisation. Two seemingly paradoxical yet interlinked processes are discernible. First, space–time compression, where hitherto separated/bounded time and space are brought together to produce both a literal and metaphorical sense of the world as 'one place' and time as an instantaneous present. Second, an increased emphasis on place and identity, diversity and difference. Globalisation therefore refers to a process where it becomes 'much more difficult for nation-states to opt out, or avoid the consequences of being drawn together into a progressively tighter configuration through the increasing volume and rapidity of the flows of money, goods, people, information, technology and images' (Featherstone 1995: 81). Greater integration of the global market simultaneously produces homogeneity and heterogeneity. Globalisation has meant the spread of the market economy, Western institutions and culture. New forms of communication enabling simultaneous transactions have created deterritorialised economies and cultures. Yet these very trends have also produced pressures for local, sub-state autonomy and identity.

This paradoxical process is emerging also from globalisation in the cultural sphere (Morley and Robins 1995). At one level, urban and suburban landscapes become more identical with familiar icons such as McDonald's golden arches ubiquitously present, and with certain media images instantly recognisable in every corner of the globe. We are witnessing a process of 'global cultural convergence, the production of universal cultural products and global market consumers' (Kenway *et al.* 1993a: 118), linked with a commodification and imagisation of culture. At the same time, globalisation induces effects of cultural specificity. There is 'a renaissance of place-bound traditions and ways of life' (Kenway *et al.* 1993a: 118), a new sense of pride and value in the recognition of difference and the revival of hitherto suppressed identities. The globalisation of culture, then, far from repressing the local and the specific, actually stimulate them. At the extremes, the contemporary condition of what Bauman (1991) refers to as 'homelessness' results in more strident assertions of a narrow sense of community among some, where difference becomes the basis for exclusion and oppression.

Alongside, and as part of, changes in the economy, therefore, are changes in cultural forms. First, in the realms of culture narrowly defined – film, music, entertainment, fashion, architecture, art. Modernist seriousness and the search for deep, often hidden meaning is contested by postmodern 'playfulness', pastiche and self-referentiality, as the possibility of providing secure and deep meanings is overwhelmed by the proliferation of signs and images. Here the playful or ludic does not signify the trivial, but an alternative strategy to transgress and dislocate meaning and power. Second, in the significance of culture generally to the economy and the social formation as a whole, where the hitherto tight boundary between the realm of culture and the realm of the socio-economic, and the dominance of the latter over the former, breaks down. Cultural goods become commodities to be consumed. Such consumer goods are 'infected with aesthetic considerations, becoming signs of style and taste, and losing their functional qualities' (Gabriel and Lang 1995: 107). Here, the cultural and the aesthetic displace, or come to be valued more highly than, the economic and the functional. Featherstone (1995: 2) argues that 'in effect, culture is now beyond the social and has become released from its traditional determinisms'. Consequently, the aesthetic and cultural displace the functional as central to economic activity, with style and design playing an increasingly significant role in ensuring consumption of products and services, and with image and lifestyle playing an increasing role in the choices of consumers. On this reading, the economy, and this includes providers of learning opportunities for adults, is increasingly recentred away from 'meeting need' towards supporting 'lifestyle practices'.

It is in this sense that some have argued that these changes are linked to the presence of a consumer society, whereby centres of production have been displaced by centres of consumption – financial services, shopping malls and superstores, entertainment complexes and theme parks (Urry 1990; Rojek 1993). Here it is suggested issues of lifestyle manifested through consumption have become central to the contemporary moment. Modernist, production-orientated identity is displaced by a postmodern consumption-orientated identity. The aesthetic, hitherto the preserve of high culture and the elite associated with that culture, now pervades everyday life and, equally, everyday life now invades high culture. The different cultural spheres lose their autonomy, as 'the aesthetic realm begins to colonise both theoretical and moral-political spheres' (Lash 1990: 11). There is a break-down in the distinction between high and popular culture. In the 'cultural economy', the relationship between consumers/audience and producers/ artists is broken down. The producer is no longer constructed as the autonomous 'genius', the legislator of 'good' taste, and the consumer is given the opportunity to actively engage in the cultural event – audience participation, interactive video, and so on. There is a consequent prolifera-tion and diversification with an emphasis on the celebration of difference and a foregrounding of multiple identities and realities. Boundaries no longer operate in quite such an excluding and exclusive way. They have not ceased to exist, but under challenge and contestation both from reconfigured forms of capital and from alternative social groupings, some boundaries have shifted and others have become more permeable.

As I have suggested, the discourses and practices of modernity are char-acterised by an emphasis on progress and faith in rationality and science as the means of its realisation. This faith, with its promise of inevitable progress in human betterment, is a feature of modernity which perhaps is most intensely questioned in the postmodern. It also illustrates the relation-ship between a poststructuralist and postmodern stance. In postmodernity, the grand narratives are greeted increasingly with 'incredulity' (Lyotard 1984). Postmodernity is a condition where people have to make their way without fixed referents and traditional anchoring points in a world charac-terised by rapid and unpredictable change, uncertainty and ambivalence, where knowledge is not only constantly changing, but is becoming more rapidly and overwhelmingly available. A modernist perspective views all this with an existential anxiety and with profound concern, a postmodern perspective as a matter of celebration of diversity and difference, of troubled pleasure (Usher and Edwards 1995; Edwards and Usher 1996).

Postmodernity has also been termed a condition of 'hypercommodifica-tion' (Crook et al. 1992), the condition where the commodity has become culturally dominant and where the dominant commodity form is the image. The communication/media revolution means that people are engulfed by images to the extent where the distinction between reality and image breaks down in a condition of 'hyperreality' (Baudrillard 1988). The hyperreal is a world of constantly proliferating images or 'simulacra' (copies detached from their originals, but meaningful despite this detachment) which become a desirable reality to be consumed, and where experience becomes contingent rather than coherent and determinate. In this process, new forms of experience proliferate, experiences that are not rooted in a stable and unified self – itself conceived as a modern patriarchal construct. Hence there is continual shaping and reshaping of subjectivity and identity. In postmodernity, therefore, sensibilities are attuned to the pleasure of new experiences, part of a constant making and remaking of a lifestyle. In the postmodern, the cultivation of desire displaces modernity's cultivation of reason.

The decentring of knowledge is accompanied therefore by a decentring or multi-centring of the self – the significance of which for the identities of workers with adults I shall return to in chapter 5. Modernity is characterised by a search for an underlying and unifying truth and certainty which will make the world and the self coherent, meaningful and masterable. In modernity, although the self constantly experiences a sense of discontinuity and fragmentation, this is regarded as an 'unnatural' condition to be remedied by such practices as counselling which enable the uncovering of a pre-existing coherent and authentic self. Postmodernity, on the contrary, is marked by 'a view of the human world as irreducibly and irrevocably pluralistic, split into a multitude of sovereign units and sites of authority' (Bauman 1991: 35). The modernist search for a true and authentic self and the fulfilment of a pre-given individual autonomy gives way to a playfulness where identity is formed and re-formed by a constantly unfolding desire realised, although never fully and finally, through lifestyle practices in a multiplicity of forms. The unified, coherent and sovereign self of modernity, the firm ground for the fixing of identity, becomes a multiple, discontinuous self traversed by multiple meanings whose identity is continually in a process of re-formation. In the postmodern, one does not experience in order to enumerate the knowledge gained or to become a 'better' person or to better become oneself. Experience leads to further experience, experiencing is itself the end, not the means to an end. It is the very openness of experience which is desirable.

> Theorists of the postmodern often talk of the ideal-type channel-hopping MTV (music television) viewer who flips through different images at such speed that she/he is unable to chain the signifiers together into a meaningful narrative, he/she merely enjoys the multiphrenic intensities and sensations of the surface of the images.
>
> (Featherstone 1991: 5)

The complexity and ambivalence that characterise the postmodern are mirrored therefore at the personal level. Identity becomes something that is continually reconstructed through self-reflexive biographies. Commentators such as Bauman and Beck have argued that in this situation individuals may still seek to construct meaningful lives, may still require the teleological certainties and comforts provided by the anchoring grand narratives of modernity. Featherstone (1995: 45) argues that in the postmodern, it is not so much that lives are totally disordered and identities totally decentred but that they have 'a more flexible generative structure which allows for a greater play of differences'. He also argues in relation to globalisation and increased intra- and transnational mobility that 'people can live happily with multiple identities' (Featherstone 1995: 9). In the face of reflexive individualisation, with teleology seemingly inappropriate, disordered lives and ambivalent identities may seem to be the new norm. At the very least, the kinds of situations people increasingly face are such as to require more flexible classifications and less highly defined boundaries.

Postmodern perspectives, then, are at one and the same time both parts of and ways of understanding the contemporary world. Reflexively there is the attempt to provide a discourse for the world they seek to explain. This is undoubtedly controversial. However, it highlights notions of decentring, ambivalence and contingency which many would argue interlink with the thrust of postmodernity in a socio-cultural and economic sense. The perspectives associated with a postmodern approach encourage us to challenge boundaries, including those of all-embracing emancipatory ideologies, and encourage us to be border-crossers (Giroux 1992). However, caution is necessary, as 'the "postmodern" discourse generates its own concept of "modernity", made of the presence of all those things for the lack of which the concept of "postmodernity" stands' (Bauman 1992: 95). In other words, postmodern discourses construct modernity in particular ways, some more inclined towards distinguishing absolute breaks than others. Attempts to distinguish the modern from the postmodern are fraught with difficulty and the construction of a discourse of postmodernity to govern the contemporary condition can be argued to displace concerns with inequality and emancipation in a period when such concerns need to be central. Postmodern discourses, therefore, are seen to address some of the consequences of changes rather than the changes themselves; 'celebrating' consumption, lifestyle and individualism and thereby providing a self-fulfilling rationale for a revitalised global capitalism – a postmodern grand narrative. In this way, postmodern discourses can become subject to post-structuralist analysis in which their many meanings are foregrounded.

Postmodernity has been deployed in a variety of ways, as an

historical period, an aesthetic style, and a change in the condition of knowledge; to conceptualise difference – a distinctive form beyond the modern – as well as similarity – a variant of the modern, or its limit form; and to describe affirmative or reactionary and critical or progressive discourses and movements.

(Smart 1992: 164)

For those for whom a postmodern discourse is interpretatively powerful, it is only through identifying such changes in this way that critical practices and possibilities can be established. This does not mean establishing firm boundaries between the modern and postmodern. Indeed Lyotard (1992) argues that the postmodern is the constantly reworked interface between the past and future, with the implication that the modern and postmodern are moments found together in dynamic tension and interaction. Further, Foucault (1986) suggests that it is wrong to think of history as discrete periods and of complete changes in these. Rather modernity and postmodernity are different attitudes and discourses present in the contemporary period. Burbules (1995) argues that the postmodern attitude is one of doubt based on 'an inability to believe' and marked by narrative tropes of irony, tragedy and parody. The postmodern marks the terrain of ambivalence and uncertainty of which it is partly a product, enhancing and opposing aspects of modernity. We may not like all the messages in the post – indeed we may feel there is too much junk mail – and certainly some are more important than others. However, it is only through a critical 'reading' that such evaluations can be made. On this basis, postmodernity cannot be simply dismissed.

THE TEXT – STRUCTURE AND READINGS

Having outlined the inter-related strands of poststructuralism and postmodernity which are woven into the rest of this text, I want now to briefly outline the senses in which I am using 'changing places' in this text and the structure of the argument which follows.

Changing Places is the title of a novel by the British author David Lodge. It tells the tale of an academic exchange between an American and British university at the end of the 1960s. The two academics involved are both white and male and the story can be read as of their respective mid-life crises. It is meant to be witty, but read in the 1990s seems somewhat crass and superficial. A similar condition can be said to exist metaphorically in many of the discourses of the education and training of adults. They are dominated by the texts of white males. They are experiencing a mid-life crisis under pressure from new right, feminist and post-colonial challenges. They also largely appear superficial by comparison with certain of the wider social and cultural literature available. This, in itself, might be a good enough reason for titling this text *Changing Places?*

However, other reasons have informed that choice. First, there are the two senses in which providers of learning opportunities are changing places in the contemporary period. Participating in them as learners or as workers, they are places in which people change through learning. However, they are also places which are subject to change. Second, there is the sense in which changing places for adults are not restricted to formal providers of learning opportunities, but increasingly come to include such other settings as the workplace, home, social movement, and so on. Third, there is the notion that discourses of 'adult education' as a place within which debates occur are subject to change as the learning of adults becomes located in different discourses. This text is both an example of and an argument for the changing discursive location of adult education and is itself a changing place for me as the author.

What follows then? First, I outline some of the changes which have contributed to the growth in interest in the notions of a learning society and lifelong learning (chapter 2). This provides a more systematic examination of certain of the claims made for postmodernity above. Particular attention is given to the economic, cultural, technological and demographic changes in the contemporary world and the ways in which those changes are constructed in particular ways through specific discourses. Second, I examine the impact of these changes on the boundaries which have been dominant in shaping the discourses and practices of adult education and lifelong learning (chapter 3). I argue that there has been a shift in discourses from a focus on inputs, on adult education and provision, towards one on outputs, on learning and the learner. This results from and in many boundaries starting to break down or become more permeable. As a field of practice, policy and study, adult education has been subject to processes of de-differentiation. New and more diverse settings are now recognised as places in which learning occurs and new metaphors are necessary to encompass these changes. I argue that a bounded field of adult education is being displaced by a more open moorland of lifelong learning – a metaphor itself located in my childhood experience of Exmoor and Dartmoor in the southwest of England. This is followed by an examination of the ways in which provision has changed to support access and participation, open and distance learning and the assessment and accreditation of outcomes in the increasing number of learning settings (chapter 4). There is an exploration of the ways in which providers of learning opportunities embrace learners and learning when the latter are separated from designated institutions. It is suggested that the notion of flexibility governing other aspects of the economy and social formation is also being developed in the provision of learning opportunities for adults with the notion of the learning organisation as a governing principle of organisational development. The implications of this for institutions and workers with adults is then examined, in particular the adoption of neo- and post-fordist models of organisational development, and the role of the reflective practitioner as a model of professional development for those working in the moorland of lifelong learning (chapter 5). Finally, I turn to the discourses of a learning society and provide a critical examination of the contemporary trends and the differing notions of a learning society which have developed alongside and as part of the trends identified earlier (chapter 6). It will be argued that, as with other discourses, those of a learning society have been subject to change and as a governing principle for lifelong learning give rise to a range of practices signifying notions of an educated society, a learning market and learning networks.

The increasingly influential discourses of a learning society harness life-long learning in ways which are certainly prejudicial to some of the equity goals of supporters of alternative visions of such a society. Lifelong learning is being galvanised predominantly to equip individuals globally to compete ever more strenuously against each other in the market for qualifications, employment and other opportunities. In other words, the currently dominant discourse of a learning society acts as a 'regime of truth' through which power is better able to be exercised in the contemporary period. Educators, therefore, need to be more cautious as to the precise form of a learning society to which they lend their support and more aware of tensions, ambivalences and contradictions in differing notions of such a social formation. Often they have failed to engage with the complexities of what they practise on the assumption of the inherent worth and good intentions of their endeavours (West 1994).

This failure of reflexivity is due in part to the modernist forms within which workers with adults, and indeed most educators, are located, which shape their identities, goals, practices and discourses. Gore (1993) argues that all pedagogies are framed within a modernist 'regime of truth', articulated in terms of universal macro-level explanations and centred on conceptions of teleological progress and goal-directed rational selves. From these perspectives, much of the learning engaged in by adults can only be considered anti-educational and something to be deplored, or un-educational and therefore beneath their concerns. The challenge of this text – and it is as much a challenge to myself as to the reader – is to engage with contemporary complexity and become more modest and maybe even less serious about the claims that we make for our practices (Jansen and Van der Veen 1992; Burbules 1995). The ambivalence in discourses of a learning society will therefore draw the text to a close, or, more accurately, will draw the text to its opening in the multiple readings to which it will be subject.

Chapter 2

Everything must change?

> Change, as Heraclitus was probably not the first to observe, is both pervasive and paradoxical. As soon as we attempt to acknowledge the rule of change by specifying its principal dimensions and fields of operation, we are left with only its empty husk: the phenomenon itself has moved on.
>
> (Crook *et al.* 1992: 220)

Change, and particularly the unpredictability of change, is often held to be a central characteristic of the contemporary world. It is also central to the growth in interest in lifelong learning and a learning society. Changes external to the world of education and training are deployed to act as rationales for changes within that world. Educational change has become a matter of increasing interest with educators positioned as change agents. This has tended to focus on change in initial schooling (Fullan 1993; Fullan with Stiegelbauer 1991), although there are some studies of processes of change in the post-school sector (Scott 1992). Change and its importance for lifelong learning is obviously not new. Since the 1960s, economic and social change has been used to argue for lifelong learning. However, it is the significance and recognition given to change in more recent years which has resulted in an increased importance for lifelong learning.

Interest in the provision of learning opportunities for adults has developed as a response to a complex series of overlapping and inter-related factors. This interest and the practices stemming from it have, in turn, acted to create the conditions in which the importance of lifelong learning has been highlighted. In other words, this interest can be seen as both a response to and a condition for some of the changes we are witnessing in the contemporary world. In many texts, it is the triumvirate of demographic, technological and economic change which is constructed as heralding the need for lifelong learning (Employment and Immigration Canada 1989a, 1989b; Training Agency 1989). In many texts and, it can be argued, in the policies of national governments, the dominant factor is usually constructed as the process of economic change and the need to promote economic competitiveness. The problem with this is that other factors become subsumed to a single form of causality in the process. This is not to deny the

importance of economic change. However, each factor has its own importance in relation to the argument for lifelong learning with differences of
emphasis and outcomes, something which simplistic forms of economic
determinism, or what is termed 'economic rationalism' in Australia (Pusey
1991), cannot fully embrace.

The attempts to characterise contemporary change are many and varied,
only some of which will be touched upon in this chapter. I have already
outlined certain of these in the discourse of postmodernity. However, there
are a myriad of overlapping concepts and debates, many of which are prefixed by a 'post'. In this situation, 'lost in the post' takes on a new
significance! In addition to poststructuralism and postmodernity, there are
also notions of post-fordism, post-industrialism, post-materialism, postfeminism and post-colonialism. There is even a developing literature on
post-postmodernism. Each in their own ways address certain dimensions of
contemporary trends. The significance of the 'post' is that in many ways
these discourses are articulating an end of something without a clear vision
or confidence in what an alternative looks like. The uncertainty and ambivalence of the contemporary world is inscribed therefore in the very discourses
developed to chart its parameters. Even where clearer alternatives seem to be
articulated, such as in conceptions of globalisation, the risk society, the
information society and the consumer society, the uncertainty surrounding
the meanings and interpretative power of each soon returns us to a more
incredulous mode. As we have seen, many of these can themselves be
constructed as aspects of postmodernity. The notion of a learning society
can itself be said to be one of these attempts at establishing a governing
principle for the contemporary world.

In different ways, many of these notions of change will be touched upon
in this chapter as contributory to the emergence of lifelong learning as
central to addressing the changes confronted by adults and the challenges
they face. The analysis here will necessarily be selective, as many texts have
been written on each of the above. In the first section of this chapter, I shall
outline a number of dimensions to change. This will be followed by an
examination of changes in the economy. In particular, I shall examine the
debates surrounding the calls for a more flexible workforce to enhance
economic competitiveness. This will be followed by a section on cultural
change, in which issues of identity and the consumer society will be
addressed. Underpinning many of the changes in the economy and culture
are changes in technology and in particular information and communications technology and the forms of globalisation it is supporting. I will
explore some of the technological changes which are contributing to an
interest in lifelong learning. Following this, I will examine the significance of
demographic changes to support for calls for lifelong learning and a learning
society. While these aspects of change are introduced separately, they are in
fact inter-related. Aspects are highlighted in each section, but they should be

read as iterative to one another. The final section of the chapter will examine the ways in which these various changes are organised into a particular discourse attempting to normalise a particular direction of change, which can be and is contested.

At times this chapter may appear to stray far from concerns with lifelong learning and a learning society, but it is central to the argument of this text that it is only through such straying that critical reflexive purchase can be gained upon the unpredictability of the changes which are taking place and the futures that are to be made. In other words, we need to change places in order to see the changes taking place in the education, training and learning of adults.

CHANGE, CHANGE, CHANGE . . .

The concept of continuing education has become one of the leading ideas in social change. It is as much a response to demands for continuous adjustment to skills and attitudes in a rapidly changing society as to the democratic requirement for social cohesion. Continuing education also fulfils individual needs for personal education strategies and fits in with the human resources development policies of companies and other organisations.

(Commission of the European Communities 1993a: 20)

In this perspective, continuing education would appear to be the answer to the contemporary period of change at the economic, social and individual levels. But in what senses? What forms of change and need are being responded to? There are five aspects to change which we can readily identify: its nature; the speed of change; the contested nature of change; the problems of conceptualising change; and changes in the self.

First, the nature of change. This is often seen purely in economic and technological terms. Shifts in the economy, the organisation and nature of work under the impact of new technology and increased global competition are examined for their significance. However, change also encompasses other features, such as environmental degradation, population migrations and political landslides, such as the collapse of Eastern European forms of state socialism. Change, often unpredictable in its consequences, is endemic therefore to the contemporary world. For adults to be able to understand and act in that world, opportunities for lifelong learning become crucial.

Second, the rate of transformation of the changes taking place. The notion of history as the progress of humanity towards prosperity, democracy and emancipation, which in different guises has underpinned much of modern political thinking, has been put in question by the increased rate of change in the contemporary world. Previously, while integral to the modern world, change was held to have a predictable quality to it, in keeping with the dominance of scientific thinking. By contrast, the increased rate of change in the contemporary world has an unpredictable quality to it which leaves many people confused and insecure as to their identities and futures, with uncertain consequences. Time is increasingly experienced as compressed, that is, there is little time available to reflect on the direction of change as the increased rate of change outpaces us. Thus, we can learn a software package for our computers, but even before we have the chance to become comfortable with using it, an updated version is available with new, improved and quicker features. The pace of change is often used to provide a basis for an argument that individuals need to become more flexible. However, a question remains as to the extent to which the rate of change outstrips an unspecified capacity among adults for flexibility. In other words, are insecurity and uncertainty the always present other side of the coin of flexibility?

The increased rate of change contrasts with the view of progressive and ordered change which is often associated with conceptions of modernity. The contemporary world is conceived to be more contingent and uncertain, a position often referred to as 'late modern' (Giddens 1990, 1991), but in this text constructed as 'postmodern'. The rate of change raises questions about the sufficiency of initial education and training for adults to be able to understand and act in the world. How best to be prepared for the personal and social uncertainty of the future becomes a significant question to which the provision of guidance and counselling and lifelong learning opportunities are seen as partial, but crucial, responses. The extent to which such provision can assist in overcoming insecurity and uncertainty, or in negotiating it more successfully, or, indeed, is part of that insecurity, is open to question.

The third dimension of change is its contestability. The processes and directions of change are contested and contestable, their significance open to debate, multiple interpretations and reinterpretation. For example, modularising aspects of the curriculum in the United Kingdom has been viewed as both a means of extending access to learning opportunities (UDACE 1989) and likely to result in the possible fragmentation of learning and assessment with consequences for the depth of learning achieved (Jarvis 1993). It is therefore necessary not only to be able to adapt to change, but also to be able to engage in the processes shaping that change. Here it is necessary to investigate those areas which are excluded from debate and contest, for example, technological change as inherently progressive, and those included, for example, the acquisition of new skills. To be able to engage in the process of contesting and making change rather than simply being or feeling subject to it, it is necessary to learn on an ongoing basis, but not simply learn to adapt. One has to learn to participate and challenge across a range of different settings and practices. Learning to learn therefore becomes central to active engagement with the contested processes of change.

> Thriving, not merely surviving, in [a situation] where change is a constant and ever present challenge ... is the most obvious sign of our lifelong learner. Not only does she possess the skills and knowledge to operate effectively and efficiently in this environment, she also has the creativity, intuition and motivation to view this challenging environment as a vehicle for her own self-improvement. Our lifelong learner stands out ... because she is able to strategically manage her own learning.
>
> (quoted in Candy *et al.* 1994: 44)

Change is not restricted to individuals. Organisations are also subject to change. For example, they often are held to have to become more efficient and competitive. It is argued that their ability to cope with and shape such processes depends upon them becoming 'learning organisations'. In the commercial environment, this is constructed as a condition for productivity, profitability and the maintenance of employment. In the non-commercial environment, this is a more generalised response to changing conditions and circumstances and the need to become more efficient. Over the last decade in the United Kingdom, the boundaries between the commercial, non-commercial, public, private and voluntary sectors themselves have been reordered and subject to change. 'Partnership' has become a governing idea as state support for various activities has been cut back or withdrawn. The significance of the notion of learning organisations itself can be contested. For instance, it can be seen as providing the opportunity for people to maximise their potential in their working lives and/or increasing produc-tivity through greater exploitation – as a form of 'empowerment' and/or an anti-union management strategy.

This leads to the fourth aspect of change impacting upon the contempo-rary world. If increased change is taken to be fundamental, but with an uncertain direction and consequences, how can we conceive the very processes of change? In other words, the very importance of change makes the analysis of its direction and significance in this and any text uncertain and contestable. In a period of uncertain change, there is a difficulty in determining which issues are central and which peripheral. There is a reflexive uncertainty about the nature of the text which resonates with the conditions that give rise to it. Discourses of lifelong learning and the learning society, therefore, tend to either postulate or assume a future arising from a certain analysis of current trends in a way which tends to marginalise alternative visions of the direction of change. In many parts of the globe, it is asserted that lifelong learning is necessary to support economic competi-tiveness and technological change. However, this marginalises questions about the costs and sustainability of such changes in terms of environmental degradation, unemployment, exploitation and poverty (Hart 1992). Yet these have become the dominant discourses, constructing an authoritative view of the 'problems' to be confronted, the 'solutions' to such problems and the usually catastrophic consequences of the failure to address them in the way put forward – the constant threat of the 'other', if nations and populations fail to submit to certain forms of change. This attempts to turn the process of change into a 'natural' process, normalising a particular view of change, rather than constructing it as the outcome of the actions and decisions of individuals, groups, organisations and states.

As we shall see in the next section, the view that global competition requires greater labour market flexibility, which has been an authoritative discourse guiding much policy in many countries of the European Union and elsewhere, excludes the possibilities of alternative ways of organising the global economy and the labour market. Also, it has constructed a view that makes the possibility of national governments intervening to regulate the market appear to be illegitimate. In such discourses, a particular view of economic change is presented as normal and inevitable, to which individual adaptation is presented as both necessary and good for the person – the alignment of subjectivity to certain goals through processes of governmentality. Lifelong learning, a way of dealing with uncertainty and change, is constructed within this discourse as an object of a particular sort, as a good thing in support of labour market policy, an adaptive process. The issues of the direction and speed of change are displaced and left largely unquestioned. In other words, the particular context gives rise to a particular discourse of lifelong learning.

However, futures are to be made and one of the ways in which they are made is in the very understanding and imagination of and desire for futures as certain directions of change. In this sense, modularisation, credit accumulation and transfer, and the accreditation of prior learning are not the results of some natural process, but stem from particular discourses of lifelong learning, access and opportunity and the powerful practices which support such developments. This openness and unpredictability in the direction of change challenges certain conventional models of scientific and social scientific understanding which attempt to explain phenomena in terms of causality. For example, this can be seen in views of the economy as functioning in the interests of specific classes, or analyses of gender inequalities based on the structural dominance of males in positions of power. Here, phenomena occur because of power and the powerful effects of factors beyond the immediate control of people. This is certainly important to the understanding of the contemporary world and changes within it. However, given that human beings can themselves change and act upon and in the world, there is also the sense in which, to paraphrase Marx, people make their own history, but not in conditions of their own choosing. There is an openness or contingency to the processes of change, if not a complete freedom. This is a complex relationship rather than one of simple cause and effect. It may be best summarised by the popular metaphor from chaos theory of the butterfly flapping its wings in the Amazon basin in Brazil 'causing' a hurricane in the Caribbean. There is a relationship, but it is not easily specified nor entirely predictable (Davies 1992). Chaos theory has become influential in the sciences and may also have much to offer those working in the social sciences and education.

However, this uncertainty over change may result in feelings of hope and feelings of despair. Hope in the sense that things can be otherwise. Despair in the sense that the unpredictable may not always be desirable. However, it would appear to be inescapable. In recent years, changes in the provision of lifelong learning – its nature, its speed, its contestation, its conception – have often polarised workers within this terrain. Some workers feel that changes, such as cutbacks in the funding of liberal adult education, are reducing opportunities for adult learners. Others feel that new opportunities and possibilities, such as offered by work-based learning and employee development schemes, are opening up opportunities. This provides the grounds for hope in relation to the opportunities created to influence change, and despair that nothing can be done to shape the 'juggernaut' of change, as Giddens (1990) refers to contemporary processes of late modernity. However, as student protests and campaigns illustrate – in the United Kingdom against aspects of the 1992 Further and Higher Education Act, in France in 1993 against reforms of higher education – contesting change is always possible, even if one can only grab the steering wheel of the juggernaut for a short while. Hope and despair need to be mixed rather than polarised if we are to move beyond zealotry and nostalgic regret in the processes of change. Reflecting on his experience in adult education, Stock (1993: 17) in some ways sums this up when he comments that 'there has been more instrumental acceptance of the social importance of education for adults than ever in history ... when the essential and basic educational structure is falling to pieces around us'. In this ambivalent situation lie opportunities and threats, pleasures and pains.

This brings me to a final aspect of change I wish to highlight. Readers of this text, like the author, are themselves subject to the processes of change highlighted above. It may even have been an influence upon your decision to pick up this text rather than a good thriller or a discussion of Hegelian philosophy. At a range of levels we are required to become lifelong learners to understand and shape the processes of change in the contemporary world. While this text focuses on the processes as they affect discourses of lifelong learning and a learning society, you will bring your own autobiographies and concerns to the issues raised. No doubt it will change the reading of this text and in the process change you. The writing of it certainly is changing me.

Being able to make sense of these changes, to reflexively understand them, to act within and on them in developing opportunities for lifelong learning is a major challenge for policy-makers and workers in this terrain. A basic premise, therefore, in situating change as central to this text is that unless we are able to understand and shape change and the meanings of change – as continually ambivalent, contingent and uncertain rather than a process of overcoming uncertainty – our capacity to work flexibly in our particular settings and with adult learners to develop their capacities to understand and shape change and the meanings of change will be severely curtailed. This is another way of saying that critical and effective workers need to be critical and effective learners (Brookfield 1993c). However, such a position is not straightforward, in particular when locating subjects within discourse. As Lee (1996: 22) argues in relation to literacy pedagogy involving discourse critique, this 'produces literate subjects capable of reflecting on the ways in which they are being positioned within discourses and the differ- ences and alternatives available. Nevertheless, the relationship between initiation and critique is a complex and problematic one.' A creative engage- ment with uncertainty is the stance adopted here as conditional for the development of the capacities to be able to locate oneself in discourses and act as a change agent, to shape and create opportunities for adult learners. However, caution is also necessary, as

> the change agent runs the risk of being rejected by the people he or she is trying to reach or silenced by other interested parties. There are also other risks less apparent: the interventionist or change agent can generate unplanned and undesirable change.
>
> (Willis 1991: 111)

Indeed, one can find oneself constructed in the 'discourses of derision' mentioned in the previous chapter. Engaging with change involves risk, ambivalence and uncertainty. Even as we engage with questions of change there are unpredictable consequences.

ECONOMIC CHANGE – FLEXIBILITY, COMPETITIVENESS, INSECURITY

This aspect of change has been the most significant in its impact upon the policies and practices of lifelong learning and is certainly the dominant discourse in promoting the need for and shaping the directions of change. However, there are different strands and emphases to discourses of economic change and different foci – changes in the macro-economy associ- ated with the globalisation of capital investment, changes in the type and organisation of work, and changes in the skills required for employment.

Within this overall terrain of economic change, two influential discourses can be discerned attempting to explain and govern trends. Each is under- pinned by a conception of changes in working and employment patterns associated with the need for increased flexibility in capital markets, produc- tion techniques and among the labour force. In many ways, flexibility and its many meanings signifies that which is held to be a necessary characteristic of economies as we move towards and into the next century. However, flexibility is most commonly addressed as an issue of implementation, of how to increase the flexibility of the labour force, whether this is happening and to what extent. There is often an implicit assumption in such debates that increasing flexibility is associated with up-skilling and multi-skilling rather than down-skilling – or, as Aronowitz and DiFazio (1994) suggest, with a displacement of skill by knowledge. The focus on implementation assumes the necessity of increasing flexibility; it is a pre-given in the situation – a necessary feature of progressive change. The wider policy and structural debates about the necessity, consequences and desirability of the changes being proposed are marginalised. Two dimensions of flexibility will be explored here. The first is constructed within a discourse of competitiveness, the second within a discourse of insecurity.

The dominant contemporary discourse of competitiveness posits increased flexibility as a desirable, even inevitable, direction for the economy to which policy should be directed. We have the view, often asserted in and through the policies of governments, that changes in the economy due to increased global competition, technological change and demographic trends demand flexible and multi-skilled workers. To be competitive companies need to respond to market changes swiftly. This requires workers to be flexible within the workplace, transferring from one task to another, and flexible between workplaces, transferring from one job to another. Through flexibility will come competitiveness, economic growth and employment.

The second, subordinate and subordinated discourse of insecurity questions the consequences of changes in working and employment patterns associated with flexibility. It is more cautious and critical, asserting that the flexibility required of the labour force is resulting in trends towards increased differentiation between a core of relatively securely employed workers and a periphery of part-time and temporarily employed and unemployed people. It is suggested that sections of the latter are becoming an 'underclass', effectively divorced from the economic and social benefits of the mainstream in the social formation. Economic development therefore requires and produces a marginalised section of the population in structural unemployment and poverty. This is something which post-Second World War Keynesian demand management and, in certain countries, the development of the welfare state were meant to overcome. The condition of those at the periphery itself becomes a constant threat to the core, who themselves become subject to insecurity, if of a different order.

Although the dominant discourse asserts that competitiveness is a condition for wealth creation and overcoming insecurity and poverty – the trickle-down effect – critics suggest that the two have a much more intimate relationship. Here the discourse of competitiveness 'succeeds' only by engendering a wider condition of insecurity within the social formation. In this sense, insecurity is a necessary condition for the success of the discourse of competitiveness within the ongoing restructuring of the global economy – 'the "discovery" of the "flexible workforce" is part of an ideological offensive which celebrates pliability and casualisation, and makes them seem inevitable' (Pollert 1988: 72). Place this alongside other economic policies, such as the creation of the Single European Market, which, Benington and Taylor (1993) comment, aims to foster competitiveness by removing 'overcapacity' in European Union industry, and other 'free trade' agreements, what are the implications and prospects for current and future labour market participants? Labour market flexibility may foster competitiveness, but on the basis of lowered conditions of employment and greater competition for the paid work that is available. 'Beggar my neighbour' becomes a literal experience for the labour force as individuals compete for the employment that is available, a position made clear in a British government consultation paper on lifelong learning – 'personal competitiveness depends increasingly on skills' (Department for Education and Employment 1995: 19). Those with the most skills and qualifications will witness an expansion of opportunity, while those with the fewest will experience a contraction of employment (Glyn 1996).

The discourse of competitiveness has dominated the thinking and policies of many governments during much of the 1980s and 1990s. Restraints on the operation of the market have been removed in order for the 'spirit of enterprise' to be unleashed. It was and remains a simple, but powerful message. Flexibility becomes an instrumental repsonse to the requirement for competitiveness. Markets have been deregulated, trade union laws enacted and managers have been given or asserted to have the 'right to manage'. In the United Kingdom, government departments themselves have been subject to 'market testing' and branches of activity have been given agency status where the government sets the policy, but no longer directly manages activities. In this process, the legitimate role of government has been redefined as providing the framework within which the market can operate most effectively. While this policy approach has resulted in the decimation of the traditional manufacturing base in many of the older industrialised countries, there has been a growth of service sector employment. Criticism has been met with assertions of the need for greater competitiveness rather than any questioning of the sustainability of competitiveness as a project.

Nor is this approach restricted to national governments. In Europe, competitiveness has also become a major concern for the European Commission. During the 1980s and 1990s, there were increasing worries about the European Union's ability to compete in the global economy. In addition to the Single European Market, the Commission directed policy towards improving member states' vocational education and training policies and reducing rigidities in the employment and labour markets. Lifelong learning is an integral component in improving the European Union's ability to compete. As one leading Commission official put it:

> Access to life-long continuing training is the key point if education and training are to have a real impact on business competitiveness. It also constitutes a major factor contributing to greater flexibility in the labour market. Access to continuing training governs the continuing development of skills in a situation marked by changes in working environments and significant changes in work organisation and production systems. . . . The twenty-first century will be based not so much on the exchange of goods as on the production, transmission and pooling of knowledge, access to theoretical and practical knowledge, and investment in human resources. The transformation of skills and qualifications will be a central issue. . . . It is becoming increasingly clear that the changing content of jobs demands multiple skills, or the acquisition of core skills. In the future, autonomy and capacity for innovation, an ability to work in groups or in networks, a concern for quality, analytical and decision making skills, as well as the capacity to learn how to learn and to pass on this knowledge will be just as important as technological skills or general knowledge.
>
> (O'Dwyer 1994: 15)

This is a position consistent with the Commission's 1995 White Paper, *Teaching and Learning: Towards a Learning Society*, which promotes policies to support competitiveness, although also with a clear concern over the social exclusion and inequality being experienced within the Union.

The discourse of competitiveness governs not only businesses, which need to be more enterprising, making the most of the opportunities offered by new technologies and new and emerging markets. The same is also true of workers and learners. People can no longer rely on stable employment in one organisation or area of work for their lifetime. They have to be prepared to move, change and develop, as employment opportunities come and go. The transferability of skill and competence and core skills have entered the vocabulary of education and training and, with that, the competences to actually transfer skills. This is not only between workplaces. Workers also have to be prepared to transfer from one job to another within the workplace. Flexible specialisation is necessary to the successful organisation and workforce. The flexibilities engendered by workers being able and willing to transfer skills, often under the threat of unemployment if this does not occur, increase the competitiveness – profitability in the private sector, efficiency in the public sector – which, in turn, results in economic growth and more opportunities for employment. The traumas of restructuring in the short term are supposedly compensated for by the longer term benefits of a healthy and expanding economy. To enable people to be flexible and competitive, opportunities for them to train and retrain have to be provided, and this has been the impetus for much of the activity and 'reform' which has taken place in the world of post-school education and training. Issues of investment and management strategies, of the precise relationship between skill levels, employment and productivity, and of incomes policy, have been ruled out of the equation as governments have sought to expand the operation of the market (Cutler 1992).

There are technological, economic and political dimensions to the discourse of competitiveness. Often the technological and economic arguments have been put forward and to the fore as a way of displacing the political agenda embedded in policy. In this way opposition to the contestable propositions of competitiveness has been marginalised in the arena of political debate. The focus is how to become more competitive and flexible, not their desirability – and who wishes to position themselves and be positioned as 'inflexible' and against 'progress'?

Technological arguments have been based on the changing nature of work and the organisation of work brought about by developments in information technology and robotics. Debates about fordist, neo-fordist and post-fordist forms of work organisation, lean production and mass customisation have ultimately rested on the implications of new technology and the requirements of firms and workers to be more flexible to respond to the diverse and changing requirements of the consumer market. For some, this is a positive move, as the compartmentalised labour of the production line, in which workers repeatedly undertake a specified task, gives way to team work with workers undertaking a variety of tasks and roles. The post-industrial artisan replaces the alienated industrial worker, giving greater job satisfaction to individuals. In this view, the introduction of new technology 'frees' the workers from arduous labour.

However, others have distinguished fordism as a method of production and Taylorism as a form of work organisation in discussing the changes taking place in the workplace. For Clarke (1996), fordism refers to a strategy of production in which there is a linear sequence of work, a moving assembly line, dedicated machinery and a maximum use of standardised parts. Taylorism, by contrast, is a management strategy in which work is sub-divided into its component parts and redesigned using work study techniques to maximise efficiency in production activities and keep close control over workers undertaking a narrow range of low-skilled tasks. Although commonly associated with fordism, Taylorist methods can be applied in small and medium-sized firms and to small batch production. It is entirely possible, therefore, to introduce advanced technological methods of production and employ Taylorist methods in the control of workers, a view often associated with neo-fordism. Aronowitz and DiFazio (1994: 193) argue that Taylorist management approaches have stripped computerisation of many of its radical possibilities. The introduction of new information and communications technologies, therefore, does not necessarily result in the organisation of the workplace on post-fordist lines, as du Gay's (1996) study of retailing demonstrates.

Within the flexible firm, core workers can expect opportunities to become multi-skilled, increasing their skills both vertically within the sector and horizontally as they learn to do jobs previously the responsibility of others. They can expect also to develop core skills, such as problem-solving and interpersonal skills facilitating working in a team. By contrast, peripheral workers will be engaged in low-skilled or narrowly skilled jobs requiring little training or retraining. Core workers could enjoy substantial autonomy in their work, whereas Taylorist principles could be applied to peripheral workers. Indeed, the control over peripheral workers could increase. This has significance for issues of gender, as it is primarily women who are employed in peripheral jobs.

Technology does not simply determine the organisation of employment and labour. It can be used in a variety of ways. The question remains as to why it is deployed in the way it is, for which an economic and political analysis is necessary. Here we return to the argument from competitiveness, a narrative grounded in a sense of fear and insecurity and the threat of the 'other' unleashed by the market. At the level of the business, companies need to deploy a variety of strategies in order to maintain productivity and compete effectively. Atkinson and Meager (1990) identify four such strategies, which they articulate in the form of flexibilities, the flexible firm being the firm of the future.

Numerical flexibility gives firms the means of increasing and decreasing their labour forces as demand for their products and/or services change. Business strategies associated with numerical flexibility include

> the use of additional or supplementary labour resources to meet changes in the level of output, such as part-time, temporary, short-term contract and casual workers, or the alteration of the working time patterns of existing labour resources to meet changes in the level of output, which might again involve the use of part-timers, or of varied shift patterns, overtime, 'annual hours' etc.
>
> (Atkinson and Meager 1990: 73)

Flexibility brings with it a casualisation of work. Other flexibilities include functional flexibility, distancing strategies and pay flexibility. Functional flexibility, associated with notions of multi-skilling, transferability and core skills, allows employers to deploy their workforce to meet the changing demands of the market. Distancing strategies replace employment relationships with commercial ones, sub-contracting the purchase of goods and services to other organisations, rather than them being integral to the business itself. Finally, there is the introduction of pay flexibility to support numerical and functional flexibility. Individual contracts and performance-related pay replace standardised national pay agreements, as part of the repetoire of human resource development practices within organisations.

While flexibility can be said to offer opportunities to many who would not otherwise have the opportunity to work, particularly women, it is also important to recognise that many flexible workers also lose out on employment rights and other benefits accruing to full-time employees. The relationship between unleashing the productive power of women in the paid economy and changes in employment and working patterns is therefore of ambiguous significance. The continued marginalisation of women within the labour force seems to be the dominant trend despite increased levels of participation.

The 1980s saw a large growth in the number of people, particularly women, employed on a temporary and part-time basis, and growth in areas of employment stereotypically associated with women, what has been termed by some the 'housewifisation' of the economy (Hart 1992). Between 1978 and 1990, male full-time employment in the United Kingdom dropped by 1,076,000, while that for women rose by 528,000. In the same period, male part-time employment rose by 280,000 and that for women by 959,000 (Unemployment Unit and Youthaid 1991). In 1992, one worker in four in Britain was part-time and 1.5 million such jobs had been created since 1980 (Hunter 1992). Women are estimated to account for 97 per cent of labour force growth between 1990 and 2001. These trends are not restricted to the United Kingdom. Between 1965 and 1991, female employment increased by thirteen million across the European Union while male employment fell by one million. Between 1980 and 1991, the growth of female employment at seven million was seven times higher than that for men. Much of this growth was in part-time employment – in 1991, 28 per cent of women workers were in part-time employment compared with only 4 per cent of men. However, 'just over one third (37 per cent) of part-time workers would prefer a full-time job' (*Bulletin from the Foundation* 1996: 1). Although 'the vast majority (89 per cent) of part-time workers in France would prefer a full-time job, only 6 per cent of part-timers in Denmark and 11 per cent in the United Kindom share this preference' (*Bulletin from the Foundation* 1996: 1).

There are also sharp differences across the Union in the activity rates for women according to educational levels. For example, in 1991, the average activity rate for women, aged 25–49 and who had completed higher education or equivalent training, was around 80 per cent or more in all member states, much the same as for men. By contrast, for women who had only basic education or less, the activity rate was less than 60 per cent in nine member states. Gender is also significant as an issue in relation to the notion of the flexible firm we discussed above. As the majority of part-time workers are women, the process of restructuring may result in a predominantly male core becoming multi-skilled and more autonomous while female workers become ever more tightly controlled as they enter the workforce. Both of these points are open to empirical test and provide important benchmarks when evaluating opportunities for lifelong learning. Gender is therefore an important dimension of discourses of flexibility in the economy. Handy comments that

> a flexilife will not look like heaven to everyone. It is, in fact, the kind of existence that the last few generations of women have been well used to, moving between work and family, mixing part-time work with home responsibilities, balancing career priorities with a concern for relationships in the home and, in many cases, having to abandon one for the other.
>
> (Handy 1985: 162)

More critically, Hart (1992) argues that the flexibility which has played a role in female labour and its devaluation is now sought from the generic worker. The dual impact is to bring more women into paid employment and demand greater flexibility from all workers.

This growth in female participation in the labour force has to be set alongside changes in the patterns of employment, in particular the loss of manufacturing jobs in the older industrialised countries. Between 1980 and 1985, the European Community countries experienced a 13 per cent drop in industrial employment. In the United Kingdom, industrial employment dropped from 47.7 per cent in 1960 to 29 per cent in 1990 (Glyn 1996). To a certain extent, this pattern was offset by growth in service sector employment, which rose from 53 per cent to 62 per cent as a proportion of the workforce across the European Union between 1980 and 1991. Similar trends can be seen in Australia. Between 1970 and 1995, employment in manufacturing fell from 24.5 per cent to 13.6 per cent, while that in services increased from 47.8 per cent to 65.7 per cent (Commission for the Future of Work 1996: 6). However, the 1990s saw the start of a decline in certain parts of the service sector as well, with an impact upon the contentment experienced by those who had largely supported the politics of the governments then in power.

The flexible firm demands flexibility from its workforce as a condition of its own competitiveness. While there are the questions of the extent of the introduction of these strategies (Phillimore 1990) and whether they are deliberate or ad hoc (O'Reilly 1992), the outcome has produced a different discourse, one of insecurity. It is to that I now wish to turn.

Galbraith writes about what he terms the 'culture of contentment' in contemporary developed capitalist economies. He argues that the majority increasingly sustain their economic prosperity and ascendency at the expense of and dependent upon the emergence of what he and others term an underclass. 'The underclass is integrally a part of a larger economic process and, more importantly, . . . it serves the living standard and the comfort of the more favoured community' (Galbraith 1992: 14). The underclass are the new poor, those for whom employment, where it is available, is at the margins of the social formation performing the tasks which the favoured majority do not want to do for themselves (Gorz 1989). They exist at the margins, sustained in their poverty by the lack of opportunities for them to be economically and socially mobile. They are the section of the labour force for whom things have been becoming worse in 'terms of conditions of work, levels of pay (relative and even absolute), and skill levels' (Glyn 1996: 5). Galbraith argues that the underclass have become a semi-permanent feature of developed economies and, as long as the majority can protect themselves from the resentment, unrest and other social problems poverty engenders, the situation will not change. In other words, the underclass are here to stay as long as the contented majority's prosperity is felt to be built upon the necessity of poverty for the minority. Despite their own insecurity and because of it, the contented majority vote in governments which are felt to protect their interests, perceived as low direct taxation and public spending. This only exacerbates the poverty of the underclass. Galbraith outlines two likely developments if current trends are allowed to persist.

> The first development, one we can already see, is resort by the contented in the larger cities to a *laarger* mentality – the hiring of personal, neighbourhood or apartment security guards or the escape to presumptively safe suburbs. . . . The second reaction is the likelihood, indeed near certainty, of what will happen if urban discontent, crime and violence increase: this will be attributed not to the social situation but to the inferior, even criminal, disposition of the people involved.
>
> (Galbraith 1992: 16)

Contentment is built upon insecurity, which is of different orders according to your position in the division of labour. Galbraith's prognosis of a contented majority and a minority underclass and how this is reproduced through an ideology of narrow self-interest and an electoral process is a bleak call to action. In many ways, it reiterates arguments elsewhere about the emergence of two-thirds–one-third social formations (Therborn 1989). It is an ethical argument for the contented electorate to pursue their longer term interests by voting for governments that increase taxation and public spending. However, whether such a strategy is sufficient or possible given structural changes to capitalism is open to question. Also, while experiencing a deterioration in relative economic position, those in low-skilled employment at the periphery have become a less numerically significant part of the labour force (Glyn 1996). Further, Galbraith's position would seem not to encompass the insecurity of employment which is resulting in a questioning of their own contentment by sections of the two-thirds rather than further attempts to defend it (Hutton 1995). What is clear is that strategies aimed at increasing flexibility and insecurity within the labour force have been central to creating the conditions for increasing economic inequality in many contemporary social formations. For some, this is structural to a new stage of capitalism.

Harvey (1991) has argued that flexibility in the economy is part of a new regime of capital accumulation which replaced the fordism of the 1910s to 1960s. Fordism, based on long-term investment in mass production systems with unionised labour and a state commitment to public services, produced the post-Second World War boom. By the late 1960s, early 1970s, as productivity and profitability stagnated, he argues, capital sought to resituate itself in the newly industrialising and developing countries which were not hampered by the 'rigidities' of union-enforced labour contracts. Governments were politically 'trapped' into supporting public services and could only raise revenue by printing money to fulfil their commitments. Inflation was built into this situation. Flexible accumulation is the strategy adopted to deal with the financial crises of states and employers as fordist strategies ran out of steam and manufacturing capital began to move away from its previously dominant sites in the Western industrialized countries. Flexible accumulation

> rests on flexibility with respect to labour processes, labour markets, products and patterns of consumption.... These enhanced powers of flexibility and mobility have allowed employers to exert stronger pressures of labour control on a workforce in any case weakened by two savage bouts of deflation, that saw unemployment rise to unprecedented post-war levels in advanced capitalist countries.
>
> (Harvey 1991: 147)

Increased flexibility has developed due to the requirement of capital accumulation, what others have called the late, consumer or multinational stage of capitalism.

Flexibility, therefore, is an attempt to resolve the problems of capital accumulation as capital becomes more internationalised and national economies more integrated into global market mechanisms. Workers in the United Kingdom, the United States and Australia now compete with those in countries such as South Korea, Thailand, Singapore and China to ensure that capital invests in their counties rather than others. Many factors play a role in investment decisions, but labour cost and skill levels are obviously important. Attempts to keep the former in check, while increasing the latter, have been part of the discourse and policies of many governments. Rather than intervening to regulate the market, many governments have intervened to make their countries or regions more attractive to the investment markets, in particular by creating a highly skilled, flexible workforce (Reich 1993).

These trends have not been experienced evenly across the globe (Massey 1991). Lash and Urry (1994) suggest that certain governments, most notably in the United Kingdom and North America, have both responded to and directed policy at increasing flexibility more enthusiastically and in different ways to others, for instance, Germany and Japan, in which social partnership, corporatism and established cultural traditions and hierarchies have a strong presence. Similarly, while the United Kingdom government adopted a stance of intervening only when the market failed to provide the necessary skills, the European Commission adopted a more pro-active stance – adding to the political tensions between the two bodies. It is important, therefore, to be aware that while national economies are increasingly embedded in the global economy, the forms of capitalism vary.

However, to compete 'successfully' in the global market does not necessarily ensure equity, and the costs have been high levels of ongoing unemployment and increased real and relative poverty (Commission on Social Justice 1993; Walker 1993). In the United Kingdom,

> average income rose in the eighties by 23 per cent in real terms; but for the bottom 10 per cent of the population, it fell by 6 per cent. The proportion of citizens living in poverty (defined as 60 per cent of average income) rose to twice the level of 30 years ago.
>
> (The *Guardian* 1992)

Poverty is a condition embracing a variety of different groups, including the elderly, one-parent families, people with disabilities and the unemployed. A 1988 study

> estimated that the numbers of people in poverty in Europe (defined as less than 50 per cent of average equivalent income for each country) had risen from 38.6 million in the period 1973–1977 (12.8 per cent of the population) to 43.9 million (13.9 per cent of the population) in 1984–1985. . . . Although elderly people still form one of the most significant groups in poverty, the unemployed and particularly the long-term unemployed now form a far greater proportion.
>
> (Benington and Taylor 1993: 126–127)

In the United States, since the early 1970s, some 30 million jobs have been created, but many of these jobs are in low-cost, low-paid services, creating a condition of 'working poverty'. Taking the value of the 1982 dollar as the standard, the average earnings of all non-supervisory employees peaked in 1978 and has been declining ever since. Or, to take another illustration, in 1994, the average earnings of seven out of ten of all hourly paid American employees was below their 1965 level. In Australia, one in nine families was living in poverty in 1994, with an increasing divide between two-income and no-income families (Commission for the Future of Work 1996).

In parallel with this process, the pressure for higher productivity squeezes many workers out of jobs. They may manage to avoid unemployment by being downwardly mobile – taking jobs previously available to less qualified workers and jobs in low-paid service industries. Elsewhere, growing numbers of unqualified and poorly educated adults are excluded from work, or at least from legal work. In its impact on labour market discipline, ongoing unemployment has acted as an important part of policies to produce a competitive business climate (Edwards 1993b). Flexibility therefore has brought greater insecurity, inequality and real and relative poverty (Hutton 1995). This trend is likely to be enhanced by concerns over budget deficits and attempts to cut the cost of the welfare state at a time when policies appear to be producing greater numbers in need of welfare support.

While Harvey puts this down to policies aimed at producing a new regime of flexible accumulation, George (1992) argues that increased unemployment is partly to do with the strategies developed to deal with the problems of 'third world' debt. Here it is the relationships in the global economy between the richer and poorer states which are central. George argues that having over-extended their lendings, banks and inter-governmental agencies have sought to protect their financial interests by forcing policies on these countries which harm not only their economies, but also those of the lending countries. To pay back debt, the International Monetary Fund and World Bank have enforced policies which require countries to generate income through exporting. This, in effect, brings these countries more centrally into the global market, but at the expense of their own domestic economies, insofar as cash crops and production for export replace the meeting of domestic economic needs.

It may be argued that this gives people in these countries a chance to gain higher standards of living through access to world markets, a position argued in relation to the Uruguay round of the GATT talks. However, this ignores the impact on both the poorer and richer economies of these policies and approaches. As well as unemployment, George outlines the ways in which the approaches adopted to debt 'boomerang' back to the richer countries in terms of environmental devastation (the Amazon rain forest is disappearing to supply richer countries with beef as a means of raising foreign currency), drugs (a valuable if illegal cash crop), immigration (as displaced and unemployed peoples migrate in search of jobs), conflict and war, and finally tax breaks to banks to help them stave off insolvency (tax-payers' money supporting the private sector). Sustained and sustainable growth and development are ruled out by the policies which are argued to produce such results, a tendency which has been enhanced by the emergence of the ex-Communist bloc countries into the global economy and their reliance on external aid and investment.

Flexibility can be seen to be based in policies adopted to sustain capital accumulation in a globalised stage of capitalism. Within this framework, post-war assumptions of full employment and comprehensive welfare provision are no longer relevant – for the moment, they are things of the past (Gaffikin and Morrissey 1992). In this sense, insecurity and poverty are integral to the introduction of flexibility into the economy. However, it is the discourse of competitiveness which governs the conception of economic change. In different ways, both competitiveness and insecurity engender a requirement for lifelong learning, but a differential requirement according to one's position in the labour market – for those at the core as a means to sustain their employability; for those at the periphery to survive the interruptions to employment. Attempts to formulate alternatives to these trends, such as that offered in Australia by the Commission for the Future of Work (1996), are marginalised.

In a wide-ranging analysis of contemporary policies, Hart is deeply critical of dominant conceptions of the economy, the way in which the relationship between the economy and education and training is conceived, and the consequences in masking the restructuring of inequality within the global drive to greater competitiveness and productivity.

> Currently predominating responses to changes in the global market system move mostly within a production-oriented paradigm of economic development, with an overwhelming emphasis on skills and techniques, preparing students for work in hierarchical organisations. Such a paradigm generates an interpretation of the current crisis which screens out the most important and most troubling aspects of this crisis: the increase in precarious, unstable work relations, the growing North/South division, the feminisation of poverty in conjunction with a new sexist division of labour, and the continued destruction of the environment.
>
> (Hart 1992: 89)

Within this critique, the challenge of the economy is not one of skills development, but the direction of economic policy itself. In other words, the challenge is one of whether the forms of economic development, of the constant process of (post-)modernisation, which have been central to both capitalist and actually existing socialist regimes, with their goal of rising standards of living in the industrialised countries, can or should be sustained due to the consequences they engender.

However, it is the requirement to increase flexibility and competitiveness which has resulted in the current focus of interest on lifelong learning and its concentration in the realms of economic policy. This is a position which is shared across the political spectrum, including by business and trade union organisations, as well as major political parties and international organisations, such as the European Commission, the Organisation for Economic Co-operation and Development, the World Bank and International Monetary Fund. However, 'despite the fact that interest in [further education and training] is driven mostly by its presumed economic importance as an investment good, surprisingly little is understood about the prerequisites to, or mechanics of, the economic payoff to [it]' (Wurzburg 1991: 2391). While wealth creation is a legitimate goal for nations, organisations and individuals, it raises important issues about how opportunities and wealth are distributed. From this perspective, lifelong learning is not simply a function of economic policy but also a key component of social policy. Thus, while economic change may have brought greater interest in lifelong learning, the particular directions of change do not necessarily support the interests of all adult learners equally.

CULTURAL CHANGE – IDENTITY, CONSUMPTION, LIFESTYLE

Economic changes both contribute to and result from cultural changes. Attempts to characterise the latter are many and varied. Here I shall focus on two major areas of debate. First, over questions of identity. Second, over questions surrounding the development of a consumer society. These are inter-related, as individualisation, lifestyle and consumption tend to support each other as dimensions of cultural change.

In his characterisation of modernity, Giddens (1990, 1991) has argued that there is a process of constantly breaking with tradition through a reflexive monitoring in an onward drive to develop 'the new'. In this process of self-constitution, modern society and the modern nation state produce more information about themselves as a condition for their ongoing development. This is true not only for social formations and nation states, but also for individuals. Modernity, therefore, signifies the loss of tradition at a personal as well as social level. Where 'in the context of a post-traditional order, the self becomes a reflexive project' (Giddens 1991: 32). In other words, who we are becomes something which we experience as a question to be answered, rather than the answers resting in a pre-given order of things.

In the contemporary context of late modernity, this process of reflexivity has been radicalised by the amount of information available, the media through which it is disseminated and constructed, such as printed text and electronic signal, and the range of options over which certain choices can and indeed have to be made. Self-identity becomes conditional upon a choice of lifestyles and lifestyle choices. This makes life planning an integral component of late modern existence. Giddens (1991: 21) argues that this situation is 'existentially troubling' as the very uncertainty and reflexivity upon which modernity is grounded means that the choices confronting people are ambiguous and insecure. The assumption of a privileged position where the rational person presented with all the choices available is able to decide which is 'in their best interests' or which 'best meets their needs' becomes problematic – the processes of reflexive self-questioning and existential anxiety becomes unstoppable. As people can never have complete information about all the conditions and possibilities of existence, they become dependent upon the expert systems which constitute the context and provide pre-packaged information for their life planning and guidance on their choices. There are puzzling options available which demand a certain amount of trust in others and ourselves, but also necessitate risk. Although Giddens sees the place and function of expert systems as part of modernity, they can perhaps be more readily seen as part of the attempt to keep the juggernaut of modernity on the road, that is, to put some closure around what is existentially troubling.

Beck's (1992) work parallels many of the concerns of Giddens, most notably in the emphasis on the individualising of identity in, what he terms, contemporary 'risk society'. Beck differs from Giddens in his view that it is only in late modernity that reflexivity develops. Beck's position has been summarised as one wherein the contemporary world is conceived as bringing not only 'commodification and the domination of techno-scientific instrumental rationality, but also opens up possibilities for individuals to reflect critically on these changes and their social conditions of existence, and hence potentially change them' (Lash and Urry 1994: 32). The risk society is one in which forms of economic modernisation result in threats to humanity – through, amongst other things, ecological degradation – just at that point where individualising processes make addressing the global collective concerns more difficult. This is significant at two levels. First, it provides a need for lifelong learning, and for understanding how and why critical reflection has become an important component of lifelong learning. Second, it provides a set of challenges for organisations and practitioners to address in engendering critical reflection on the risk society. Jansen and Van der Veen's (1992) assessment of Beck's position suggests that lifelong learning has a greater importance to reflexive modernity, but a more modest role than is sometimes suggested, as the challenges are so great. Providers of learning opportunities for adults 'will be both more modest about the autonomous contribution [they] can make to social problems and less convinced of a role as the messenger for all-embracing liberating ideologies' (Jansen and Van der Veen 1992: 285).

To a certain degree, Giddens' and Beck's view of identity are shared by writers on postmodernity, but there are differences of emphasis and explanation. For postmodernists, the notions of 'lifestyle' and 'image', and the proliferation and circulation of the latter through the media, are the means by which an identity, a self-image, is constructed. Image here is important in two senses, as a form of communication through the media and as an expression of identity. Images help people to constitute an identity, a self-image. The economic and the functional are displaced by the cultural and the aesthetic. Life itself is said to have become subject to aestheticisation, where identity is formed and re-formed by constantly unfolding desires expressed in lifestyle choices, including those surrounding what, where and how we learn. The increased volatility of image results in an increased volatility of identity – 'as the pace, extension, and complexity of modern societies accelerate, identity becomes more and more unstable, more and more fragile' (Kellner 1993: 143). Governmentality becomes more problematic and greater emphasis is given to the exercise of pastoral power.

The particular emphasis on consumption, lifestyle and image associated with the electronic media and neo- and post-fordist forms of production, distribution and consumption engenders new forms and possibilities for identity. The image gains greater cultural significance even as images are commodified and consumed – 'the effect is to make it seem as if we are living in a world of ephemeral created images' (Harvey 1991: 289). Thus, while a postmodern perspective on identity shares the reflexivity of a modern view, the former 'tends more to be constructed from the images of leisure and consumption and tends to be more unstable and subject to change' (Kellner 1993: 153). Here, the uncertainties and anxieties of troubled identity provide the possibility of excitement and disturbing pleasure in the consumption of images that never fully satisfy, and in the constant forming and re-forming of multiple identities (Usher and Edwards 1995; Edwards 1996).

There is clearly a radical difference between the modern view of the reflexive, yet transcendental self, for whom the finding of a stable identity is a normative goal, and the postmodern perspective of the self subject to images, through which there is a disturbingly pleasurable construction of multiple identities. The dispersal and diversification which characterise globalisation are echoed in the proliferation of world views, belief systems and styles. This is seen as something to be celebrated rather than regretted, a form of opportunity rather than loss. By some, it is a world characterised as one of rapid change and bewildering yet pleasurable uncertainty, wherein there is a proliferation of micro-narratives, localised knowledges and pastiche. For others (Giroux 1994), the multiplicity of meanings have to be situated within power relations of dominance/subordination – contingency does not abolish the unequal effects of power.

Key to the adoption of lifestyle practices in the construction of self-identity is the adoption of a learning mode towards life and explicit notions of 'learning through life'. The culture industries both serve this learning – educating the consumer – and make it necessary – we are bombarded with images we are asked to identify with through experience and we must learn to interpret them. Problems arise when such positions are extended to the population as a whole. However, we need to evaluate carefully the significance of consumer culture to the contemporary period (Field 1994; McRobbie 1994).

Consumption is not an activity or category which figures highly on the list of educators' 'good things' with which to be involved. Indeed consumption, with its connotations of the frivolous, seems to be surrounded by an aura of disapproval. Any interest in it seems to signal a concern with surface rather than depth, with 'false consciousness' rather than 'authentic' understanding, with markets rather than public service. There is an acceptance that consumption figures importantly in people's lives, but it is usually accompanied by a wish that it did not, particularly in relation to education and training. Mostly, it is suggested that its importance is due to the seductive images purveyed by advertising and the media, images – spectacles – which manipulate people away from their 'true' interests or needs. The fact that such seduction is claimed in a period in which greater numbers of people are receiving greater amounts of education and training says little for the educators' or education's assumed effectiveness as a guarantor of enlightenment of course! However, while the view of the self manipulated by images to consume more is a popular one, it is also argued that to constitute a self-identity in the contemporary period is to construe one's life precisely in terms of consumption choices.

The distaste for consumption is also expressed in the view that with its foregrounding there is a loss of concern for oppressed groups. However, it is also the case that many groups construct 'empowerment' as involving the increased consumption of goods, services and images. This cannot and should not be explained simply as a manifestation of false consciousness, the duping of the masses – a deeply embedded but patronising position which some radicals share with conservative critics of the contemporary world. Further, whilst not all may consume equally, all are affected by consumer culture and consumptionist discourse and images.

There is considerable agreement about the contemporary significance of consumption as a socio-cultural activity and it is often highlighted as an integral part of globalisation and the world-wide reorganisation of capitalism. Bauman (1992) talks of the development of a post full-employment consumer society as one of the main characteristics of postmodernity. He argues that consumer behaviour rather than work or productive activity has become the cognitive and moral focus of life, the integrative bond of a social formation in which consumption rather than production is the fulcrum of individual and social existence. In the West at least, capitalism has come to work through the idea of individual freedom and the freedom to consume rather than through repression. The historical emphasis on self-denial and the deferral of gratification has been overlayed and displaced by the pursuit of desire through the consumption of commodities and services, including learning opportunities, and the rise of new social groups. This imaginative pleasure-seeking, 'the disposition to live out desires, fantasies and day-dreams, or the capacity to spend a good deal of time in pursuit of them, may vary among different social groups' (Featherstone 1995: 24).

Featherstone (1991), borrowing from Bourdieu, links postmodern lifestyle practices to what he terms the 'new middle class' (in contrast with the 'old' or settled bourgeoisie). This class fraction is constituted by the new cultural intermediaries, the helping professions, the post-industrial middle class, with their bases in, for example, the media, education, finance and advertising. These groups tend to be well educated, reasonably affluent, predominantly urban, possessing a counter-cultural informality and oppositional stance to the established order. He argues that it is this class fraction which is centrally concerned with the production and dissemination of consumer culture, imagery and information. This is not a view shared by all. Urry (1995: 227) drawing upon research elsewhere, outlines three broad middle-class lifestyles: 'the ascetic among public sector welfare professionals; the postmodern among private sector professionals and specialists; and the indistinct among managers and government bureaucrats'.

Such distinctions are also situated within general trends. Urry (1995) argues therefore that deferred gratification and the governing of work and leisure by clock time were practices associated with attitudes and dispositions shaped by reason and discipline. Forms of identity required by the 'organised' capitalism of modernity were predominantly derived from work. Postmodernity and contemporary 'disorganised' capitalism encourage and require consumption, and people who develop their identities through consumption. There is an emphasis on those aspects of consumer culture which favour the aestheticisation of life, where the 'good' life is construed in terms of taste, style and sensibility. This is linked to the view that there is no pre-defined singular self, but only shifting and multiple identities. Life becomes an endless pursuit of new experiences, values and styles in which 'experience' is not passive acceptance, but, stemming from its root 'per', 'means to try, to test, to risk' (Featherstone 1995: 152) and where 'consuming can be a passionate experience, an expressive act' (Tomlinson 1990: 17). However, as Gabriel and Lang (1995: 190) point out, the very casualisation of work in disorganised capitalism can also result in a casualisation of consumption for certain people – 'consumers will lead precarious and uneven existences, one day enjoying unexpected booms and the next sinking to bare existence'. Disturbing pleasures may become more disturbing than pleasurable!

The postmodern is not so much one particular style, as a range of styles which have in common eclecticism and the privileging of the cultural and aesthetic. This aestheticisation of everyday life has, among other things, the consequence of de-differentiating or undermining the boundaries between high and mass culture and, with that, boundaries between education and entertainment, and education and leisure. Everything, including the past, becomes available for recycling, an archive to be raided, from which new experiences and meanings can be constructed. Certain sites, such as shopping malls, museums and heritage parks, become centres of aesthetic consumption, in which leisure becomes consumption and consumption a form of leisure activity. Here, as Rojek (1993: 133) argues, 'leisure and tourism are now equivalent to mere consumption activity. The modernist quest for authenticity and self-realisation has come to an end.' The pejorative 'mere' assumes the validity of the modernist quest and ignores its socio-economic base in the nineteenth-century bourgeois culture of Western Europe and North America rather than the populist experience of travel and leisure in late twentieth-century social formations (Urry 1990). Authentic consumption is restricted to the 'educated and enlightened' minority!

Alongside the emphasis placed on the economic dimensions of the cultural is the foregrounding of the cultural dimension of the economic; the symbolisation and use of material goods as communicators, not just utilities. Discussing the retail industry, du Gay (1996: 164) notes that rather than a simple penetration of the market into all areas of social and cultural life, there are possibilities for 'the socialisation and culturalisation of market relations within its own borders'. More generally, Featherstone (1991) talks of an economy of cultural goods located within market principles of supply and demand, and operating within the sphere of lifestyles and identities. Consumer culture, then, implies a structured set of values, attitudes and behaviour, which constitutes a coherent means of communication; a differentiation between people, with goods and services acting as markers of difference. This position follows the argument by Baudrillard (1981) that objects of consumption act as signs, so that when we consume we are consuming sign values, or meanings. Furthermore, we consume meanings in order to differentiate ourselves from others – in effect we consume difference. Consumer objects act as a classification system that codes behaviour and structures the social. Political economy, with its privileging of production, is subordinated to a general political economy of the sign based on consumption. Bourdieu (1984) also argues that consumers actively use goods and services to establish and demarcate a distinctive social space. There is a 'shift in patterns of differentiation from the social to the cultural sphere, from life-chances to lifestyles, from production to consumption' (Crook *et al.* 1992: 133). Consumer culture is therefore an economy of signs in which individuals and groups communicate messages about social position and worth. Consumption is a signifying system that differentiates selves wherein identity is constructed through consuming experiences and symbols. As Tomlinson (1990: 30) argues, 'meaning and consciousness are vitally linked to relations of consumption and . . . we respond to images in many aspects of our daily lives'.

There are resonances to be found between developments in consumer culture and the growth in interest in lifelong learning. Field (1994) has pointed to a number of factors which emphasise the need to take proper account of consumption. First, long-term changes in affluence in general enable adults in richer social formations to exercise greater choice in the purchase of goods and services. Second, the notion of citizens as consumers stands at the heart of much contemporary policy development. This is part of an ideological shift where the supply of lifelong learning is governed by a consumer orientation and a growing private sector of providers of opportunities. Linked to this is the widespread development of videos, audio-cassettes and increasingly sophisticated multi-media computer programmes which commercially provide adults with a range of self-study options not previously available. Third, education activities have become consumer goods in themselves, purchased as a result of choice by agents in a marketplace wherein educational goods and services compete. Related to this, the boundaries between education and other fields of activity, such as the media and entertainment, have become blurred. People learn increasingly from television programmes aimed at entertaining, and educational activities are geared now as much to ensuring consumer satisfaction by producing outcomes previously only associated with entertainment. Nor is this a marginal trend, as the United Kingdom government's Technology Foresight Programme, designed to map the directions for the funding of research, makes clear (Office of Science and Technology 1995) – 'there will be much greater *convergence of leisure and learning activities*, partly through new technology and partly as a result of changes on the supply side' (emphasis in the original). Fourth, contemporary culture is marked by individualisation and this is also a characteristic of trends in lifelong learning. In order to explore the relationship between consumerism, individualisation and lifelong learning, we need to look much more at areas such as personal development and creativity as cultural practices. There has been a huge growth in courses offering the possibility of new identities: assertiveness training, do-it-yourself, creative writing, interpersonal skills, counselling, and so on. As Tomlinson (1990: 6) argues, 'it is in the sphere of consumption that many will seek to express this sense of freedom, this personal power, their status aspirations'. In relation to this, lifelong learning is increasingly orientated towards the recognition that adults can continue to change throughout their lives, a recognition that is reinforced in the postmodern emphasis on the ephemerality of identities. At the same time, this also reinforces the point that it is now very difficult, if not impossible, to draw a firm boundary between education and consumption. Fifth, Field emphasises the need to take on board the notion of learning as enjoyable experiences. To talk of such events being enjoyable is to foreground the place of play and desire. It is to foreground the ludic or playful quality of experience and construct learning as something to be consumed in an active sense. This is a basis for a learning approach to life disembedded from modernist assumptions about education and enlightenment.

Whilst the language of consumerism undoubtedly jars among many educators and trainers, patterns of participation in lifelong learning and the increased diversity of learning opportunities cannot be understood, even in part, without reference to it. Learning opportunities have to compete for the consumer's income and their scarce leisure time, even as consumption is accorded increasing cultural significance. More than this, we need to consider the education and training of adults in relation to a cultural economy of signs, where learners' choices can be examined as social and individual communicative acts. Here learning acts as a marker, part of the process by which individuals differentiate themselves from one another and group and are grouped around certain identities. For the adult, it is only important for the learning to be considered education if to be an 'educated person' is important to their identity, if it acts as a means of distinguishing themselves from certain others and including themselves with other 'educated people'. This, in itself, can be differentiated on the basis of the construction of the multiple meanings of 'education', for instance, the 'sentimental education' of the nineteenth century or the 'vocational competence' of the contemporary United Kingdom. Similar differentiations of identity can be made around the notions of 'student' and 'learner' (Edwards 1996).

Many see the individualism engendered by and through an emphasis on lifestyle and individual responsibility as undermining the possibilities for collective forms of transformation. This echoes long-standing debates on the extent to which individualism is transformative and/or subordinating (Keddie 1980; Edwards 1991a). However, such inequalities can only be understood and challenged, not by simply rejecting consumer culture, but by engaging with consumption as a complex and multi-dimensional process which can be active, critical and generative as well as passive and reproductive. In particular, we need to understand the significance of cultural changes and the multiple meanings of consumer behaviour, the role that consumer choices have in certain social practices wherein meanings and self-identity are developed. Featherstone (1995: 24) points out that 'consumption is eminently social, relational and active rather than private, atomic or passive'. This challenges paradigms of consumption such as marxism, where it is seen as a reflex of production, and the Frankfurt School, where it is seen as alienated consciousness, the source of manipulation and passivity. Rather than simply being victims of consumer culture, 'consumers can resist the dominant economic order, even as they consume its outputs, its commodities and its images' (Gabriel and Lang 1995: 139). The intentions of producers are not necessarily what is entailed in the practices of consumers.

Any discourse of lifelong learning which excludes consumer culture fails to engage with the very everyday existence of adults in the contemporary period. However, it also has to be recognised that engagement with consumption as a dimension of cultural change also has the danger of normalising certain processes and practices which exclude the development of certain forms of lifelong learning even as they engender others.

In summary, therefore, notions of cultural change have a number of dimensions. First, in the realms of culture itself – fashion, entertainment, film, and so on. Second, in the significance of culture to the social formation as a whole. In the contemporary period, the separate realm of culture has come to influence the social formation and economy more generally wherein the aesthetic values which previously pervaded the arena of culture alone now pervade everyday life. Thus, the cultural industries, such as entertainment, the media, education itself, have all become more significant in contemporary social formations. Choices about the clothes we wear, the food we eat, how we decorate our homes and maybe even the learning we undertake are choices of 'taste', and taste is educated through the media, advertising industry, and so on, as well as the more formal provision of education and training. For those with the cultural and economic capital, lifestyle practices and image are fundamental to such changes, in which 'the cultivation of personality is a vocation' (Hunter 1993: 184), possibly making greater use of self-directed mass-produced guides to self-improvement than more conventional forms of education and training. Those excluded from the realms of choice find themselves increasingly subject to marginalisation, although not completely divorced from lifestyle practices in the construction of self-identity.

The significance of an increased emphasis on cultural change for the development of an interest in lifelong learning is two-fold. First, taste needs to be constantly re-educated to fuel the desires of consumers to consume new goods and services as they become available. To be able to cope with these choices, to make informed choices, consumers need to be constantly learning and services need to be offered to help them make those choices. Second, learning opportunities themselves become subject to the cultural imperative, creating new market genres such as info-tainment and edu-tainment (Kenway *et al.* 1993b). Learning opportunities not only service the requirements of the consumer society, but also they are part of it. This is witnessed in the increased use of discourses of and concern for the 'customer' rather than, for example, the 'student' or 'client'. Cultural change results in a greater emphasis on the individual as a consumer of products and services, including those of education and training. A certain form of power is thereby transferred to individuals as consumers, a process enhanced in education and training by the introduction of, for instance, vouchers for individuals, graduate taxes and career development loans. As Chadwick suggests from his study of employee development initiatives in industry, success

> means offering greater power and control to individuals over their lives. This can only be done at the expense of existing groups and institutions. Neither industry nor education can be expected to comply readily with any diminution of their powers.
>
> (Chadwick 1993: 24)

This brief exploration of cultural change suggests that adults are subject to: an explosion of information and knowledge, thereby placing greater emphasis on the process of learning, which is ongoing, rather than the content of learning, which, dependent on what is learnt, will go out of date (Husen 1986); increased responsibility for choices about identity and lifestyle as individuals, placing greater emphasis on life planning and guidance and counselling.

Individuals are expected to take responsibility for their own lives and to make the right decisions to further their own career chances, while at the same time being dependent on conditions that they can hardly see through, and certainly not determine.

(Jansen and Van der Veen 1992: 279)

However, the issues raised by discourses of cultural change have had a limited explicit impact on the discourses of lifelong learning. Their impact is there, but it is seen as something largely to be regretted, rather than with which to engage. However, it is played out in a number of significant ways. First, in the way in which greater importance is given to lifelong learning and particularly the cultivation of taste in the construction of lifestyles. Second, the emphasis on ephemerality and fragmentation provides a link with a certain democratic tradition of tolerance and difference. Third, the instability introduced by cultural change is reinforced by groups which challenge dominant norms of knowledge, values and practices. The certainty surrounding canons of knowledge and 'ways of doing things' is undermined, providing opportunities for diversity, for new and innovative practices. This both provides a condition for and is an outcome of rethinking the challenges of marginalised groups (Westwood 1991). The possibility is raised of new and multiple forms of lifelong learning. Fourth, the organisation of lifelong learning opportunities is reconfigured, with a wider range being provided and increasing emphasis being placed on satisfying the desires of the consumers. There is a thrust towards reconstituting formal providers of education and training as businesses with a greater emphasis on marketing (Tuckett 1991b; Kenway *et al.* 1993a; Tett 1993). Fifth, as Field (1994) suggests, there is a growth in the interest in self-improvement manuals and therapies aimed at supporting the development of certain lifestyles. Thus, cultural change does not only result in greater interest in lifelong learning, it also has an impact on the types of opportunities developed and ways in which opportunities are to be structured and delivered.

TECHNOLOGICAL CHANGE – GLOBALISATION, FIXES, FAXES

It is often argued that underpinning many of the aspects of economic and cultural change outlined above are changes in and the deployment of information and communications technology. This can lead to arguments from technological determinism. However, the particular changes in technology that occur are themselves embedded in certain economic and cultural changes; they are an outcome of change as well as contributors to these complex and multi-faceted processes.

In relation to the economy, it has been the impact of technology upon the existence and nature of employment which has been pivotal. While, as Clarke (1996) suggests, there were arguments between those who suggested that the new technologies would predominantly destroy employment

(Jenkins and Sherman 1979) and those who suggested that employment would be created, it was generally accepted that more employment would be lost by not introducing new technologies than by introducing them. Glyn (1996: 2) argues that it is 'absolutely wrong' to blame the introduction of technology for the unprecedented loss of jobs in recent years. In addition to issues of job creation and loss, questions are raised as to whether the skills changes associated with changes in technology are a condition for up-skilling, de-skilling or multi-skilling (Robins and Webster 1986). The impact of technology and its application in the economy has varied across sectors and by size of company. In the United Kingdom, studies indicate that between 1981 and 1987 the introduction of micro-electronics into manufacturing industries resulted in the net loss of 214,000 jobs (313,000 were lost and 99,000 new ones were created). Thus, while technological change has been central to the discourse of competitiveness, new forms of employment and ways of organising work, it has also contributed to the economic insecurity of the workforce.

The dominant discourse has constructed technological change in relation to the economy and the requirement for competitiveness in the global economy. New technology is the spur to increased productivity. However, there are important issues about the ways it is introduced, through negotiation or imposition – questions of whether the human dimensions of technology are encompassed within considerations of change, embraced in the German notion of *technik* (Lash and Urry 1994). Where social partnership or stakeholder notions prevail, 'more participation by employees and their representatives in introducing and applying new technology can help reap the full benefits of modernisation' (European Foundation for the Improvement of Living and Working Conditions 1990: 1). Advances in technology tend to be held to be inherently beneficial and progressive, almost inevitable. Thus, the countries of the European Union are encouraged to maximise the economic opportunities arising from the introduction of new technology by increasing the participation of employees in the planning and implementation of its development through a structured process of human resource development. Some countries and employers are more inclined to do this than others. However, alternative practices are possible. For Robins and Webster (1986: 42), the linking of technological change to the economy has as its objective 'to re-establish social control and discipline, and to create a submissive and flexible workforce'. Here different technologies are taken to provide the conditions for different forms of management control of the labour force (Rosen and Baroudi 1992). This, however, is not inevitable and can be contested.

In relation to cultural change, it is the impact of communications technology, such as personal computers, satellites, the Internet and jet airlines, which has had a significant impact. Goods, services and people are able to move around the globe much quicker than in previous periods. Information and images are brought into our homes. Events have a more instant impact. As suggested in the previous chapter, space–time becomes compressed. In the home, as consumers of products and services and in the forms of leisure and entertainment available to many people, technology plays a significant role in cultural change. With this comes the need to be able to understand and use the new technology. It is no good introducing new kitchen appliances, computer software, laser disc players, fax machines, automatic bank telling, and so on, unless people are able to use them, and this involves learning. As the rate of technological change has increased and as technologically sophisticated objects have become prevalent in increasing areas of people's lives, so the need for learning to continue has also increased. In 1990, just under 22 per cent of households in Britain had a home computer, the percentage ranging from 45 per cent for professional economically active heads of households to 5 per cent for economically inactive heads of households (Central Statistical Office 1993: 141). In Australia, 29 per cent of households had a personal computer in 1993 (Australian Bureau of Statistics 1995). Domestic space has become more technologised, supporting changes in household practices and relationships and new activities. However, the differential impact of technological change is also significant not only by class, but also by gender (Kirkup and Jones 1996).

Caution is necessary, therefore, towards any discourse which attempts to present technological change as a neutral, almost 'natural', universal process leading to an 'information society' or 'post-industrial society' (McNeil 1991; Webster 1994). This is often presented as though there is no choice to be made over such changes and tends to under-emphasise the processes of geographical relocation of industry around the globe rather than its removal from history (Soja 1989). As such, technology can appear to have a dynamic of its own, free from human intervention: 'the exploitation of new (information) technology is seen as part of the march of "progress" – a progress that is necessary and inevitable and in which we must acquiesce' (Robins and Webster 1986: 37). This, in itself, tends to result in the decisions which support such changes being excluded from scrutiny and contest. While technological change has increased the requirement for lifelong learning, therefore, for many, and this includes some who participated in technological change as a condition for employment – in the financial services, for instance – that has meant learning about unemployment.

Technological change is not new, but the speed at which it takes place has resulted in a greater integration of the globe than was the case even fifteen years ago. The nature of it has also altered under the increased influence of computers and micro-technology. The impact of information and communication technology is significant in the possibilities it has raised for revolutionising the organisation of communication, production, distribution and consumption and the range of products and services available. There is a 'chronic intensification of patterns of interconnectedness mediated by the modern communications industry and new information technology. Distant localities are now interlinked as never before. Globalisation has reordered both time and space and has "shrunk the globe"' (Held 1993: 5). In the process, new relationships between space and place are made possible. New technologies

> through their capacity to transgress frontiers and subvert boundaries ... are implicated in a complex interplay of deterritorialisation and reterritorialisation. ... Things are no longer defined and distinguished in the ways that they once were, by their boundaries, borders or frontiers. ... We can say that the very idea of boundary – the frontier boundary of the nation state, for example, or the physical boundaries of urban structures – has been rendered problematical.
>
> (Morley and Robins 1995: 75)

The development of technology under conditions of flexible accumulation is resulting in the reorganisation of space–time at many levels and in many ways. For instance, whereas the early processes of modernisation brought people together in large-scale industries in a particular part of the globe – Western Europe and North America – the speed of communication and transportation now enables industries to be spread around the globe, exploiting the relatively low production costs and skill bases of newly industrialising countries. At the same time, the processes of urbanisation which were entailed by industrialisation and mass production – the need for a secure and readily available supply of labour – are being challenged by technological change, for instance, in the possibilities for the increasing use of distancing strategies in the organisation of businesses. In Europe, the geographical distances between paid work and unpaid work and leisure are increased for many by the possibilities provided by developments in communication and transport. This reduces the need for the concentration of populations into a few urban conglomerations. Physical distances increase, but people, goods and services are brought together. At its most extreme, this now allows the possibility for certain groups of people not to have to visit a workplace at all. They may live some distance from their employers, but technology – faxes, modems, mobile telephones – enable them to have all their activities based within their own homes. The very notion of the employer and workplace being geographically unified is lost. People are able to work at a distance from their employers, but none the less to be in constant contact and, therefore, available to them.

This reorganisation of space–time within the nation state is part of a global reorganisation of space–time. Coca-Cola, for example, now refers to itself as a multi-local rather than a multi-national, both global and local (Featherstone 1995). Such trends are uneven and look different from different vantage points. For instance, China is currently going through a massive process of industrialisation in which the migration from the rural to urban areas in the period from the mid-1980s to mid-1990s has been esti-mated at 90 million people (BBC2 1994). However, this process of industrialisation is dependent on the technological changes which enable information, goods and services to be distributed to a global marketplace.

In relation to lifelong learning, technological change plays a dual role. It both creates a condition for lifelong learning and it also helps to support it by providing new possibilities for the design, production and delivery of learning opportunities through flexible, open and distance approaches. For example, with the introduction of video recorders we need to be able to learn how to use them, but once we have, we can also use videos to learn about other things which may interest us. Similarly with computers. Once we have learned how to use them, we can use software packages to learn about other things, from solving complex manufacturing problems to learning to play chess. The very learning about new technologies and how to use them can help to build the confidence to go on to further learning. Here tech-nology becomes a powerful tool which can also undermine the necessity for a mediator between the learner and what they wish to learn. A survey of further education colleges in the United Kingdom on the use of radio and television programmes on courses discovered that both teaching staff and learners found they contributed to learning, but for different reasons. 'Teachers tended to think in terms of classroom practice and broadcasting was able to make lessons more interesting. Learners talked more about inde-pendent use of tapes for study and the flexibility of recordings' (FEU 1994: 14). Such findings provide grounds for the development of learning resource centres and the development of self-directed learning.

Technology, and particularly its use in forms of flexible, open and distance learning, supported by the discourses of 'educational technology' (Laurillard 1993), may be seen as a condition for increasing and widening access to learning and for the learner to become more 'autonomous'. Here technological change can be said to be supporting the individualising tendencies discussed in the previous section. For some, the use of technology in the delivery of learning programmes increases not so much the autonomy of the learner as their isolation. For others, autonomy is a way of making attractive to people the need to accept and adapt to a particular kind of technological change – new technology 'frees' us. In other words, autonomy is a way of discursively normalising technological adaptation over which one is given little substantive control.

Alongside individualising tendencies, Lyotard (1984) argues that informa-tion technology also redefines knowledge, whereby the logic of computers commodifies knowledge into information. Through the use of, for instance, computers, CD-ROMs, e-mail and the Internet, individuals can access infor-mation, interact with it and with others without attending centres of learning. It is suggested that a consequence of this is that educative processes are displaced and reconstituted as a relationship between producer and consumer in which information/knowledge is exchanged on the basis of the value it has to the consumer-as-learner and learner-as-consumer. However, as so often, there are countervailing tendencies. Here it is possible for information and communications technology to mediate new forms of sociality and networks through, for instance, computer conferencing, thereby reconstituting sociality to include global relationships. The formation of virtual networks means that in addition to individualising tendencies, there are different opportunities to bring people together in new forms of gatherings (Maffesoli 1996). Similarly, the view of critics that interaction with information technology is a form of passive consumption is challenged by the increasing levels of interactivity involved. Different subjectivities may result, raising challenges for the contemporary world, metaphorically captured in notions of the 'cyborg', 'cyberpunk' or 'alien' (Green and Bigum 1993), where difference is not necessarily deficiency.

A further consequence of technological change is that it provides the possibility for new centres and forms of knowledge production and distribution. The impact upon universities is particularly significant here. Universities would appear to be losing their privileged status as primary producers of knowledge as they become part of a wider learning market, which includes the research and development departments of large organisations, think tanks and consultancies. Plant (1995) argues that universities are less able to control access to knowledge, when it increasingly takes the form of information circulating through networks which evade the control of educational institutions and when its value as a product of 'educated' minds is challenged. It may be little wonder then that a sense of crisis pervades the terrain of education, just at that point when participation and lifelong learning are constituted as necessary conditions for social and economic life.

Technologically mediated images and information also have consequences for conceptions of literacy, for both current and future adult learners. Technological change produces new media, such as video, interactive computer programs, virtual reality, from and through which one is required to 'read' and learn. This involves an extension of traditional discourses of literacy (Archer and Costello 1990; McNeil 1991) to include more than books. For current adult learners, it necessitates acquiring the skills to operate and 'read' these media. This is one of the reasons for an increased emphasis on the development of computer literacy in the curricula. Further, as Mace (1992: 174) suggests, helping learners to 'read' television seems 'to be an obvious part of any literacy curriculum which enables students to explore and reflect on their intellectual interests as critical participants in the cultural environment they inhabit'. In other words, media literacy is as significant as traditional notions of literacy.

However, as with more conventional discourses of literacy, the ways in which this is constructed are themselves important (Lee and Wickert 1995).

For some, literacy is more a human right than a set of skills (Limage 1993). The many forms of literacy can both promote technological determinism – it is a set of skills to enable adaptation – or provide the possibility to challenge the inevitability of the direction, pace and consequences of technological change. It is as much a cultural activity of interpretation as a set of skills. Learning to learn using new technologies has a wider significance than simply being able to use and 'read' the technology effectively. In many countries, this adds a significant concern to that which already exists over the more conventional literacy difficulties experienced by adults. There are significant sections of the social formation, therefore, for whom technological change may represent yet a further barrier to social and economic participation.

For future cohorts of adults the issues may alter, as they may well have had experience of the new media through their initial education. This partly depends upon the pace and direction of technological change in the near future, but the computer literacy requirements of many adults at present may not be relevant to that first generation of adults for whom information technology has been a part of their initial education and training. However, this will not reduce the requirement for what some have called a pedagogy of multiliteracies (New London Group 1995), the latter having a basis in the globalised diversity which goes far wider than the requirement to negotiate the mediated meanings of technology.

Technological change is far more complex and ambiguous than is often suggested, with differing implications for lifelong learning. Discourses which portray such changes as neutral, something which needs to be adapted to in order to ensure economic competitiveness, can be challenged. They can be challenged in relation to the necessity, direction and speed of such changes and the differential impact they have on adults and the differing possibilities of participating in shaping technological change. However, adaptation to technological change would appear to be the dominant experience for many adults rather than participating in and shaping the processes of change.

On the one hand, we have discourses of an information society and technological utopia. For instance, Halal and Liebowitz (1994: 26) suggest that as 'the technology for acquiring and distributing knowledge permeates home, work and all other locations, all social functions should be integrated into a seamless web of learning. Everyday living will then take place in an electronic school without walls.' However, more critical and cautious evaluations are also available. In relation to the applications of new technology in flexible, open and distance learning, Kirkup and Jones (1996: 289) argue they have 'not yet proved effective enough to replace many well-established teaching and learning activities (for example, the use of the postal system), and may never do so. Nor have the technical resources become socially ubiquitous.' The significance of technological change for lifelong learning therefore has to be situated within the context of unequal social formations and the contestation of the future.

DEMOGRAPHIC CHANGE – TIMEBOMBS, THIRD-AGERS, PANTHERS

The demographic structure of the population played a significant role in the 1980s in the United Kingdom and elsewhere, leading to concern that the drop in the numbers of young people coming through the education system would result in a shortage of labour in the economy and students in higher education. The discourse of the 'demographic timebomb' aligned with the concerns for economic competitiveness provided strong support for increasing the opportunities available for adults to become lifelong learners. It came to the fore at a time when it was argued that an increasingly quali- fied labour force was necessary to meet the 'needs' of employers. Employers were encouraged therefore to increase their recruitment of adults from 'under-utilised' groups, such as the long-term unemployed, women returners, minority ethnic groups, people with disabilities and older workers (Training Agency 1989). They were also encouraged to increase the training available to employees to enable individuals to change their roles as skill demands changed.

Similarly, higher education was encouraged to increase its intake of mature students. As with employers, it was held that due to demographic pressures this increase in participation would result also in the widening of access to include groups previously excluded from higher education. At the time, however, any adult over 21 years old could have been considered as marginal in relation to conventional higher education. Changes in funding, institutional self-interest and the commitment of those trying to expand opportunities for adult learners resulted in a massive expansion of higher education during the 1980s and early 1990s. This expansion was also witnessed elsewhere in the industrialised world (McCormick 1989; Minichiello 1992).

In the United Kingdom, the discourse of the demographic timebomb focused on the drop in the numbers of 16 to 19 year olds by 21 per cent or around 2.5 million between 1985 and 2001 (HMSO 1991) and the fact that in 1991, '80 per cent of the workforce in the year 2000 are at work already' (Tuckett 1991b: 12). Alongside the drop in the percentage of young people is a growth in the proportion living to greater ages. Between 1991 and 2031, it is estimated that the numbers of over 65 year olds in the United Kingdom will rise from 10.6 million to 14.6 million (Central Statistical Office 1993: 15). The overall ageing of the population can be seen in the increased proportion of over 40 year olds – in 1991, 44.4 per cent; in 2001, 46.1 per cent; in 2011, 49.9 per cent. While these shifts are significant, how significant and in what ways is an issue which is contested. For instance, should more

resources be shifted in favour of older adults, and, if so, how? It is also interesting to note that within overall demographic changes, women become an
increasing proportion as the population ages. Further, Central Statistical
Office figures (1993: 16) demonstrate the ethnic dimensions to demography,
with the white ethnic group having a smaller proportion of under 16 year
olds and a larger number of over 60 year olds than some other groups. This
has implications for the learning opportunities developed across the age
range, as there will be a much bigger number of older adults from minority
ethnic groups in the years to come for whom the provision of learning
opportunities will be important if equality of opportunity is to be pursued
(Dadzie 1993).

The trend towards an ageing population is something which is shared to a
greater or lesser extent in most of the major industrialised and industrialising countries. For instance, between 1980 and 2020, the proportion of the
population over 65 years old will rise from 13.96 per cent to 19.45 per cent in
France, from 13.13 per cent to 17.8 per cent in Greece and from 11.29 per
cent to 16.16 per cent in the United States (Schuller 1993). Over the same
period, the proportion of over 60 year olds will rise from 7.3 per cent to 16.4
per cent in China, from 5.3 per cent to 11.4 per cent in India, and from 5.6
per cent to 11 per cent in Colombia. By contrast, in Kenya and
Mozambique the proportion of over 60 year olds remains fairly static, rising
from 3 per cent to 3.7 per cent in the former and 5.4 per cent to 5.6 per cent
in the latter. However, Schuller (1993: 2) cautions against generalisations
based on proportions of the population, as in some countries, particularly in
Africa, 'the total population is increasing so fast, the actual numbers [sic] of
older people is rising sharply even though they do not form a growing
percentage of the population'.

The concern over demography in the United Kingdom initially produced
an emphasis on increasing the numbers of adult returners in higher education, with particular emphasis on occupationally relevant higher education
(Jordinson 1990). However, while increased access did take place, and not
simply to higher education, the demographic timebomb failed to materialise
in the way that it had been expected. A number of reasons help to explain
this failure. First, it was due to the class composition of the cohort of young
people coming through the initial education system during this period.
While the proportion of young people overall fell, there was a greater
percentage of middle- and upper-class youngsters amongst that cohort
(Smithers and Robinson 1989). As most major studies have demonstrated
class to be a key factor in people continuing to participate in education and
training (McGivney 1990; Sargant 1990, 1991; Maguire et al. 1993), the fall
in numbers applying for access to higher education did not occur as
expected. Higher education expanded and more adults participated, but not
simply due to demography. Second, there was also the continuation of high
levels of unemployment. Economic growth did not bring sufficient

expansion of employment to enable a return to the full employment patterns experienced in the older industrialised countries of the 1950s and 1960s. The demand for labour was insufficient even for the lower numbers of young people entering the labour market. Explanations for this vary, but Glyn (1996) argues that it is the expansion of demand for work which has outstripped supply rather than too weak a supply of employment. Whatever the causes, during the 1980s and 1990s, there was a continuation of significant levels of youth unemployment throughout the older industrialised countries, but particularly in countries such as Spain, Italy, France and New Zealand. In the United Kingdom, youth unemployment and the poor quality of much government-funded training are thought to have been significant factors in contributing to the overall expansion of participation in post-compulsory education and training.

While demographic change was a significant spur to increasing and widening access for adult learners, it does not appear to have proved as significant as was thought initially and was far more complex in its impact. For instance, as well as differential demographic changes on the basis of class, there were also differences between ethnic groups. While the argument for lifelong learning due to demographic change was based on a generalised summary of population trends, different arguments may have been developed if there had been a more detailed focus on class composition and ethnic background (Dadzie 1993). In the process, the discourse of the demographic timebomb has largely been displaced with concern now shifting to considerations of how to support an ageing population. Here the discourse of economic insecurity is being utilised to promote a condition of fear over what will be available to older adults, the third age, over time. The aim is to increase individual and familial preparation and responsibility for one's old age, as a condition for curtailing publicly provided pensions and services, and for cutting direct taxation.

This is in stark contrast to the discourse of the timebomb, in which the emphasis was on demography as it affected the labour market and primarily on the demography of youth and younger adults. Less concern was focused on the demographic implications of an ageing population as it affected middle- and older-aged adults. However, for many in the United Kingdom and elsewhere, paid working life is finishing in the fifties through early retirement, unemployment and redundancy. 'In the UK, economic activity rates for men aged sixty to sixty four have decreased from over 80 per cent in 1971 to barely over 50 per cent two decades later' (Schuller and Bostyn 1993: 366). More people are living longer and longevity is itself extending, as health care and education improve, partly through technological change. What, then, are the lifelong learning implications of what has been termed the 'grey revolution'? Do these increasingly large sections of the adult community also have an entitlement to learning opportunities? What type of learning opportunities and provided by whom? How will they be enabled to make use of the new information and communications technologies? People who have paid taxes for much of their lives might well expect certain services, including education and training services, to be available to them at a cost they can afford. They can be a significant political force in their electoral and campaigning behaviour. It is suggested that organised and politicised third agers could become a 'grey panther' movement, echoing the radical activist group of the 1960s in the United States, the Black Panthers. Here the notion of timebomb may take on different connotations!

We also need to be cautious about homogenising middle-aged and older adults into a single grouping. There may be as many differences between 50 and 80 year olds as there are between 20 and 50 year olds. Generational differences exist within overall demographic changes. As van Tilburg (1993) suggests, commenting on her work with women in the Netherlands, there are significant generational differences between those who experienced the occupation of the Second World War and those born afterwards. There is an experiential and historical dimension to demography which, among other things, impacts upon people's attitudes towards education and training and, with that, the possibilities for lifelong learning and the types and forms of opportunities that need to be developed. A 50 year old who left school at 14 and lived through the Depression of the 1930s and the Second World War will have a very different perspective from a 50 year old who completed their education in the late 1950s and experienced the economic prosperity of the 1960s and early 1970s. Tennant (1988) also draws out the issue of generations when providing a critique of some of the models of adult development as ahistorical.

Similarly, the length of initial education, itself an important factor in continued participation as an adult, will have important consequences for the potential for and forms of lifelong learning necessary for different generations of adults. A 1990 survey in the United Kingdom showed '81 per cent of those aged 65 or over and 77 per cent of those aged 55–64 have not studied since completing their full-time education' (Schuller and Bostyn 1993: 370). In addition, there are the physiological changes that occur with age, although caution is necessary as these can be constructed as a 'norm' of ageing and development which ignores the specific historical, geographical, cultural and technological contexts which give rise to specific processes of ageing and responses to it. In examining the demography of older adults, there are also important considerations of gender, as more women than men are living longer and their longevity is greater than men's (Arber and Ginn 1992). Given differential gender experiences – for instance, domestic work and finance – what are or will be the specific requirements of elderly women and men?

Once again, therefore, while demographic change has provided a condition for a general interest in lifelong learning, in examining demography in more detail we have uncovered a more complex situation which provides the grounds for a variety of arguments over access to learning opportunities for different sections of the adult population. While the focus of much debate has been and remains on demographic change and lifelong learning for those groups who are or wish to be active in the labour market, for those older adults no longer active in the labour market or active in the voluntary sector of the economy the possibilities for continuing to learn have not received so much attention. The third agers have been marginalised by dominant discourses of demographic timebombs and economic imperatives. When third age interests have been articulated, this has usually been in terms of the 'burden' of how to support future cohorts of older adults. In other words, the timebomb is reconfigured as stemming not so much from the shortage of young labour market entrants, as from the increasing number of people exiting from or not part of the labour market.

Attempts to address this issue have occurred largely at the margins of policy and practitioner debate (Carnegie Inquiry 1993; Schuller and Bostyn 1993). In other words, if the education and training of adults are at the margins of discourses of education and training, the position of older adults is at the margin of the margins. Self-organised activities by older adults, such as the University of the Third Age and other forms of less formal provision, thereby receive limited recognition within discourses of change and lifelong learning (Minichiello 1992; Pilley 1993). While demographic change has been constructed as a condition for an interest in lifelong learning, it is a particular discourse, one which is open to challenge. There are alternative perspectives regarding demography and lifelong learning, as a focus on the third age and grey panthers suggests. Like other aspects of change, demography has been important to the interest in lifelong learning, but its precise significance can be interpreted in a number of ways.

CONTESTING CHANGE – CULTURAL RESTORATIONISTS, MODERNISERS, PROGRESSIVES

Change is not a 'natural' process, but is the result of decisions and actions taken and positions adopted throughout the social formation and within the institutions of the state. The changes outlined above are not coherent, monolithic or predictable. They are themselves subject to contestation. In the different discourses of change, we are faced with the issue of whose perspective and knowledge is being pursued. Which is the most powerful discourse in shaping change and with what consequences? How is that manifested in practice? For instance, what values are embedded in criteria of quality and funding arrangements? Change and its impact are produced and distributed unevenly around the globe and the perspective I have outlined is largely a construct of the debates in the richer, older industrialised countries, perspectives which are criticised rightly for their Eurocentrism and the way the concerns of the other parts of the globe are marginalised (Joseph *et al*.

1990). Also, change impacts differentially upon groups within the older industrialised countries, so discourses of change also inscribe particular perspectives of, for instance, class, gender, 'race', age, geography.

Each of the above forms of change – economic, cultural, technological, demographic – has been and can be used to promote certain priorities within a generalised growth in interest in lifelong learning. These are set out in Table 2.1. While not necessarily implying each other, these different discourses of change have been bound together by, among others, governments, policy-makers, the media, educators and trainers to produce a powerful discourse which has been highly influential in promoting a specific form of interest in lifelong learning. In this discourse, change requires the provision of lifelong learning opportunities for the economically active with particular emphasis on science and technology and the attributes to be flexible within the labour market, for which the individual is largely responsible. The general possibilities are welded into a particular discourse of change which supports an interest in lifelong learning, but a particular form of interest with particular consequences. This has been used to guide the policies and practices of lifelong learning to produce a market in learning opportunities to meet the 'needs' of employers and individuals active in the labour market – employed and unwaged.

Different groups have taken different positions on how the interest in lifelong learning is to be developed. This produces different discourses of change with differing implications for lifelong learning. These differences are contested at a variety of levels – institutional, local, regional, national, international – and within a range of groups and organisations – employers' groups, trade unions, professional bodies. The state itself is not immune from such contestation, with various government departments taking differing perspectives on policy development which either directly or indirectly impact upon opportunities for lifelong learning.

In his analysis of the evolution of the 1988 Education Reform Act in the United Kingdom, Ball (1990a), drawing on earlier work by Raymond Williams, traces three broad strands of influence on policy development.

Table 2.1 Change, education and training

Change	Education and training response
Economic	Lifelong learning opportunities relevant to the 'needs' of the economy to ensure competitiveness.
Cultural	Greater emphasis on the individual as the consumer of educational and training products and a learning approach to 'life'.
Technological	More science and technology provision for all age groups.
Demographic	More varied provision for adults throughout their lifespan.

Each of these strands – cultural restorationists, modernisers and progressives – constructs a particular discourse of change, thereby identifying both
particular problems and policy solutions to be adopted. These discourses
can also be identified in the influences on policy development in relation to
lifelong learning (see Table 2.2). Each offers an analysis of what is considered wrong with current practices, what the purpose of provision for adults
is, the modes of controlling provision, and styles of practice associated with
the provision of learning opportunities.

It would be comforting if it was possible to assign each of these strands
of influence to a particular discourse of lifelong learning and a learning
society. However, this would be misplaced. The different strands of influence

Table 2.2 Contesting provision for adult learners

	Cultural restorationists	Modernisers	Progressives
Form of analysis	Provision too permissive. National culture and academ-ic standards under threat.	Provision too staid, academic and anti-industrial. National economic performance under threat.	Provision too staid, reinforcing dominant interests. Rights and equity under threat.
Definition of provision	The academic, the cultivation of literary and aesthetic sensibilities and the reproduction of culture. Moral subordination.	The needs of industry and the economy. Applied knowledge, flexible skills, correct attitudes.	The needs of citizens. The cultivation of critical skills, knowledge and understanding to function in a complex social formation. Moral questioning.
Modes of control	Stronger state control over institutions and curriculum. Proscription of non-subjects and `politicised' curriculum.	Consumer control/ influence, with employers in positions of critical influence. Respon-sive to the requirements of the market.	Learner control/influence. Forms of democratic accountability. Responsive to the requirements of the community.
Styles of practice	Formal relationships between tutors and learners. Summative assessment and selection. Competitive individualism and an emphasis on cognitive skills.	Innovation, shift of emphasis from teaching to learning. Formative assess-ment and develop-ment. Co-operation, group work and an emphasis on process, social skills and ways of knowing.	Learner-centredness. Negotiated curriculum. Emphasis on formative assessment where required. Co-operation, group work and an emphasis on process and `empowerment'.

Source: Adapted from Ball 1990a

may agree about certain aspects of change. For instance, cultural restorationists and progressives may agree about the 'damaging' influence of the media and the development of a consumer society, even if the roots of their concerns and how to deal with them differ. They may at times form alliances in the defence of academic 'freedom' and forms of knowledge against the influence of governments promoting skills more relevant to the requirements of employers. Similarly, within the strands of influence there are differing perspectives. For instance, progressives may include liberals, marxists, socialists, feminists, critical pedagogues, postmodernists, post-colonialists, each with their own particular views on what constitutes democracy and responsiveness to the community, or even on the 'community' to which it is necessary to respond. On what is traditionally constructed as the political 'Left', it is sometimes felt that more energy is spent disagreeing with each other rather than focusing on the opposing political forces. As with all typologies, therefore, caution is necessary.

> Abstract accounts tend towards tidy generalities and often fail to capture the messy realities of influence, pressure, dogma, expediency, conflict, compromise, intransigence, resistance, error, opposition and pragmatism in the policy process. It is easy to be simple, neat and superficial and to gloss over these awkward realities. It is difficult to retain messiness and complexity and still be penetrating.
>
> (Ball 1990a: 9)

Actual policies, therefore, may well incorporate different aspects of influence, rather than having the clear direction and goals they may present themselves as having. For instance, the 1992 Further and Higher Education Act in the United Kingdom aimed to provide 'parity of esteem' between academic and vocational qualifications. However, in excluding certain forms of non-vocational adult education as 'leisure' from funding, in some ways, it reinscribed the division it aimed to overcome. More recent (1996) proposals to revamp the 14–19 qualifications structure are yet another attempt to create parity of esteem, the success or failure of which will be watched with interest, as will the access and progression of adults over 19 who also take these qualifications.

It is on such ambiguities and messiness that alliances can exist, for instance, between modernisers and progressives against more restorationist forms of provision and approaches. As suggested in chapter 1, a poststructuralist stance provides the possibility of understanding and engaging in these processes as well as contributing to them. Both modernisers in the Department for Education and Employment in the United Kingdom and progressive adult educators and trainers support greater recognition for learning from experience, even while differences over the significance of such approaches continue to exist. There is likely to be disagreement between them over whether opportunities are opened up to all through a market approach or one based on more equitable principles. Similarly, both modernising and cultural restorationist trends can exist within government and state institutions. For instance, in the United Kingdom in the late 1980s, it is suggested that while restorationist influences were dominant in the former Department of Education and Science, modernising influences were to the fore at the former Employment Department. It is for such reasons that many despaired at the apparent different directions of state policy. The merging of the two Departments into the Department for Education and Employment in 1995 provided at least the possibility for overcoming such tensions and/or them being fought out in changed circumstances.

Discourses of change are deeply ambiguous and ambivalent. Yet they are also immensely powerful in influencing the nature, direction, pace and understanding of change. In promoting change as central to contemporary existence, they already assume and introduce an uncertainty and unpredictability into that condition. In destabilising tradition and established economic and socio-cultural norms, they provide both possibilities and threats. In this chapter, I have provided an analysis of the ways in which specific discourses of change have been constructed to provide the basis for a growing interest in lifelong learning and a learning society. Here lifelong learning and the provision of learning opportunities are constructed as a mechanism to service change taking place elsewhere in the economy and social formation. It is now time to examine some of the changes to which the discourses of adult education and lifelong learning themselves have been subject. Changes in these discourses are not simply a passive response to change, but are subject to and part of the processes of change.

Chapter 3

Boundaries, field and moorland

The previous chapter focused on different discourses of change as they have been deployed to support an interest in lifelong learning and a learning society. It was suggested that the provision of lifelong learning opportunities for adults is viewed primarily as a mechanism to service changes going on elsewhere in the economy and social formation. In this chapter, the focus will be more specifically on the changes to which discourses of adult education, training and lifelong learning have been subject, and some of the consequences of those changes. However, as I have suggested, conceptualising changes in discourses in conditions of unpredictable change represents a challenge in itself.

This chapter will examine the changing discourses framing lifelong learning and learning opportunities for adults. In particular, I want to suggest that there has been a shift in the discourses from a focus on the provision of education and training for adults to one which focuses on learners and learning. Indeed, the discourse of 'lifelong learning' deployed here signifies that shift and reflexively challenges and displaces the traditional discourses of 'adult education'. This has important implications for formal institutions of education and training, as their privileged status is brought into question by such a shift, even if they retain significant power. While a focus on 'adult learning' was formulated initially to provide the basis for a specific and bounded provision for adults as distinct from younger people, the shift towards a focus on learning has actually undermined the requirement for the privileging of certain settings. A differentiated and bounded field of adult education is being made problematical and displaced by a de-differentiated and more diverse moorland of lifelong learning. Here 'moorland' signifies a rich metaphorical space of exploration, about and upon which some discourses are stronger than others, with effects of re-differentiation. However, its resonance may be somewhat restricted due to its locatedness within the English autobiography of the author, signifying particular meanings and possibilities. Alternative metaphors may be necessary therefore to signify the meaning of moorland in other contexts.

This chapter will explore the ways in which a shift from a field to moorland discourse expands the settings in which adults can be said to learn, as well as the possible implications of the breaking down and moving of established institutional, policy and conceptual boundaries. In relation to practice, the changing boundaries between institutions, within institutions and between institutions and learners will be explored. The ways in which those boundaries are reconfigured as, for instance, more adults participate in school classes, further and higher education, or undertake learning in their own homes will be examined. The chapter will turn then to the question of boundaries in policy and the possibilities for coherence in supporting the development of a learning society at a range of levels – local, national, international. It will explore the problems raised by policy development based on departmental responsibility and the shift from a social to economic framework in constructing policy on lifelong learning. I will then turn to adult education as a field of study and suggest that in terms of its 'object of knowledge' and in its forms of knowledge production de-differentiation is at work. This will be reflexively exemplified through a discussion of the boundaries between 'education', 'training' and 'leisure'. These are important concepts within the field of adult education, not least as they are inscribed in policy and the funding of learning opportunities by the state. The problematic nature of these distinctions and the ways in which the boundaries which have traditionally been drawn around each of these areas are shifting and/or breaking down will be explored. The basis for the analysis in this chapter is the attempt to think differently the discourses that have framed and could frame lifelong learning and a learning society and to suggest that the very discourse of lifelong learning contributes to the processes of de-differentiation at work. It signifies the changing place of adult learners and learning, as the relationship between boundaries and space is reconfigured in contemporary times.

DE-DIFFERENTIATION, FIELD AND MOORLAND

One way of characterising the changes taking place, particularly in the older industrialised countries, is as a process of de-differentiation in increasingly globalised conditions. Differentiation depends upon establishing clear demarcations around fields of practice, which can be acted upon, fields of policy, which can be managed rationally, and fields of study, establishing what can be discussed legitimately. While demarcations have always been subject to challenge, the extent and nature of the challenge to the differentiation central to the governance of the modern nation state leads many to argue that in the contemporary world not only are the boundaries shifting and becoming more permeable, but the structuring metaphors of boundedness are themselves questionable (Morley and Robins 1995). Such metaphors include the notion of field, such as adult education as a field of practice, policy and study. It is suggested that what are needed are new metaphors and it is here that the notion of moorland is suggested as more resonant and resourceful in relation to understanding the processes of de-differentiation. Moorlands are open spaces ungovernable by the imperatives of technical instrumental rationality, although still spaces inscribed with exercises of power and attempts to place boundaries in the way of walkers on that terrain. On the moorland, there is more open-ended exploration, a searching for new routes to travel through a complex and uncertain ecology and archaeology. Discourses of lifelong learning both contribute to de-differentiation, attempting to normalise a position which elides boundaries, and reflect de-differentiation at work in the practices of lifelong learning. Here, rather than seeing de-differentiation in polarised opposition to differentiation – an aspect of binary logic which reflexively differentiation signifies – the former is constructed as the 'other' of the latter. There is an ongoing interplay between differentiation and de-differentiation, with the latter subverting the possibilities for governmentality sustained in attempts to differentiate the social formation.

Any consideration of lifelong learning as a condition for a learning society immediately confronts the issue of the nature and extent of what is to be encapsulated. While compulsory education is clearly demarcated by a set of institutional arrangements for a particular age group, this is not the case with adults. Boundaries provide the grounds for bringing a certain order to the apparently chaotic, unpredictable and changing activities in which adult learners engage. They provide the basis for deciding what is to be included and what is to be excluded. This process of boundary-setting is part of the wider processes of differentiation in modern social formations. 'The modern period was one of vertical and horizontal differentiation, the development of many separate institutional, normative and aesthetic spheres, each with their specific conventions and modes of evaluation and with multiple separations (and legislating hierarchies) . . .' (Lash and Urry 1994: 272). Differentiation is the process whereby responsibility for specific functions is hived off to specific institutions. At the level of the state, for instance, in a differentiated approach a Department for Education has responsibility for education, a Department of Health for health, and so on. In institutions of education and training, departments of geography will be separate from those of health education. In employers, the training department will have a separate function to the personnel department.

Differentiation is held to be rational and effective in the management of complex modern social formations. What it entails is being able to place certain institutionalised boundaries around areas of activity. In this way, boundaries are powerful in deciding what constitutes 'the field'. Who has the power to set boundaries and what boundaries are set have powerful effects. This makes boundaries controversial and subject to debate, linking the world of ideas and practice to the world of politics and policy-making. Traditionally in education and training, this process of boundary-setting conceived post-compulsory education and training involving different sets of institutional arrangements for different groups of learners and different forms of learning. Thus, higher education was for young people to learn academic disciplines and professions, further education was for young people to learn technical skills, and adult education was for adults to undertake general and recreational education – the 'great tradition' of liberal adult education. The field of adult education was constituted dominantly through the discourses of the great tradition. In the process, certain parts of the full range of actual adult learning activity were lost or marginalised so that, for instance, the major participation of adults in further education provision was not embraced as part of the discourses governing the field. This has, in a sense, 'bound and gagged' the development of practice, policy and study in relation to lifelong learning, providing a straitjacket which, for some, has become a comfortable security and, for others, an intolerable restriction. Speaking of Australia, for instance, Foley and Morris (1995: 109) comment that the 'too easy acceptance of this [English great tradition] view has retarded the development of a body of Australian adult education theory firmly rooted in local practice'. In North America, it is argued that the search for academic respectability and a professional identity resulted in the construction of adult education as a specific form of practice which excluded whole arenas of adult learning (Brookfield 1989; Briton 1996).

The provision of learning opportunities for adults has a long and diverse history with a wide range of providers, including the churches, trade unions, co-operative guilds, temperance organisations (Keane 1988). However, for much of this century in the United Kingdom, this diversity has not been reflected in the discourses which dominated debates. With the development of state support for organisations providing learning opportunities for adults, particularly following the end of the First World War, learning opportunities became associated largely with a few relatively discrete forms of organised learning. These were provided through the Local Education Authority or Regional Council Adult Education Services or Institutes, the pre-1992 universities' extra-mural departments and the Workers' Education Association. From the Second World War until the 1970s, this triangle of organisations was constructed as the field of lifelong learning, or, as it is more usually put, 'adult education'. The boundaries of lifelong learning were defined by the state through its funding of these recognised settings for adult learning and the practitioners and policy-makers associated with those settings provided the discourses by which the field was constructed and understood. In other words, the field of adult education and the institutional concerns of adult educators were the dominant discourses in the moorland of lifelong learning. These particular forms of privileged institutional discourse dominated and set the terms for contesting the terrain of debate and understanding of what was constituted as a field. The fields of policy and practice were focused primarily on these institutional arrangements, as was the field of study.

In a provocative and polemical analysis of the history of adult education in the United Kingdom, Bell (1996) argues that the focus of much professional and academic discourse has marginalised the interests of the majority of adult learners who are more concerned with issues of consumer choice than emancipation. For Bell, it is not the liberal discourse which has marginalised the diversity of lifelong learning, but the radical adult education discourse with its focus on education for social change or transformation. While this indicates one of the struggles within the field of adult education over values and purposes, it remains none the less positioned within the privileged institutional sites mentioned above. This argument over the privileging of certain forms of provision in the discourses of adult education is also supported by examinations of the history of the literature (Chase 1995). In the history of adult education in the United States, Hugo (1990) suggests also there is a distinct gender bias towards the deeds and writings of male adult educators, largely because they occupied the sites of power within certain privileged settings of adult education. In addition, the development of adult education as embracing all adults over time displaced and marginalised the discourses and practices of 'workers' education' with its espoused focus on the working class – although the notion of 'workers', in turn, has been problematised in recent times as signifying the male breadwinner (Pateman 1989). Thus, a set of boundaries constructed the field, boundaries which came to be based upon the institutional settings of particular forms of adult education. This marginalised forms of adult learning taking place elsewhere, such as in the workplace, the home, local clubs, and lifelong learning as a terrain of practice, policy and study.

Two linked characteristics were constructed to mark the boundary of the field of adult education. First, there was the purpose of adult education. This was to support individuals and groups who had benefited least from previous initial education – to promote personal and social autonomy and emancipation through forms of development associated with the liberal education of the arts, humanities and certain of the social sciences. Here, many adult educators paradoxically took up the mantle of liberal education established in the elite public schools and universities of Victorian England (Sanderson 1993), even though it was precisely such elitism that many saw adult education as contesting and combating. It also had the consequence of sustaining a boundary between liberal adult education and vocational training. Participation and equality became guiding features of the discourses of adult education, with occasional concerns over the restricted numbers actually engaging in adult education and the privileged social profile of the majority of its participants (Ward and Taylor 1986; McGivney 1990; Sargant 1991). 'After fifty years of celebrating the merits of study for its own sake, it was disquieting to confront evidence that black and working-class people wanted clear, instrumental outcomes from their studies, and that many found adult education centres unwelcoming places' (Tuckett 1991a: 25).

The second characteristic was the distinctiveness of adults as 'learners'. A range of practices and discourses, in particular emphasising life experience and the processes of teaching and learning necessary for working with adults, produced an emphasis on learners and learning. Group and discussion work with more active participation and 'democratic' organisation of the learning setting and less power invested in the tutor characterised the specifics of adults as learners (Brookfield 1993b). Attempts were and continue to be made to differentiate adult learning from that of children and adolescents, as a basis for establishing a boundary between adult education and other forms of provision. 'The fact that most education is still so linked [to childhood and adolescence] has led some adult educators to define the nature of their enterprise in terms of the atypical nature of their students' (Squires 1987: 178).

Pivotal to this task of distinguishing adult learning from that of children has been the concept of andragogy. In contrast to pedagogy, which is defined as the art and science of teaching children, andragogy is constructed around the specific attributes of adults and the process of helping adults to learn. This conception of andragogy was put forward by Knowles (1970) and has continued to be influential. Knowles identifies four major characteristics of adults associated with increasing maturity: (a) the self-concept moves from dependency towards self-direction; (b) experience becomes an increasing resource for learning; (c) learning is increasingly directed towards social roles (e.g. in the workplace, neighbourhood, parenting); (d) learning becomes less subject-centred and increasingly problem-centred. Thus, the literature on adult learning is permeated with notions of self-direction, experiential learning, problem-based learning, and so on.

Andragogy has been the subject of dispute and controversy since its popular formulation in the 1970s (Day and Baskett 1982; Davenport and Davenport 1985; Davenport 1993). Knowles (1979) has modified his position, viewing andragogy as not in opposition to pedagogy, but as there being a continuum between the two. However, as Davenport (1993: 116) argues, 'emerging research results do not appear to support Knowles' conceptualisation of andragogy as a theory or proven method. Some adult educators even argue that adult education should simply drop the word from its lexicon.' Collins (1991) argues that the emphasis on developing techniques to facilitate adult learning – andragogical methods – has undermined the critical and emancipatory potential of adult education. However, andragogy has refused to go away. Even as Knowles' conception was being subject to critique, alternative formulations were being attempted. For instance, Mezirow (1983), drawing on the work of Habermas, formulated a conception of a distinct andragogical practice based on a concept of perspective transformation. This enables adults to enhance their capacity to function as self-directed learners through a process of critical reflectivity. In many ways, Mezirow is combining the two characteristics which have been deployed to construct a specific field of adult education; perspective transformation is a specifically adult form of learning with an emancipatory purpose. As with Knowles, there has been much debate surrounding the adequacy of Mezirow's conception of andragogy (Collard and Law 1989; Mezirow 1989; Hart 1990).

While andragogy was put forward to distinguish adult learning and provide a unifying concept for the field of adult education, it came under siege even as the practices of adult education and their role and significance for the social formation came into focus. In other words, discourses of andragogy can be seen as an attempt to put or keep a boundary around particular forms of provision during a period when those forms start to be questioned in terms of their adequacy. Hanson (1996) argues that the major theories put forward to distinguish adult learning from that of younger people are not sustainable and suggests the need for a more pragmatic and modest approach. Mackeracher (1994) has drawn out the gender differences which are marginalised in the discussion of andragogy as a generalisable and universal theory of adult learning. She argues that women tend to be 'relational learners' while men are more inclined to be 'autonomous learners'. Where autonomous learning is assumed to be the norm, women may find themselves in difficulties, from which are constructed deficits.

There is a further dimension to the centrality given to Knowles' conception of andragogy within North American and United Kingdom debates that is worth mentioning. This focus has marginalised the traditions of thought and discourses of adult learning formulated elsewhere (van Gent 1991). Particular discourses of andragogy, with a set of assumptions based in American/Anglo culture, have marginalised alternative perspectives within these countries and have dominated the field of adult education internationally. This reflects and enhances the established links between adult education and adult educators in the United Kingdom and North America at the expense of continental European countries and other nations – a linkage which still inhibits the theory and practice of lifelong learning within and across the European Union. In his survey of various concepts of andragogy, Savićević (1991) demonstrates how andragogy was formulated in institutions of higher education in continental Europe to provide the boundaries for a specific academic discipline as much as for a specific form of practice with adults. Knowles' focus on the distinctiveness of adult learning is not part of these traditions. The boundaries of the discourse constructing the field therefore need to be constantly foregrounded. Hall (1994: 190), in particular, draws attention to the ways in which the issues and concerns of the first world frame the discourses of research in this field, asking the question, 'what are the mechanism by which uneven power relations are reproduced in our own adult education discourse often in spite of our own intentions?'

The emancipatory purpose of adult education and its implications for adult learning have been much influenced by the work of the Brazilian, Paulo Freire (1978; Mayo 1993; McLaren and Leonard 1993; hooks 1994). Progressives from a wide spectrum – christian socialists, marxists, feminists, postmodernists and post-colonialists – have drawn upon Freire's work to support their own positions and practices. For Freire, the distinction between andragogy and pedagogy as specific to a certain age group of learners is lost. By contrast, it is the purposes and outcomes of the learning which are significant and result in and from specific practices of teaching and learning. In his work on literacy in developing countries, Freire (1978: 46) argued that a 'banking' conception of education was dominant in which 'knowledge is a gift bestowed by by those who consider themselves knowledgeable upon those whom they consider to know nothing'. This is the pedagogy of the oppressed, a pedagogy of domestication. By contrast, he argued for forms of 'conscientisation', an education based on problem-posing, dialogue and social action, in which education itself would become a 'practice of freedom'. By focusing on the actual problems faced by people in literacy groups, 'reading the word' would also involve 'reading the world' and provide a consciousness to engender social action to improve conditions. Freire's work has become influential among those workers with adults who construct their role as producing progressive social change. In its emphasis on problem-posing, dialogue and the active role of the learner in learning, it also shares and supports other progressive and modernising discourses.

However, it also has not been without its critics. For instance, in outlining the similarities and differences in Freire's thought and certain strands of feminist pedagogy, Weiler (1991) emphasises that while both share a progressive political commitment in their work, Freire's claims for universal goals of emancipation ignore the historical and contextual specifics of oppression, which require a grounded conception of pedagogy. This reflects the experience of a women's consciousness-raising group which uncovered diversity, difference and conflict among women in their experience of oppression with consequences for the possibilities for progressive social change. Weiler argues that it is only through working with difference that an emancipatory pedagogy can be produced, a claim which also resonates with Gore's (1993) position that the claims of critical pedagogy need to be more firmly grounded in specific contexts.

The notion of andragogy as a unifying discourse for establishing the boundaries to the field of adult education has fallen into the background in recent years as its institutional basis has been subject to greater scrutiny. It is certainly questionable that there is a hard and fast distinction between adult learning and that of younger people. The distinction is itself a product of certain psychological discourses of maturation and decline which have come to be challenged. An irony is that many of the ideas adopted as specific to adults in the discourses of andragogy in the 1960s and 1970s in the United Kingdom and North America resonated with those of progressive educators of children. The coherence of adults as a homogeneous group with a distinct and common form of learning has become questionable. Similarly, although emancipatory purposes continue to play a role in the discourses of many adult educators and feminists, critical pedagogues and post-colonial writers, they do not demarcate a specific and bounded adult educational field. The class, gender and age assumptions and ethnocentricism of many of the concepts deployed in the construction of a field of adult education need to be constantly addressed and the consequences of their adoption examined.

However, many of the concepts from such discourses have remained and remain influential and have been sustained in the wider discourses of life-long learning. For instance, the concept of self-direction (Brookfield 1993a) and the centrality given to experience (Kolb 1984; Boud *et al.* 1985, 1993; Weil and McGill 1989) continue to play a central role in the discourses of lifelong learning in the attempt to provide a basis for distinguishing a specific boundary for practice with adults.

The irony of the discourses of adult education as an emancipatory practice and the focus on learning is that while they have been deployed to construct a boundary, actually they have helped to undermine the possibility of differentiating adult education as a specific bounded form of practice. The settings in which adults learn and from which progressive social change can be engendered are far wider than the formal institutionalised provision of adult education. Discourses of adult learning thereby help to undermine the dominant discourses of adult education from within which initially they were largely conceived. This is particularly marked as the discourse shifts from adult learning to lifelong learning. The focus on learning gives rise to the possibility for a discourse of lifelong learning, in the process of which the discourse of adult education is displaced. This has two principal consequences for the boundaries of adult education. First, they begin to shift to encompass the much wider moorland of lifelong learning and, in the process, reinscribe fresh boundaries. Second, certain boundaries become more permeable, or break down subject to the processes of de-differentiation (Lash 1990, Crook *et al.* 1992). These processes are inter-related and reconfigure the terrain of practice, policy and study to which boundary-crossing becomes central – a point to which I will return in chapter 5.

Much of the above is based on analysis framed within the context of the United Kingdom. As suggested in chapter 1, direct national comparisons are inappropriate, but resonances may be found elsewhere. Due recognition needs to be given to the various traditions of the provision of learning opportunities and discourses of adult education that exist within Europe and elsewhere. As the discussion of andragogy demonstrated, adult learning as it is constructed in the United Kingdom cannot be directly mapped onto debates in other European countries. If we take Sweden as an example, post-Second World War state support for adult education embraced a wider range of provision than that in England and Wales, including study circles, folk high schools, formal adult education and employment training (Abrahamsson 1993). However, even here the dominant discourses of adult education tended to focus on the provision of the study circles and the folk high schools in the support of adults who had not achieved their full potential in their initial education. Shifts in emphasis during the late 1980s and early 1990s towards funding occupationally relevant learning and away from earmarked funds for more general adult educational activities have tended, therefore, to be constructed as a threat. In fact, such shifts have complex and contradictory meanings, embracing new possibilities for learning in the process of marginalising others. Thus, while certain of the traditions in the provision of learning opportunities for adults may not have had as discrete a set of institutional bases as in the United Kingdom, privileged sites and discourses – of the study circle and the folk high school – none the less developed.

The wider and less clearly demarcated moorland of lifelong learning results in and from an elision of the boundaries established around specific forms of learning and institutional arrangements. Discourses of lifelong learning and learning opportunities subsume traditionally conceived adult education as part of the moorland. They embrace adult learning wherever it takes place. It is often argued that the distinctions marking the field of adult education – between different forms of provision, between education, training and leisure – do not make sense for adult learners themselves and inhibit access and progression to opportunities. Such boundaries are elided by placing the emphasis on learning, wherever and however it takes place, and the outcomes of that learning. In other words, while discourses of adult education are about forms of provision, those of lifelong learning are about learners. The cultural shift identified previously, placing greater emphasis on individual responsibility for life courses, is also to be found, therefore, in the shift towards conceptualising learning opportunities for adults within a discourse of lifelong learning. Similarly, there is a shift from a focus on the producers to the consumers of learning opportunities. While the shift in discourse opens up a de-differentiated, wider moorland of lifelong learning, it also involves a reconfiguration of what takes place on the terrain. In similar vein, the discourse of lifelong learning gives fresh impetus to notions of a learning society, but reconfigured from a concern with the provision of recurrent education (Abrahamsson 1993) towards supporting diverse learning and learners.

It was the conception of lifelong learning as recurrent education which influenced many of the policies towards adult education in continental

Europe during the 1960s and 1970s. In the 1980s, it has been commented that there has been a shift in concern within discourses of lifelong learning away from access and equity towards vocational relevance. What has not been commented on as extensively is the shift within discourses of lifelong learning from a framing of provision towards a framing of the learner and their responsibility for their own learning. In this sense, while debates have tended to focus on the vocationalising of adult education, a more significant shift may actually be the individualising of lifelong learning (McNair 1996) and its reconstruction as part of lifestyle practices and consumer culture (Edwards and Usher 1997a, 1997b), in which the identity of 'lifestyle learner' overlays and displaces that of 'educated person'.

Since the 1970s, the field of adult education has been subject to increasing processes of challenge. First, the policy frameworks governing the terrain have shifted with an emphasis on economic rather than social policy. Second, the institutionalised boundaries of the field have been challenged. Third, the practices in the field have been subject to disruption, with an emphasis on access and progression through assessment and accreditation. Fourth, the discourses have been and are in a continual process of being reformulated. This challenging and/or shifting of boundaries has occurred between and within institutions and adult learners, within policy formation and within the study of lifelong learning.

There are different ways of evaluating the significance of the shift towards lifelong learning. On the one hand, in encompassing a wider moorland of adult learning, discourses of lifelong learning can attempt to encompass diversity and difference, in which unhelpful distinctions between, for instance, education and training, vocational and non-vocational learning, further and higher education, can be overcome. In other words, boundaries melt and permeability is possible, thereby helping to overcome physical and cultural barriers and inequality. This provides the possibilities of higher education being offered in further education colleges, workplace learning being integrated into that of education and training institutions, informal experiential learning being assessed and accredited – all of which are actually occurring. On the other hand, given the ambivalence of change and Foucault's view that everything is dangerous, the discursive move can be said to itself marginalise significant shifts in what is available to whom. In other words, the boundaries are moved to, for instance, give greater emphasis to the vocational and the credentialising of learning, the outcome of which is uncertain. The possibilities for contesting these shifts may be made more difficult as the discourses of lifelong learning marginalise the significance of the boundaries through which inclusion and exclusion are exercised. While lifelong learning suggests an expansiveness and openness, therefore, its form and characteristics are themselves contested. The most powerful discourses of lifelong learning are those linked to the dominant conception of change, outlined in the previous chapter, promoted by governments and policy-makers of the most developed countries. Thus, the unfreezing of meaning imparted by a discourse of lifelong learning has been channelled into particular directions which tend to selectively support forms of learning that have labour market and economic relevance. Permeability may be increased, but only within the boundaries of lifelong learning and forms of provision relevant to the dominantly conceived directions of change. Complexity and ambivalence openly haunt the moorland whereon direction is uncertain and fog always possible.

Such shifts are never complete or irrevocable. However, discourses of lifelong learning have contributed to the displacement of adult education as the dominant discourse and also a reconfiguration of what constitutes a learning society. The focus on learners and learning both acts to undermine the boundaries around specific arrangements for organising learning and is itself a response to a position in which such boundaries are seen to be problematic. Lifelong learning removes the concern with adults from the margins, as its practices become part of the 'mainstream'. The focus on adult learning as a means of sustaining a specific discourse and practice of adult education has subverted the rationale for that very provision. This has given rise to a discourse of lifelong learning to which the traditionally differentiated structures and provision of learning opportunities are conceived as lacking relevance. In summary, therefore, I am suggesting that a discourse of adult education with a focus on certain providers of learning opportunities – inputs – through which the field was constructed and the boundaries of that field were maintained is being challenged and displaced by a discourse of lifelong learning. The latter focuses on learners and learning – outputs – and a construct of moorland upon which boundaries are permeable and shifting.

As with all interpretative frameworks, questions of the permeability or shifting of boundaries can provide a tidier picture of the processes at work than may be the case. They are rightly subject to challenge. They may also have a cultural specificity, as the precise construction of discourses of 'adult education', 'adult learning', 'lifelong learning' and a 'learning society' may have different meanings and each can be contested. If the Inuit have numerous words for 'snow', then workers with adult learners also have many meanings for 'lifelong learning'. Similarly, alternative formulations may be found. Discourses of 'recurrent education' (Tuijnman and Bengstsson 1991; Chadwick 1993) , and indeed 'lifelong education' (Faure et al. 1972; Gelphi 1985) and 'permanent education' (Pantzar 1993), suggest different histories and traditions in the provision of learning opportunities for adults – the first emphasising a more limited and instrumental set of arrangements than the latter two with their holistic and humanistic ideals. It is necessary to be sensitive to discursive and practical differences even while recognising that the full range of those differences cannot be encompassed in a single text. In a sense, the metaphor of the moorland opens up this realm of diversity as part of the terrain to be explored. It does not do away with boundaries, but it does allow for a reconfiguration of what those boundaries may be and the work they do in a period of de-differentiation and globalisation. There are many parts of a moorland, only some of which are contained within this text.

DE-DIFFERENTIATION IN PRACTICE

There are four aspects surrounding the de-differentiation of the boundaries of practice to be explored in this section. First, the boundaries between different formal providers of learning opportunities, that is, those institutions whose sole task is organising the provision of education and training. This in itself raises questions about what constitutes the 'formal sector'. Second, the boundaries between formal and non-formal providers of learning opportunities – institutions, groups and organisations that provide learning opportunities as part of their function. Third, there are the boundaries between learning organised by institutions for others and informal learning organised by individuals and groups for themselves. Fourth, there are the boundaries between learning as a dedicated activity and incidental learning which takes place as a result of other activities. It will be suggested that each of these boundaries is becoming problematic and subject to processes of de-differentiation.

In 1993 in the United Kingdom, adults over 21 years old constituted over half of those studying in further education colleges and over 25 year olds constituted over half of the students in higher education institutions. This foregrounds the question of the adequacy of any notion of the boundaries of adult learning being confined to specific institutional arrangements for adult education (Field 1991). Nor are such trends confined to the United Kingdom. Adult participation in equivalent institutions elsewhere has also become highly significant. In Australia in 1993, 83 per cent of higher education students were over 25 years old (Australian Bureau of Statistics 1995). As adults participate in a wider range of institutionally organised learning, staff in those institutions have to address a much wider range of learner groups in terms of age and experience. Further and higher education can no longer be assumed to be the institutional bases for a certain – young – age cohort. In many areas, the distinct organisations of adult education have themselves been subsumed into the provision of further or community education, thereby formalising certain processes of de-differentiation.

Boundaries have also broken down between institutions in other ways. For instance, in the types of learning they offer and the currency of the curriculum provided by credits and qualifications. Further education in the United Kingdom is not restricted to vocational education and training. It also offers academic and leisure provision, and, in franchise arrangements with universities, encompasses some higher education provision. This is also true of community colleges in North America and has a longer history than in the United Kingdom. Many colleges provide forms of liberal adult education. Higher education institutions may well provide forms of access courses and the accreditation/recognition of prior learning to enable adults to take degrees. Forms of continuing education to enable students to update their skills and professional skills, knowledge and understanding have also been developed. In more traditional adult education, more emphasis is placed on the provision of certificated and vocational courses to enable adults to develop or update their labour market skills and competences.

Within formal institutions there has also been a challenge to traditional boundaries. Modularisation of the curriculum, credit accumulation and transfer, and flexible forms of delivery break down the boundaries between full- and part-time courses and reconfigure relationships between institutions and learners and what it means to be a 'student' (Edwards 1996). Demarcations between categories of staff break down as people are asked to take on new tasks and responsibilities. Teaching staff may themselves play a variety of roles including, and increasingly, liaising with employers (Chappell and Melville 1995). This blurring of boundaries in staff roles and functions signifies for some a form of de-skilling and increasing productivity – more through 'the system' for less. For others, it entails the multi-skilling of staff and raises issues about the extent to which neo- and/or post-fordism is/are also (a) feature(s) of organizational change in formal institutions of education and training (Edwards 1993a). I shall return to this issue in chapter 5.

It is not solely in the post-compulsory sphere of education and training that the differentiated boundaries of institutions based on servicing particular age groups with particular types of learning opportunities have become problematic. Forms of community education and family literacy schemes have resulted in the breaking down of the boundaries between initial and post-initial education and training. For instance, there were 14,000 adults learning in Scottish schools in 1991 (Tett 1993). Not only does community education involve adults participating in schools, it also involves the 'blurring of boundaries between educational establishments and their surrounding communities, as well as between teachers and students and work and leisure' (Hargreaves, quoted in Martin 1993: 192). In this sense, discourses of community education themselves help undermine the boundaries around a specific institutionalised arrangement for adult education. However, such discourses tend to remain focused on provision and the institutional position of community schools and community colleges, a perspective which Martin (1993: 192) associates with the universal model of community education – the non-selective provision of opportunities for all age groups and social classes. He contrasts this model with the reformist model, with a focus on the primary school, home and neighbourhood and a strategy of selective intervention to assist disadvantaged groups, and the radical model, focused on working-class action groups with a strategy of issue-based education and social action. These contrasting models – signifying different ways in which the notion of 'community' is constructed and bounded, with questions of who is included and excluded within the practices of community education – lead us into the second aspect of de-differentiation. This is the question of boundaries as it applies to formal and non-formal provision.

Increasing recognition is being given to the role of non-formal providers, and particularly employers, in providing settings in which learning takes place, which can be assessed and accredited (Metcalfe 1992a, 1992b). For instance 'higher learning' is not necessarily the preserve of higher education institutions, but can take place in employer training and employee development schemes. Whyte and Crombie (1995: 96) report that in Australia in 1993, participation by adults in formal education courses was 28 per cent, while that in firms was 27 per cent. Similarly, many voluntary groups and campaigning groups, such as Greenpeace, provide learning opportunities, not only to assist in their own organisation, but also to help in the achievement of their goals. Increasing recognition in recent years has been given to the significant amount and forms of learning that are engaged in by adults in such organisations. There have also been an increasing number of private organisations engaging in the provision of opportunities supported by funds from the state, employers and from individuals. In many instances, such organisations have crossed the boundary between formal and informal, as they are in certain areas providing similar services to those that were conceived to be the confines of the more narrowly defined field. Giving due recognition to learning in non-formal settings has become of increasing importance to formal providers of education and training. As they have lost their monopoly in providing learning opportunities, they have moved towards providing forms of assessment and accreditation to encompass learning in the various settings within which it takes place. There have been moves also by formal institutions to continue to provide opportunities for adults to learn in these various settings through the development of forms of distance, open, work-based and flexible learning. Here institutional boundaries are not crossed by adults entering a physical environment, but are mediated by forms of learning conducive to the learner's non-formal setting. I shall examine this two-pronged approach to bridging boundaries in more detail in the next chapter.

De-differentiation provides the grounds for a variety of relationships between formal and non-formal provision with varied and contested relationships between groups of learners and providers of learning opportunities. It also raises questions of the boundaries between learning that is organised by providers and informal learning that is organised by learners, such as through cookery and do-it-yourself manuals, or as part of local community activities and action (Deem 1993; Lovett 1993; Welton 1993b).

This boundary was highlighted in the work of Tough in the 1970s. Tough (1993) conducted surveys of adults and discovered a high percentage were engaging in 'learning projects' which involved no contact with specific organisations. People used the resources and learning strategies available to them in their communities – people, books, radio, television – to undertake their projects. They were also focused on personal development issues rather than vocational skills and/or social action. In many ways, Tough's analysis is consistent with the view of a shift towards a consumer culture and learning as an aspect of lifestyle discussed in the previous chapter (Field 1994; Bell 1996). Here informal, self-organised learning outside of the boundaries of institutions is constructed as the primary learning activity of adults in the social formation.

Tough's work has been both influential and controversial. It has been argued his samples were unrepresentative and, as such, ignored the impact of such factors as class, gender and 'race' upon learning. The research also fails to give due attention to the importance of resources being available for people to be able to undertake their learning projects. However, it remains significant in questioning the boundary between institutionally organised learning and adult learners, insofar as learning rests with the individual and groups rather than with institutions. Thus, home-based 'leisure' activities may well entail learning, even if not as a specific 'project'. In the United Kingdom in the 1980s, patterns of participation in such activities such as watching television, listening to the radio or gardening generally rose (Central Statistical Office 1993). This included reading books, suggesting concerns over literacy and the impact of other media may have been over-emphasised as part of the discourse of 'failure' adopted in relation to formal providers of learning opportunities. The emphasis on the individual in Tough's work is consistent with a discourse of lifelong learning. It also sits within cultural changes which place greater responsibility for lifestyle on the individual, thereby contributing to and reflecting the wider individualising processes of the contemporary period in certain parts of the globe. In other words, the harnessing of adults as 'learners' rather than 'students' can be seen as part of the reflexive responsibility for the self and of learning to learn in different settings – a harnessing which is central to the development of certain conceptions of a learning society. In this sense, discourses of life-long learning and adults-as-learners need to be situated within the contested processes of change, rather than as a neutral or 'natural' description of what adults do.

This also highlights the importance of the role of both the broadcast media and the increasing range of consumables available for self-use and informal learning, such as videos, computer programs and CD-ROMs. The possibility of undertaking learning projects is obviously greatly enhanced insofar as adults do not have to attend specific institutions. Here the notions of 'edu-tainment' and 'info-cation' enter the discourse to encompass the hybridity of education, entertainment and the media. As I have suggested, the growth and development of the latter provide the possibility for formal institutions to be by-passed on a far more significant scale than might have been the case previously. The scale and range of materials now available in certain parts of the globe are far more significant and of far greater variety than was previously the case. When roughly 99 per cent of households possess a television and 72 per cent and 80 per cent a video recorder, as was the case in Britain in 1990 and Australia in 1993 respectively (Central Statistical Office 1993: 14; Australian Bureau of Statistics 1995: 166), the potential resources available to adults from which to learn are expanded significantly. However, a question remains about the extent to which those resources are constructed as being used for 'learning'. In a survey of adults in the United Kingdom, Sargant (1991) found that only 26 per cent classified themselves as 'learning' at home from a book and a mere 2 per cent as 'learning' at home from television. This suggests a disjunction between the discourses of those concerned with lifelong learning and adults themselves, in which certain types of experience are constructed as learning rather than, or as well as, in other ways, such as leisure, entertainment or even 'vegging out'. Learning is given an elasticity of meaning in certain discourses which may not be apparent in the discourses of many adults.

It is therefore no coincidence that the discourses and practices of 'experiential learning' and 'learning from experience' have developed and extended their reach as the focus has shifted towards lifelong learning. Such notions construct a range of non-formal and informal experiences as learning. However, in a sense, they remain conceptually loose, for what learning is not experiential in some form? Even formal study entails a certain form of experience for the learner. However, this does not stop it from being powerful. Experiential learning has been deployed to undermine the boundaries between adults and institutions, producing a greater permeability, improving access through assessment and accreditation, and enhancing what are understood as legitimate forms of learning. The extent of that permeability, however, is not limitless and needs to be examined, as only certain forms of learning tend to be given recognition by providers of learning opportunities and employers. The powerful function of assessment and accreditation is not lost through recognition of experiential learning and, in some ways, may be said to extend the exercise of governmentality (Usher and Edwards 1994). Adults may therefore be required to demonstrate specified competences and/or learning outcomes for the boundaries to melt. In this sense, learners may be able only to commodify certain of their experiences as learning in exchange for qualifications, that which is valued in assessment and accreditation procedures (Usher 1993a). This usefully illustrates the ambivalence in the processes of de-differentiation whereby as certain boundaries shift, become more permeable and break down, fresh forms of re-differentiation are inscribed.

This is also true for the boundaries between informal and incidental learning (Marsick and Watkins 1990). Incidental learning, like experiential learning, recognises that much learning can take place even when it is not specifically planned. Learning can be a by-product of other activities. Examples include learning from mistakes or from social interaction. Once again, there is the question of whether such activities are constructed within a discourse of learning or not. For the individuals concerned, incidental learning may simply be tacit understandings and actions and not considered as learning. There are boundaries between such activities and learning. For institutions and adults seeking to make boundaries more permeable, the construction of these activities as incidental learning may provide the poss-ibility for those individuals to be brought within the orbit of the institutionalised provision of opportunity, to become part of a learning society.

Examination of de-differentiation in some of the practices of lifelong learning reveals a central paradox. On the one hand, the discourse of life-long learning undermines many of the pre-existing boundaries of the field of adult education. On the other, it is formal providers of learning opportu-nities who largely seek to construct adults' experiences as 'learning'. This suggests the boundaries of the field are being extended rather than being completely undermined. In other words, a process of recuperation is possible, wherein discourses of lifelong learning can be said to extend insti-tutional boundaries and the governance of 'experience' rather than simply supporting the alternative spaces within and from which adults' experiences are framed. Field (1995: 153) suggests that as 'boundaries become more permeable, it is far easier for knowledge to flow, and this creates enormous potential for learning'. However, the issues of boundaries and de-differentiation are ones of complexity, ambivalence and change. Central to that complexity is the policy framework within and through which lifelong learning is constructed.

DE-DIFFERENTIATION IN POLICY

Generalised discussions of policy can be deeply misleading, as there are differences within and between nations and cultures in their structures and processes of policy formation. Sub-national and supra-national levels of the state, as well as non-governmental organisations and individual institutions, all have a role in the complexity of policy formation, decision-making and implementation. Once again, while attention will be drawn to contrasting positions and possible resonances, it is issues as they have been formulated in the United Kingdom which will be foregrounded here. This in itself raises issues, as the situation within the four nations of the United Kingdom – England, Northern Ireland, Scotland, Wales – is not always the same and variations exist within the nations, for instance, between different Local Education Authorities/Regional Councils, Training and Enterprise Councils/Local Enterprise Companies. In addition, within the European

Union the role of the European Commission and Union-wide legislation is increasingly influential.

Two inter-related aspects of de-differentiation in policy will be discussed here. First, the responsibilities of state departments for lifelong learning. Second, whether lifelong learning is conceived as a dimension of economic and/or social policy. However, this does not exhaust the possibilities for analysis.

After the Second World War, the field of adult education was largely demarcated by specific institutional arrangements in the United Kingdom. At that time, the focus of the state was on building the compulsory sector of education as part of the process of constructing the welfare state – assuming and seeking to suppress conflict and/or build a consensual society. The importance of adult education was limited. The then Ministry of Labour did have responsibility for adult (re)training, but it was the Ministry of Education which provided the dominant policy focus and discursive tradition with the provision of non-vocational adult education as its primary concern. This reflected the view of a social formation in which initial education and training were sufficient to the needs of the individual throughout their lifespan in a period of large-scale, low-skilled employment and gender differentiation. The provision of lifelong learning opportunities was not considered a necessity for the state and, therefore, was not in need of coherent support. Responsibility was devolved to local government and the Responsible Bodies, that is, the extra-mural departments of the 'old' (pre-1992) universities and the Workers' Education Association. In policy terms, the field of adult education was encompassed by a department with specific responsibilities for liberal or general education, a position which was replicated at other levels of the state, wherein specific responsibilities fell within the boundaries of specific departments. Differentiation in the structures of policy formation governed policy implementation.

In 1996, the boundaries between the departments of state continue to exist, but they have been reconfigured and the influence of policy across organisational boundaries is more apparent. In the United Kingdom, policy in relation to lifelong learning has brought together previously separated strands. In 1995, the then Department for Education and the Employment Department merged to become the Department for Education and Employment. In Scotland, the new department was called the Scottish Office Education and Industry Department, reflecting the trend towards de-differentiation, although of a different form to elsewhere in the United Kingdom. Similar trends have been witnessed elsewhere. In Australia, for instance, policy is governed at the federal level by the Department of Employment, Education, Training and Youth Affairs. However, this does not exhaust the extent of the influence of policy on lifelong learning. For example, in the United Kingdom, Department of Social Security regulations on receipt of benefits and participation in training affect the learning opportunities available to the unwaged. Department of Transport policies and their impact on public transport impact upon the mobility and availability of opportunities. Department of Health policies contribute to forms of learning – nurse education and health education – and help to determine who is healthy enough to engage in different forms of learning. Department for National Heritage policies support the cultural and historical legacy which adults visit in large numbers. Policy towards lifelong learning is developed within an overlapping and not necessarily co-ordinated series of policy bases within the nation state.

This is in part due to a distinction between the direct and indirect outcomes of policy. Many departments of state do not focus on the implications for adult learners of their policies, but none the less have an impact upon the practices of lifelong learning. While many adults pursue their own independent learning outside the gambit of direct policy influence, indirectly that policy powerfully influences what is available to whom and how. For instance, cuts in expenditure on libraries can reduce the current books and services available from which adults are freely able to learn. Alternatively, the role of libraries can be expanded by directing funding towards services provided through the introduction of information and communications technologies. Similarly, increases in television licence fees or the cost of heating may affect what people are able to afford in pursuing their own interests in their homes. In other words, the 'private' life of the individual or family is not separated from the effects of 'public' policy, but, at least partly, is constituted in particular forms by it. As such, 'policy constitutes all who come within its reach as potential political actors who can open this area to a politics of voice and representation' (Yeatman 1994a: 110).

What is at stake here is the extent to which national policy is or can be co-ordinated in the provision of opportunities for adults, the extent to which the overlapping boundaries of state departmental influence are able to offer coherence for adult learners, to insert the structured heterogeneity of difference into policy processes and outcomes. For while de-differentiation has taken place, it has taken particular and restricted forms. It is through focusing on the indirect as well as direct outcomes of policy that the potential for further de-differentiation comes to the fore. Here there is a paradox in policy as an aspect of governmentality in the modern nation state. A coherent policy would appear to require de-differentiation, but the processes of rationalisation in the bureaucratic state require differentiation.

Tuckett (1996) suggests that the United Kingdom government has constantly failed to come up with a coherent policy and firm legislative base for lifelong learning. Instead it has instigated a range of initiatives directed at providers of learning opportunities and employers to support specific areas of work within the field – REPLAN for unwaged adults, Investors in People for employers. In his discussion of labour market policy, Haughton (1993: 138–139) also draws attention to lack of coherence in policy due to its formulation based on differentiated departmental boundaries – 'policies to combat skills problems need to be formulated coherently and consistently across traditional government department boundaries, since the problems themselves are so multifaceted and inter-linked, often lying outside the labour market as such'. Here the United Kingdom, and particularly England and Wales, is often contrasted with Scotland and other northern European and some third world countries.

The contrast with Scotland rests on the relative autonomy of the Scottish Office Education and Industry Department in framing and implementing policies agreed nationally. Scotland has a certain amount of discretion in the interpretation and implementation of policy, as indeed do Wales and Northern Ireland. In 1975, Scotland produced the Alexander Report (Scottish Education Department 1975). This was the basis for the national provision of community education linking adult and initial education. However, even here, although the boundaries vary with those elsewhere in the United Kingdom, they none the less remain and overlap. The Alexander Report, like the similar Russell Report (1973) in England and Wales, was restricted to reviewing policy in relation to adult non-vocational education. Thus, the direct and indirect policies relating to other spheres of lifelong learning were not embraced as a matter of policy coherence across forms of provision and departments of state.

Elsewhere in Europe it is often suggested that policy is more coherent and provision better. Certain countries, particularly in Scandinavia, have for a long period been held up as models for the provision of adult education. Here, for certain periods, particularly in the 1960s and 1970s, legislation was guided by a policy of redressing educational disadvantage and inequality with specific Acts for the provision of adult education (Nordhaug 1986; Rubenson 1993). In Sweden during the 1970s, large resources were allocated towards the provision of liberal adult educational opportunities through ideologically varied folk high schools – providing for those who had not completed secondary education – and study circles – in which groups of adults were able to meet in each other's homes. State support was available to a wide range of organisations, including churches, trade unions and temperance societies. The state supported a diverse range of liberal adult education opportunities. Yet although this diversity may have resulted from a certain coherence in policy, whether it provided coherence in provision or overcame the inequities in the system is less clear. Even in Sweden, a relatively coherent adult education policy did not embrace the full moorland of lifelong learning. Boundaries remained, most notably in the separation of state policy in relation to the labour market from that of liberal adult education. How the latter was meant to address educational inequalities without addressing the former is a somewhat startling omission, although reflecting the modernist optimism in the emancipatory capacity of education and its social policy basis in that period. As Nordhaug (1989) suggests of Norway, where similar policies to Sweden were pursued, the goal of redressing inequality was not achieved despite state support. More generally, it is suggested that welfare state policies have benefited the middle classes more than the poorer and most marginalised sections of the social formation.

Lack of policy coherence is not restricted, therefore, to the United Kingdom. A 1992 report on the provision of learning opportunities for adults found that across the European Union there was a lack of coherence in policy at national, regional and local level (Wouters 1992). This was felt to be a major barrier to provision and echoed earlier findings to the same effect (Himmelstrup *et al.* 1981). Similarly, a more focused report on vocational education and training in France, Germany, Italy and the Netherlands found that provision for continuing education was 'generally diverse and uncoordinated' (FEU 1992: 73). Even at its best, the provision of learning opportunities for adults is co-ordinated insufficiently to maximise access, participation and progression. In Japan, where support for learning to sustain economic competitiveness is held up as an example and threat to populations elsewhere in the globe, lack of policy coherence is still found to be a problem (McCormick 1989).

Many post-colonial countries initially produced national plans for adult education in support of economic development and nation-building. For a large number, this involved provision for adults who had not experienced initial education or had experienced it only to a limited extent. Particular emphasis was placed on literacy and other basic skills, including health education, often as an aspect of population management. The consequences of and responses to colonialism resulted in very specific goals for adults' education. However, lack of resources meant that in many countries these goals could never fully or even partially be achieved. Often reliant on forms of aid from the first world, more restricted and focused projects, often linked to dimensions of community development, have tended to predominate in the provision of learning opportunities for adults.

This brief survey illustrates both the problem of differentiation in policy for the provision of lifelong learning and the general consensus over the value of policy coherence. Policy coherence provides the boundaries for a field which can be rationally managed. In many ways, boundedness is both a product of and produces a form of technical rationality. Yet, as indicated in the discussion of the direct and indirect consequences of policy, a moorland of lifelong learning is far more complex and diverse than is suggested by the metaphor of a field of adult education. It is questionable therefore whether policy coherence is even an achievable goal. In the United Kingdom and Australia, where attempts have been made to extend the boundaries by establishing a department of state with a wider remit than education, the influence of other departmental policies on lifelong learning is still apparent. Co-ordination across all the different departments of state, effectively combining aspects of economic and social policy, would seem somewhat unrealistic given their different foci and priorities and the sheer complexity of governance in contemporary social formations. While policy coherence is discursively constituted as more desirable than its other – incoherence – this marginalises and suppresses the very complexity it seeks to embrace.

This assumes, of course, a position in which the state takes an active role to provide policy coherence in support of lifelong learning. However, under the influence of new right thinking, the trend in government in the United Kingdom has been to leave this more to a market regulated by centrally established funding and quality criteria – an administered market. Similar trends can also be seen in many countries. First, in the greater emphasis on lifelong learning for the labour market. Second, in the nation state's withdrawal from responsibility for establishing a coherent framework for the managed provision of education and training of adults (Kivinen and Rinne 1993). In Sweden, 'the "grand plan" of coherent strategy of recurrent education has seen its best days. Collectively organised solutions backed by overall organisationally pre-fabricated patterns are no more in service' (Abrahamsson 1993: 67).

This redrawing of the relations between the state and civil society has been marked by a shift towards the market rather than state as responsible for the provision of learning opportunities as part of a general shift in the discourses of the state from welfare to competition and performativity (Lyotard 1984; Yeatman 1994a). This is part of and a response to some of the wider processes of globalisation. Nation states are losing effective and exclusive 'control' of their economies and cultures, and their ability to use this control politically for the fulfilment of collective goals of social betterment. One powerful response has been an ideological reluctance by governments to engage in programmatic interventions to achieve such goals. The result is an increasing withdrawal from and reconfiguring of the boundaries of civil society by the state and with that a greater part of the social formation being subject to certain market mechanisms. The state cannot manage lifelong learning rationally, so it is left to an administered market in its diverse forms to provide any coherence. The former Employment Department (1993: 5) in the United Kingdom illustrated this position admirably – 'national development work will only be supported centrally where it is clear there is a market failure preventing the private sector from undertaking development of wider, general benefit'. Responding to market failure rather than a more active interventionist role is constructed as the function of national government. Any coherence is to be provided not through policy focused on providers but by the market in qualifications (Employment Department 1993; Fennell 1994).

The discussion so far has been about the nation state as the primary focus of policy. This is understandable given the powerful role it continues to have. Even if the nation state does not take direct responsibility for providing coherence, the process of delegation to other bodies, such as Funding Councils, Local Education Authorities/Regional Councils, Training and Enterprise Councils/Local Enterprise Companies, comes from national government and may be returned to it through changes in policy and legislation. While some have proposed market responses to questions over the adequacy and ability of the nation state to provide coherence, others have suggested coherence needs to be sought at a different level of the state (McNay 1991). This takes us into the question of boundaries between policy at those different levels – institutional, local, regional, national, supranational. If the boundaries within one level of the state are problematic, the fact that there are many organisations engaging in relevant policy development and implementation makes the scene even more complex. Within the context of the European Union, some argue that a combination of European and local/regional policy is necessary (Cripps and Ward 1993). However, given national sensibilities and interests, the possible diffusion of the responsibilities of the nation state beyond certain limits seems unlikely. Within the state, different organisations can adopt different policies with implication for access and participation. For instance, in 1994, the Further Education Funding Council for England adopted a policy of full fee concessions for unemployed adults attending courses. By contrast, most Local Education Authority-funded provision only offered partial fee reductions.

At the various levels of policy, the problems of boundaries and coherence are as prevalent as at the level of the nation state. At the local level, the field of lifelong learning is not encompassed simply by local/regional authorities and responsible bodies. Training and Enterprise Councils/Local Enterprise Companies play an important role. The policies of individual institutions, employers, trade unions and voluntary groups, whose funding may partly come from the state, will influence outcomes. Multinational companies may have world-wide policies which may affect both their employees' entitlement to training and employee development. At the supra-national level, European Union countries are subject increasingly to legislation taken at a European level and the policies and sources of funding made available through the European Commission. Most notably, this has impacted on provision for the unemployed, regional development and women returning to the labour market, where funding has contributed significantly to the development of opportunities.

More fundamental to this discussion is the question of the actual possibility for policy coherence in relation to the moorland of lifelong learning given the number and diversity of the organisations and learners involved. Coherence in policy on lifelong learning would seem to be an impossibility, even as it is discursively constituted as desirable. Even where attempts are made to realise policy in relation to a specific bounded field of adult education, the direct and indirect effects of policies adopted elsewhere will have unexpected and often undesirable consequences. Policies on open and distance learning or the provision of learning opportunities for unemployed adults – where boundaries are drawn in respect of a specific form of provision or group of adults – may produce some positive results, but how do they cohere within the whole 'system'? For instance, even while there is policy support for adult participation in economically relevant learning by governments, cuts in funding to local/regional authorities to support policy goals of lowering inflation and overcoming budget deficits have meant that certain forms of grant awards have been withdrawn (NAEGA 1994). We are left with the impression of the 'messiness and complexity' mentioned by Ball (1990a) as an inherent part of policy influence, formation and implementation.

To suggest this seems to fly in the face of the normative goal of rational management which underpins dominant discourses on policy, to which differentiation and coherence are central. However, to ask who is or should be responsible for the production of a coherent policy on lifelong learning, or even the bounded provision of 'vocational education and training' or 'adult education', does not provide a clear answer. Within the complex network of states, institutions and organisations involved in the provision of learning opportunities, policy coherence does not appear to be a feasible task. It is for such reasons that many governments have moved towards market 'solutions'. As the state is unable to produce the policy coherence necessary for the provision of lifelong learning opportunities, a market responding to consumer demand is held to be more successful. Even if one rejects market responses, it may be that a continued argument for coherence in policies on lifelong learning is simply impossible given the range of variables involved. In a period of increasing de-differentiation, the possibility of policy coherence, or even, as some have argued naively, its achievement, is highly questionable. It remains, however, as a continuingly powerful modernist discourse of the role of the nation state in the governability and governance of the social formation – managed and manageable (Miller and Rose 1993). Such discourses are a powerful form of 'witchcraft' which suggests a beneficial neutrality in the possibility of making provision work better while marginalising the complexities and inequalities it produces (Stronach 1989). De-differentiation and a discourse of a moorland exposes the witchcraft of policy coherence and the impossibility of the rational management of change in a period in which change is less predictable. Here it is interesting to note the shift in some management discourses away from technical rational models to approaches based on craft and artistry.

Differentiated state responsibility for lifelong learning opportunities in terms of both specific departmental responsibilities and responsibilities at different levels of policy is clearly problematic. Discourses, such as those of 'adult education', 'vocational education' or 'training', may result in and from certain boundaries in policy-making and the institutional bases of policy-making, but they do not and cannot embrace the full moorland of lifelong learning. The latter would appear to involve an inconceivable co-ordination of policy-making given its own 'incoherence'. Boundaries place barriers in the way of permeability, access and progression and fail to support the wider moorland of lifelong learning. However, the discourse of moorland fore-grounds the terrain as ungovernable in conventional policy terms. Within market-orientated governments, this is manifested in the view that governments 'distort' the market through the use of policy instruments. However, certain boundaries may be necessary to maintain the legitimacy of governments and organisations as somehow in control of events rather than simply subject to them – normalising a particular order of things through the deployment of a discourse of policy coherence. These boundaries may be necessary also to counteract the 'distorting' effects of the market on issues of equality and exclusion. In this, the boundaries inscribed in state policy become powerful governors of the life opportunities of adults, even as their control is exposed as largely reactive and limiting, and the boundaries as constructs of discourse rather than resting in the phenomena themselves. In other words, governments may not be able to provide a coherent policy for the total provision of learning opportunities for all adults. However, they none the less are powerful in steering and influencing the directions of change and development. A more modest and de-differentiated policy towards lifelong learning may therefore legitimately direct resources to certain forms of provision and/or certain groups of learners. This may sit uneasily with the universal claims of many educators, but signifies a discourse that locates the particular groups and settings of particular forms of practice within a moorland of difference.

Boundaries in policy have so far been explored in relation to the institutional sites of responsibility for policy-making. Linked to this is the question of what guides policy. What assumptions are there in the policy goals set and what are those goals? Who sets the goals? In the previous chapter, attention was drawn to the influence of cultural restorationists, modernisers and progressives on policy. Are these influences embedded in public policy and, if so, in what ways? What forms of provision are promoted through public policy? To what extent is de-differentiation a process to be found here?

The overall public policy framework governing the terrain of lifelong learning is fundamental to the types of provision supported through public funds. This links to the discussion of economic change, as there has been a clear shift in the last twenty years from conceiving lifelong learning predominantly within a social policy framework towards a more explicit economic policy framework. This is true across a range of countries. In the immediate post-war period, adult education was conceived largely within a social policy perspective, contributing to the improvement of general social conditions. In the United Kingdom, this was an aspect of the development of the welfare state, effectively inscribing a liberal progressive ethos into the provision for adult education. This overlayed a more social redistributary conception of adult education to promote greater equity, which has continued to challenge the welfarist model (Thompson 1980; Lovett 1988). The latter is embedded in a discourse of the 'adult education movement', which initially aligned itself to working-class interests. In more recent years, this has widened, diversified and in some ways fragmented as the white male boundaries of what it meant to be 'working class' or 'oppressed' have been exposed and the interests of women and minority ethnic groups asserted.

Also in recent years, and with greater significance, the social policy framework governing the field of adult education has been challenged by a market model. In the process, the welfarist model of adult education contributing to social improvement has been displaced by a market model as a condition for economic competitiveness. Such shifts have been identified in many countries (Arvidson 1993; Rubenson 1993). In this way, it can be argued that a social redistributive movement has been overlayed and displaced by a liberal progressive service which, in turn, has been overlayed and displaced by a market-orientated business. In the process, public policy has shifted from an emphasis on social improvement secure in its economic prosperity to one of economic competitiveness insecure about economic improvement.

Quigley (1993) suggests that it is a shift towards a market model within social policy that is reshaping the provision of learning opportunities for adults. However, an alternative formulation is that there has been a shift in public policy from conceiving education as part of social policy to constructing it more specifically as an aspect of economic policy. While the economy produced sufficient surplus through taxation, the field of education and training and its relationship with the economy could be left to employers, trade unions and individuals. However, as the economic competitiveness of certain countries deteriorated, it became more important for consideration and action to be taken to provide learning opportunities to more satisfactorily meet the perceived needs of the economy – even if the policy is directed at encouraging employers and individuals to take greater responsibility for lifelong learning. Much of the policy focus for lifelong learning shifted from the social policy domain to the economic – and a market model within that domain – causing much discomfort to many practitioners who situate themselves within a social policy framework – either a liberal welfare or social redistribution discourse. Here is yet another paradox. The state takes a greater interest in lifelong learning as part of economic policy, but, under the influence of new right thinking, devolves the responsibility for the effective development of opportunities onto an administered market.

Traces of different policy discourses can be found in actual policies rather than the clear differentiations suggested by typologies. For instance, within the discussion of the economic competitiveness of the European Union in the 1990s there was concern also for social exclusion, suggesting a related social policy focus (Commission of the European Communities 1993b, 1995). While the policy framework is primarily economic, there is potential for a de-differentiated perspective in public policy in which the economic and social dimensions are addressed together rather than separately – 'education and training should be looked at from the point of view of both social values and economic objectives' (*Le Magazine for Education, Training and Youth in Europe* 1996: 6). Similarly, support for equal opportunities and/or the targeting of specific 'under-represented' groups may still be an important goal of policy even within a framework positing economic goals and market 'solutions', as has been the case in much modernising discourse. For instance, in 1994–5, despite the increased marketisation of provision, the Welsh Further Education Funding Council developed an enhancement to the funding formula to 'include an element which would encourage institutions to attract students from neighbourhoods which were under-represented in post-school education' (*Adults Learning* 1994: 138). Boundaries between different policy frameworks may not be as clear as is often suggested. Indeed differentiated discourses of social and economic policy marginalise the social aspects of economic policy and the economic aspects of social policy and raise the issue of the need for a revitalised debate concerning a political economy of lifelong learning.

There are many policy discourses within the moorland of lifelong learning, and the discourse of moorland foregrounds the relevance of those policies to lifelong learning. Many working within a liberal service model of adult education would also construct themselves as contributing to the social redistributive goals of an adult education movement. Similarly, there is no necessity that lifelong learning as a dimension of economic policy should be provided through a business model based on market principles. Economic change can be a planned or structured process in which, for instance, learning opportunities are provided as a service by the state for the well-being of the community and economy as a whole. This is often suggested to be the case in Germany and Japan, although there remain questions of who is constituted as part of the 'community'. For alternative approaches to be developed requires forms of cultural and political change.

The links between the different forms of provision and the purposes they seek to fulfil have been the subject of much debate. Some have sought to criticise the de-radicalising effects on the provision of learning opportunities for adults, as it became a concern of institutions operating within a public policy framework. Others have celebrated the support that public policy can provide, but are concerned about the impact of market approaches. In examining specific developments in the moorland of lifelong learning, we need to look at the explicit and implicit economic, social and political purposes and consequences, and the ways in which different forms of provision enmesh with each other. The attention given by policy-making bodies to lifelong learning, as a dimension of economic policy and market-orientated social policy, already assumes and produces certain explicit and implicit social, economic and political outcomes. The boundaries between policy strands cannot be clearly differentiated from each other in the sense that is often suggested. Such boundaries may exist more on the basis of differentiated departmental competition within the state for status and funds than in the actual policy issues themselves. Boundaries and differentiation and therefore permeability and de-differentiation are the outcomes of and contribute to political contestation, an effect of which is re-differentiation. Each department produces a discourse of policy issues from its own institutional base with its own concerns and 'solutions'. What the United Kingdom and other governments are doing in shifting towards market-led policies is to emphasise the importance of learning by giving learners entitlements to obtain guidance and learning opportunities through such approaches as vouchers, career development loans, or graduate taxes. However, this is set within a specific set of vocationally relevant limits. In other words, even as the moorland is opened up with a focus on learners and learning, fresh constraints and boundaries are reinscribed. There is constant movement in these processes and the attempt to differentiate a field of provision in policy is constantly de-differentiated by the paradoxes and ambiguities of this process and the fact that policy implementation is not a fully rational process.

Policies based on differentiation define a certain field of learning opportunities, create boundaries between the responsibilities which are the state's and those which belong elsewhere, and attempt to sustain boundaries between different forms of provision. However, within a discourse of lifelong learning there is a shifting of and across such boundaries. It is the learning, not who provides it, which becomes most important. The moorland of lifelong learning, therefore, is unstable, with the features changing according to light and weather conditions. While policy attempts to operate within a process of boundary-setting in terms of institutional arrangements and goals – to rationally manage a field – these boundaries are subject to continual shifts which may or may not increase and result from de-differentiation. A specific policy in support of lifelong learning will not embrace the full moorland of learning opportunities for adults. Boundaries will be re-differentiated in the process of formulating policies, even as discourses of lifelong learning de-differentiate any such attempts at boundary maintenance.

DE-DIFFERENTIATING THE SUBJECT

Earlier I suggested that the notion of andragogy as a distinct field of adult education was, at least partly, developed to provide the base for the study of adult education within institutions of higher education. The creation of an institutional and professional base and status for adult education as a professional field of practice depended upon establishing adult education as a bounded subject of study and research. One of the characteristics of a profession is argued to be its 'expert knowledge', and this is provided traditionally through academic study at the higher education – and often post-graduate – level. Talking of the twentieth-century professional, Aronowitz and DiFazio (1994: 209) argue that 'the core required courses signify to the rest of the profession that the student has undergone an adequate intellectual preparation and . . . has been properly initiated into the values and tradition of the profession'. Adult education as an institutionalised form of provision is given a power base, however limited, through the construction of a cadre of professional adult educators and a canonical body of adult education knowledge. It is the framing of the latter within a technical rational paradigm that not only makes professionalisation possible, but also restricts what can be constructed as 'adult education' properly speaking (Briton 1996). Without canonical knowledge, adult education remains – and some may argue, should have remained – a voluntarist terrain of activity outside the realm of public policy and professionalisation. Alternatively, it is situated within a realm of salaried work, part of public sector trade unionism.

Debates about whether adult education could be constituted as a discipline or field of study have been part of the struggle for legitimacy. Disciplinary knowledge is developed within the differentiated subjects within universities, initially of the natural and human sciences, but then becoming paradigmatic of the social sciences and humanities as well. Disciplines depend upon constructing distinctive methods directed at and constructing specific 'objects of knowledge' and forms of subjectivity – the subject discipline also disciplining the subject (Edwards and Usher 1994a). For instance, in studying philosophy one is disciplined into the ways of knowing and bodies of knowledge associated with being a philosopher.

The application of disciplinary criteria to the social sciences was always problematic – and indeed is problematic for the natural sciences as well – as the possibilities of working within a distinctive methodology came to be questioned. A diversity of methodologies developed within disciplines and, with that, the disciplinary boundaries came to be challenged. While the traditional disciplines still remain powerful, none the less in recent years there has been the growth and development of multi-disciplinary, inter-disciplinary and trans-disciplinary subjects more generally. Courses abound in media studies, women's studies, bio-chemistry, environmental science, cultural studies, and so on. Fields of study sit alongside and in some ways displace disciplines. It is important to note, however, that while fields of study de-differentiate disciplines, they none the less are constructed as bounded subjects.

Education is a good example of this process. Constructed as a field of study from a range of disciplines, including philosophy, history, psychology and sociology, it provided the basis for the expert knowledge of the emerging education profession. It has also had an uneasy status in universities as an 'applied', non-disciplinary area. If this uneasy status as a field of study has been true for education as a whole, it has been even more the case for adult education. What constitutes adult education as a bounded field of study within education? As we saw, the distinctiveness of adults as learners and a distinctive set of institutionalised practices were key to this process, but the basis for that boundary is itself being challenged, as is adult education as a field of study. For many, this is a point of regret, but there is a reflexive lack of engagement with the multi-disciplinary construction of itself as an object of knowledge which internally undermines claims to distinctiveness as a bounded field of study. The strength of the disciplinary processes on the subjectivities of the professional adult educator, therefore, may be more limited, or more diverse given its multi-disciplinary terrain as a field, or, in the light of the argument above, a moorland of study.

The production of knowledge generally is moving in directions of de-differentiation and, in a sense, those who have been involved in the academic study of adult education could be ground-breakers drawing upon different methods, forms of analysis and bodies of knowledge to produce a different object of knowledge – a moorland of lifelong learning. To a certain extent, this is already happening and this text is a reflexive example of such processes, drawing as it does on a range of academic and non-academic literature from a range of countries and a range of subjects. In this way, in examining the terrain of study, it exemplifies reflexively the permeability of boundaries across different academic bodies of knowledge, across academic and other forms of knowledge available through a variety of media, and the influences of globalisation on what can be included in and excluded from such a text. What this suggests is that both the process of knowledge production and the object of knowledge are being de-differentiated with the boundaries of the terrain of study as a field breaking down and the methodological approaches becoming more diverse and eclectic – dare one say, in the discussion of education, ill-disciplined! What this means and what this text exemplifies is a changing of the subject in the many senses of the latter. This is both a response and a contribution to change, raising and reflecting questions about what, if anything, is the field of adult education and who are the adult educators, once a universal canon of knowledge is no longer constructed as a basis of *the* profession. Diversity of knowledge and diversity of subjectivity would appear to mark the moorland of lifelong learning. The danger of such processes is that those concerned with the moorland of lifelong learning may lose a specific and collective base of study in universities. With that may disappear the notion of adult educators as a profession with expert knowledge. The possibilities include engaging with a more diverse range of knowledge, learners, settings and practices and producing more complex, ambivalent and culturally located knowledges of that moorland. Rather than a bounded field of professional adult educators, there is the possibility of a wider, more diverse cadre of 'cultural workers' (Giroux 1992).

These are complex issues in themselves with uncertain directions and consequences. What I want to do is attempt an analysis which reflexively illustrates the significance of some of what I have just argued. De-differentiation undercuts the boundaries of adult education as a field of study and provides a possibility for a richer terrain of study, including concepts drawn from a range of locations and, with that, different objects of knowledge. Central to the processes of differentiation are the concepts of 'education', 'training' and 'leisure'. These are integral to the construction of the field of adult education and adult education as a field, and are also very influential in policy. Traditionally, adult education has demarcated itself as a field of study from training and leisure. Drawing on earlier work (Edwards and Usher 1997a), I want to argue that these conceptual boundaries, and the practices and policies they reflect and reinforce, are breaking down and shifting. Attempts to analyse this within adult education as a field of study have tended to be defensive and nostalgic, failing to come to terms with the significance of the processes at play. The analysis here draws upon discourses other than those of adult education and offers a suggestive, if more ambivalent, understanding of what is taking place in the moorland of study and the terrain of study as a moorland.

Much has been written on the question of the boundaries between 'education', 'training' and 'leisure' (Dearden 1984; Kenney and Reid 1986; Young 1993; Campanelli *et al.* 1994). The debate is highly significant as the values placed on each and the boundaries between them affect not only the forms of learning opportunity available to adults, but also who is given responsibility for delivering and funding those opportunities. Within conditions of differentiation, education, training and leisure are constructed as offering separate and specific forms of provision. Education is constructed as providing for the general development of individuals and is primarily a responsibility of the state. Training provides (mostly young) people with employment and job-related skills and is primarily the responsibility of employers. Leisure provides adults with recreational pursuits, the funding for which comes, at least partly, if not totally, from individuals.

In the contemporary world, these boundaries have been subject to a range of challenges, shifting and/or becoming more permeable. First, in terms of changes within the boundaries. Second, in terms of the boundaries themselves. Third, in the categorising of certain forms of learning within specific boundaries. In this respect, discourses of lifelong learning have engendered a more diverse, complex scene, eliding the conventional boundaries within fields of study.

Changes within the boundaries of education, training and leisure have taken place on the basis of each area's own sets of contested concepts and histories. Within education, the process of general development may involve a range of practices. For instance, the inculcation of certain disciplines of knowledge, the development of basic skills, personal 'growth', the skills, knowledge and understanding necessary for professional work and the attributes of citizenship. It may be all or part of these. A wide range of learning opportunities therefore might be said to be, in some senses, educational and produce an 'educated person'.

Equally, training has a range of meanings and has been subject to change. Providing skills or competences for specific tasks may remain an important part of much training, but forms of development associated with, for instance, inter-personal skills, team work and multi-skilling may involve processes which were not traditionally within the boundaries of training. Professional training involves the acquisition of personal attributes and expert knowledge that also strain narrow conceptions of training. As do cross-national comparisons, where the knowledge base for technical and trade qualifications may be given much greater emphasis in certain countries (Germany) than elsewhere (the United Kingdom) (Lane 1993; Smithers 1993). Narrow discourses of training have been challenged by those of 'human resource development' and the development of 'human potential' in which less clearly demarcated notions of training are linked to personnel practices of appraisal and staff development. These are processes to which staff within education and training institutions are themselves subject (Ball 1990a, 1990b). Despite these changes, however, different discourses of training among professionals, employers and participants are still apparent. A major investigation of the concept of training in the United Kingdom found that

> the general population uses the term *training* to refer to a much narrower set of activities than those understood by training professionals . . . that for most people *training* is that which happens on formal courses . . . that employers have a narrower definition of training than employees in that activities which are not employer initiated/funded tend to be excluded . . . that activities included in the definition of training will vary across subgroups of the population . . . that activities which are self-initiated and/or self-funded are less likely to be included than those which are initiated and/or funded by an employer . . . that there is a fuzzy boundary between training and education for most people.
>
> (Campanelli *et al.* 1994)

Unsurprisingly, there is no single discourse of training. What is interesting is the continuing strength of discourses based on differentiation, although the 'fuzzy boundary' between education and training is suggestive of forms of de-differentiation. This demonstrates the discursive dislocation between different groups and that the discourse of the de-differentiated moorland of lifelong learning may be powerful in some ways, but lack influence in others.

Leisure is another area of dispute. Like consumption, it is also an arena of debate which educators and trainers have tended to avoid in the attempt to delineate their practices as 'serious' and therefore worthy of concern and funding rather than 'recreational'. Leisure can be conceived in a number of ways. Three will be outlined here.

First, it is conceived in terms of leisure time, a period free from and outside the labours and boundaries of work, in particular paid work. The gender assumptions contained in this discourse have been challenged and unpaid work is now often incorporated into the discussion of leisure time (Allison and Duncan 1992). Also, women tend to have less leisure time than men (Lowe 1991). This conception is still based on the assumption that leisure is something continuous with and supplemental to work, whether paid or unpaid. Second, leisure is associated with certain kinds of activity, for instance, rock climbing, playing cards or learning to paint. Here it is the nature of the activity rather than the relationship to work which defines leisure. However, this conception is itself problematic since the differentiation of activities upon which it is based, and the notion that some activities are inherently part of the realm of leisure, is not sustainable. Activities may be leisure for one person, but work for another. Third, leisure can be conceived as to do with the way any activity, including work, is approached. A leisurely approach combines certain attitudes and behaviour, such as taking one's time, going at one's own pace, and forms of experience which might stretch across a spectrum from bland satisfaction to optimal intensity that balances challenges and skills (Csikszentmihalyi and Csikszentmihalyi 1992). Optimal experience is held to develop out of play, which in the modernist differentiation between work and leisure is understood as belonging entirely to the realm of leisure. Play is consequently a manifestation of deviant attitudes and behaviour in the realm of work (Mitchell 1992). This deviancy is also manifested in the perspective on leisurely attitudes and behaviour in discourses of education and training – often associated with ill-disciplined, apathetic and unserious approaches.

In one sense, leisure could be understood as a situation where there is a leisurely approach to a leisure activity that happens outside of work time. On the face of it, this seems to provide a firm set of boundaries for leisure. Yet these boundaries break down very easily and are themselves subject to contradictory tensions. Leisure time can be used for activities more associated with work, such as DIY. Leisure activities can equally be work for others, such as amateur and professional sports. Leisureliness can be pursued in all dimensions of life, including work and learning. This perhaps suggests that any attempt to impose boundaries, to differentiate leisure, is as problematic as differentiating a field of education and/or training.

This indicates that the differentiation between leisure and adult education as a bounded field is not as secure as is sometimes suggested. Here analyses drawn from leisure studies and cultural studies become important and influential in helping to understand the processes at work – bodies of knowledge from outside the 'field' of adult education. Rojek (1993, 1995) argues that modern leisure can be likened to a grid imposed on life in which leisure becomes moral regulation cloaked in an ideology of freedom, choice and life-satisfaction. In this sense, leisure becomes an essential element of the social order and functions to maintain the well-being of the individual and social formation. Leisure is considered

> a legitimate and progressive feature of civilized social life. It [modernity] identifies leisure with social integration, with enhancing the well-being of society. To this end leisure time and leisure space are allocated where leisure identities, associations and practices can develop. Finally, it installs and maintains a formal and informal system of policing which aims to ensure that leisure practice is orderly and decent.
>
> (Rojek 1995: 39–40)

Leisure is a civilising influence, an aspect of 'progress', as the more leisure a social formation has the more progressive and civilised it must be and vice versa. However, leisure activities are bounded in both space and time. They can only occur in certain places, such as cinemas and sports arenas, and in periods of free time, such as holidays and weekends. There must not be too much of it and it should not interfere with work. Furthermore, only certain forms of identity, association and practice are appropriate and these are enforced either through the sanctions of the law or through mores of 'civilised behaviour'. Leisure is tied to policy goals of producing a healthy and responsible population; a form of provision aimed at producing personal improvement, health and a certain acceptance of social place – a view consistent with the discourses of cultural restorationists. Bounded leisure time to pursue certain goals is therefore part of a specific socio-cultural context.

In this discourse, leisure is seen both as a central means of life-satisfaction, of expressing freedom and choice, and as closely bounded and strictly policed. It is subordinated to work despite its status as a civilising process. Work is the dominant part of a work–leisure binary and central to individual identity. Leisure is a reward for work, but never at the expense of wealth creation and always subject to reason. Reason is the means of ascertaining which pleasures are good and which bad. This ensures that 'mindless' activities, unruly passions and pleasures are not allowed to assert themselves. Leisure is a form of 'rational recreation' aimed at moral governance, arousing and cultivating particular attitudes and behaviour as part of the cultivation of reason, order and consent. 'Typical forms of rational recreation were physical exercise, educational instruction, craft, musical instruction, excursions and hygiene, temperance and self-control in the poor' (Rojek 1993: 34). Rather than being differentiated from leisure, in these discourses, adult education is part of a tradition of rational recreation. The governmentality of the 'educated person' embraces forms of leisure as well as education and adult education as leisure. Self-improvement and self-development through participation in adult education have been and continue to be central to the arguments for continuing state support for its activities.

However, as Rojek points out, modernity has another side. Here modernity is characterised by disorder rather than order, change rather than stability, conflict rather than harmony. In this sense, leisure is reconstructed as directed by desire rather than reason, transgressive and subversive rather than contained and containable within socially accepted boundaries. Goalless rather than teleological, leisure becomes discontinuous from and not subordinate to work. With these forms of leisure, people's everyday routines of living, including forms of rational recreation, seem banal and boring and are experienced as anti-climactic. As Debord (1983) argues in his critique of the 'society of the spectacle', people have the capacity for diversion and subversion through irony and humour, part of a leisurely attitude and behaviour – the 'other' of modern forms of leisure.

> The subjectivity which produces, consumes, and is itself produced and consumed by the spectacle is already busy looting it as well. It does not passively consume and obediently produce as the spectacle ostensibly intends: it sabotages, steals, plays in the supermarkets and sleeps on the production line.
>
> (Plant 1992: 88)

In other words, transgression against the regulation of the modern moral order through leisurely attitudes, behaviour and lifestyle practices is always possible.

It is this 'other' of modernity which is foregrounded in a postmodern and de-differentiated view of leisure. Leisure comes to be seen more in terms of play and desire, with a greater role attributed to social actors and an emphasis on a leisurely stance in all aspects of life. Rojek (1995) suggests that leisure has become a constant supplier of symbols and images to be consumed, and through which daily existence is negotiated. A 'playful' or 'ludic' attitude and behaviour are integral to disrupting the banality of everyday existence. To be playful is not simply to relinquish oneself to the 'joys' of capitalism and consumerism, but it is rather to adopt a stance of subversion through playfulness to all aspects of life, including education and training. In other words, play is a serious business, not confined to leisure time and pre-defined leisure activities. In the postmodern, there is a leisurely, challenging stance to life, within which the consumption of goods, services, images and meanings is central. Even if not fulfilling the teleology of rationality and self-improvement of modernity, leisure is still a vital factor in the creation (and re-creation) of self-identity. This suggests that leisure and playfulness become central to activities within contemporary social formations, including those of lifelong learning. De-differentiation within leisure results from and in a de-differentiation between leisure, education and training. The latter two increasingly become geared to and indistinguishable from leisure forms.

If both adult education and leisure are inter-related, is the distinction between them as forms of free association taking place at a time free from labour also subject to challenge? What of the boundary between leisure and work? Research appears to illustrate the more complex patterns of de-differentiation I have outlined. For instance, research on the provision of 'leisure opportunities' for the unwaged found that

> the whole concept of 'leisure time' and hence 'leisure interests' proved difficult for many participants to make sense of. For a large number, leisure is something that exists only in relation to work and something that often needs to be paid for . . . the process and outcomes of the project's overall Leisure approach call into question the whole distinction between Leisure and Work.
>
> (Johnston *et al.* 1989: 32–33)

This differentiation has also been challenged by research into workplace culture. Research on practices in a restaurant found that

> even poorly paid staff were 'free' to organise their activities according to their own designs. Indeed much of the 'work' of the staff consisted of socialising with customers who were their friends from outside. The staff did not even use phrases such as 'going to work'. For most of them it was a 'way of life' resulting from the physical proximity of employee and consumer, of work and leisure.
>
> (Lash and Urry 1994: 199)

Differentiations between work and leisure therefore prove to be as problematic as differentiations between leisure and adult education. Leisureliness of a playful and performative character can suffuse other areas of activity. Here work itself may take on the forms of self-expression which Worpole (1991) associates solely with leisure time. The view of service industry employees as simply exploited ignores the cultural dimensions in which encounters with customers 'are shown to have a performative character and thus one can think of this kind of workplace as a stage, as a dramatic setting for certain kinds of performance, involving a mix of mental, manual and emotional labour' (Lash and Urry 1994: 202).

Worpole's position is clear and clearly modernist. Leisure is free association occupying a sphere separate from, yet subordinate to, work. Within this discourse, leisure is understood as a form of self-improvement threatened by trends towards consumerism – and the unspoken possibility that adult education centres could be closed and reopened as heritage centres, which people would visit to see where adults used to learn whilst they themselves learn through multi-media technology in their homes and workplaces. From a progressive critique, Worpole is asserting the need to reassert rational recreation to govern a bounded field of leisure, of which adult education is a part. It is clear that within both modern and postmodern discourses of leisure, adult education and lifelong learning are implicated. They cannot be differentiated in quite the way adult educators often would appear to want.

In examining discourses of leisure, therefore, it is important to recognise that different conceptions overlay and attempt to displace, rather than completely replace, one another. More 'serious' conceptions of leisure and notions of creativity and self-expression exist alongside more consumer-orientated and playful practices. Further, while under conditions of boundary maintenance distinctions between work and leisure time were clear, with adult education positioned within leisure, the very notion of leisure time has become problematic. For instance, many unwaged people have time, but not the resources to enable them to make much use of it for leisure activities. Also, many use leisure time to pursue interests relevant to their work – paid and unpaid – and as we have seen may indeed define their leisure activities as being hard 'at work'.

These changes within boundaries both have contributed to and reflect the challenging of the boundaries between the three areas to produce an ambivalence in the way in which provision can be conceived – as education, training or leisure. Forms of education can be conceived as training, or leisure, or both. To learn philosophy also trains a person to think philosophically and for many adults is very pleasurable and undertaken in leisure time. Similarly with training, a person may take a course in health and safety which develops their overall understanding of issues, and which in a different context might be part of a leisure pursuit. Leisure activities such as sport may also constitute the training of the body into specific activities and an education about the body. How do we construct the keep-fit sessions for workers and managers which begin the working shift in many Japanese-owned companies? Or the events and packs organised and produced for parent-governors of schools to help them with their roles and responsibilities? Or a visit to a heritage centre or theme park?

The attempts to put boundaries around forms of learning on the basis of certain discourses of provision immediately undermine themselves. For the adult concerned the learning may be educational, it may train them, it may be leisurely, or it may be any combination of these. To invoke differentiations, such as that between vocational and non-vocational education inscribed in much contemporary policy, is clearly unhelpful to adults negotiating the moorland of lifelong learning. In a sense, the process of boundary confusion within and between education, training and leisure is reflected in the growing number of categories developed to describe and conceptualise specific institutional bases, types of learning and modes of delivery. For example, common categories we now find in discourses of lifelong learning include vocational education, non-vocational education, vocational education and training, adult continuing education, continuing education and training, continuing vocational education, continuing professional development, training, human resource development, employee development schemes, open and distance learning, flexible learning, recurrent education, lifelong education, as well as more conventional notions of further education, higher education and adult education. Each modifies the boundaries within and between education, training and leisure, attempting to differentiate the field of practice they encompass. Each can be located within a discourse of the moorland of lifelong learning as a terrain of study.

Once again, it is sometimes suggested that such differentiations are not so apparent in certain continental European countries. Differences in language and culture mean that concepts cannot necessarily be translated in a straightforward manner. For instance, although the German concept of *Bildung* and the Swedish notion of *bildning* are closely allied to English notions of education, they are somewhat wider, encompassing a sense of cultural cultivation. In Sweden, it is the notion of *utbildning* which is used as a synonym for education, even though the English concept embraces more than the Swedish. In his discussion of conceptual and policy issues, Abrahamsson comments that

> when educators and teachers in the the UK or North America quarrel about the education and training dichotomy, Swedes have their conceptual fight on *bildning* vs *utbildning*. . . it is possible to add the prefixes *ungdoms-*, *vuxen-* and *yrkes-* to *utbildning*, which add up to *ungdomsutbildning* (youth education), *vuxenutbildning* (adult education) and *yrkesutbildning* (vocational education). . . . The word *bildning* is instead united with *folk* (people), *arbetare* (workers) and *sjalv* (self) . . .
>
> (Abrahamsson 1993: 47)

So debates take on a different form according to the language and culture within which one is working. However, the issue of boundaries remains powerful within the different contexts.

> The view that continuing vocational education forms part of the delivery system for adult education, as is the case with occupational training for the unemployed, is generally accepted in France, the Netherlands, the Nordic countries, and parts of North America; in Germany, Japan, the United Kingdom, and other countries the 'territorial struggle' in the field of adult education is being continued by some writers . . .
>
> (Tuijnman 1991: 146)

While situating certain learning opportunities within specific discourses may seem somewhat arbitrary on the above account, they are in fact strategic to the conceptual and indeed policy discourses traversing the moorland of lifelong learning at any point in time and place. This discursive ambivalence provides limited but important possibilities for provision to be reformulated within the prevailing frameworks at the time. For instance, in recent years in the United Kingdom, the policy emphasis on vocationally relevant opportunities and academic entry into higher education has meant that funding has been targeted to support certain forms of provision. In response to this, learning opportunities which may not have previously been categorised as 'vocational' have been reformulated as such in order to become eligible for funding support. Such categorisations do not simply signify a certain form of provision, but also situate it within a specific discourse. For instance, forms of non-certificated non-vocational learning, such as cake decorating, may become certificated if that becomes a means of gaining state funding for putting on courses in an area. In the process, it may shift from being conceived as non-vocational to vocational becoming part of the policy established to support that area of learning. This has happened in the United Kingdom. Such reframings may or may not have an impact upon the learning opportunity itself, possibly introducing forms of assessment and accreditation or some changes to the curriculum, and possibly influencing the nature of participation as a result. However, it is the ambivalence in the categorising of provision which is significant, because it allows learning opportunities to rest within a variety of frameworks and a wider and shifting moorland of study. Questions of status and funding are tied into the situating of forms of learning within specific discourses and able to operate across rather than within conceptual, policy and political boundaries.

In examining the concepts of education, training and leisure, I have both focused on activities and drawn in forms of analysis from outside the traditional field of study of adult education. I have attempted to both exemplify de-differentiation and illuminate the consequences. Such processes are necessary if we are to study the moorland of lifelong learning and lifelong learning as a moorland – they are part of the discursive shift and give further impetus to it. This is not entirely comfortable or uncontroversial. There is certainly continuing travel and destinations may only be temporary and provisional. In addition, there will be many more types of discourse on and about the moorland, only some of which we may encounter and with which we may engage. Rather than being dismissed as not part of the field – as is often the case with discourses of, for instance, training, human resource management, economics – they also travel and inscribe parts of the moorland and there is the requirement for dialogue on all sides to map the ever-changing terrain. However, this argument will not stop the attempts to reinscribe differentiation into the terrain of study, even as it continues to be de-differentiated.

At the start of this chapter I suggested there are clear difficulties in attempting to put boundaries around the moorland of lifelong learning, to construct a clearly demarcated field of practice, policy and study. I have examined this difficulty across a range of factors. For a period after the Second World War, a relatively settled set of practices and discourses evolved which were pursued at the margins of public policy and academic study. This was the basis for the bounded field of adult education. As public policy has taken a greater interest in the moorland of lifelong learning amidst wider changes in the social formation, so those practices and discourses have been disrupted and in many cases de-differentiated. As well as being unsettling and troubling, this disruption also opens up different possibilities. In this sense, discourses of the moorland of lifelong learning are very much part of the processes and senses of change outlined earlier. In this, the emphasis has shifted away from a focus on the provider towards one on the learner and learning in the anticipation that this will result in a greater permeability of boundaries for adults. The question remains as to whether and how the de-differentiation in the practices and discourses of lifelong learning undermines and/or masks a shift in boundaries. The increased difference it opens up does not signify necessarily greater equity. In the next chapter, I will explore how this issue is manifested in some of the changing practices in the practices of lifelong learning which respond to conditions of de-differentiation. Such responses also contribute to the processes identified, as does the adoption of a discourse of a moorland of lifelong learning rather than a field of adult education.

Chapter 4

Flexible friends?

Since the learning needs of adults are highly differentiated, the strategies to be followed will have to be diversified as well. How can a flexible yet comprehensive approach to skills formation be developed?

(Tuijnman and Van der Kamp 1992: vii)

If adults are to be lifelong learners and lifelong learning is to be given value, yet the boundaries within which that learning takes place are not set and are subject to change, how then are providers of learning opportunities able to provide access and progression, and to which groups of adult learners? What consequences are there for the formal providers of learning opportunities for adults in the changing discourses of lifelong learning? These are some of the questions to be examined in this chapter.

I have suggested in the exploration of change that notions of flexibility have come to the fore as a discourse governing the economy, organisations and individuals. Flexibility has been deployed by a range of bodies in a range of modernising and progressive discourses to construct the need for change from established practices. Becoming flexible has contributed and responded to the processes of de-differentiation outlined in the previous chapter. In this sense, the lifelong learner is the flexible self-reflexive subject of the postmodern attitude, able to negotiate the unpredictable changes of the contemporary period.

To support lifelong learning, it has become necessary for the provision of learning opportunities to be 'reformed'. On the one hand, this has taken place under conditions of the 'discourse of derision' (Ball 1990a), the undermining of the professional as having a legitimate voice in the formulation of policies relevant to their arena of practice. On the other hand, the discourse of flexibility has been deployed in relation to providers of learning opportunities, in which the requirement for providers to be more responsive to the 'needs' of individuals and employers is posited. Flexibility, therefore, has become central to the governance of changes in the provision of learning opportunities for adults, almost a unifying principle in the restructuring of practices. As such, it foregrounds the already existing 'non-traditional' provision, that is, not involving full-time attendance at an institution, and acts as a constant pressure upon institutions and practitioners to respond to changing and diverse requirements. Flexibility has become a norm to be pursued, invested with positive value. By contrast, any failure to increase flexibility is invested with perspectives on the self-interestedness of professionals and their lack of accountability. Discourses of flexibility establish flexibility as central to their regime of truth.

Alongside and as part of these discourses of flexibility, in the United Kingdom there has been an emphasis on 'relevance'. In line with the dominant economic discourse of change, the relevance of provision is evaluated according to the contribution it makes to the skills of the workforce to support enterprise and competitiveness. Flexibility and relevance, therefore, act as powerful conditioners of institutional responses to the requirement to sustain or increase levels of participation, supporting lifelong learning and a learning society. Numerous reports and documents have been produced on how providers of learning opportunities can change to become more flexible in order to extend more learning opportunities to more adults (FEU 1987a, 1993; McGivney 1991). Improved marketing (FEU 1990), the provision of guidance and counselling (UDACE 1986; Oakeshott 1990; *Adults Learning* 1991b; Cooper 1996), outreach work (Portwood 1988; Kinneavy 1989) and networking (UDACE 1990) have all been put forward as ways in which providers can support lifelong learning more effectively. Largely constituted within a technical rationalist discourse, these texts tend to focus on how to become more flexible in various ways as a means of extending participation and relevance.

A wide range of powerful influences – policy, managerial, financial, intellectual, social, political – have been deployed in the United Kingdom to engender greater flexibility in organisational and staff practices. In the process, formal providers have started to take on the characteristics of the flexible firm and become more like learning organisations. Specific institutions and sectors have had flexibility deployed against them as a challenge over their failure to support lifelong learning and their failure to change. The number and range of such discourses have tended to multiply in proportion to the decreased resources in real terms available to formal providers of learning opportunities relative to the numbers of learners they are meant to serve. Flexibility thereby becomes a discursive strategy to deal with less resources and yet do more, increasing the pressure on all concerned and intensifying workloads. Flexibility governs the promotion of access while cutting real costs – finding more 'efficient' ways of expanding provision.

Many of the changes being experienced within the provision of learning opportunities are being governed by an emphasis on learning – supporting learning in various settings and recognising it through assessment and accreditation procedures – and a shift towards a consumer-orientated model in the provision of learning opportunities. Formal institutions are losing their monopoly, if not their privileged status, as settings for learning and there are increased inter-institutional links. The use of open and distance learning and modularisation of the curriculum are necessary to fill the 'gaps' identified in the individual's 'portfolio of learning'. Trends are towards flexibility through such practices as the accreditation (recognition) of prior learning, credit accumulation and transfer, workplace learning, criterion-referenced assessment and student-centred learning. The diversity of providers and provision necessitates increased guidance and counselling to enable individuals to make the best choices possible, negotiate their way through the increasingly complex moorland of opportunities and provide some coherence to an increasingly diverse curriculum offering (Cooper 1996). Performance indicators act as a measurement of success and a basis for future funding and planning of provision. These are being implemented unevenly and an important question involves assessing the differential effects on the adults who are held to benefit from such changes. While access, participation and progression are central to the discourses of providers of learning opportunities, adults themselves are increasingly subject to processes of individualisation and familialisation – consumers in the market in learning opportunities – a process with important economic, social and cultural consequences.

In this chapter, I shall focus on three aspects of the development of practices aimed at supporting lifelong learning – the development of open and distance learning, the moves towards outcomes-based assessment and accreditation, and the reconstitution of workplaces as learning organisations. These emerge as major trends in supporting learners on the wider moorland of lifelong learning. First, however, I want to explore the question of who participates in what forms of learning opportunities, the factors which bear upon adults' participation in learning and the ways in which these are discursively constituted. If flexibility is to be effective in supporting lifelong learning, then the factors which impact upon who participates in what becomes important, for while increased flexibility may expand opportunity, to whom remains a central issue. The ways in which flexibility may develop to widen opportunity depend upon the ways in which non-participation is constructed. Having explored this issue, the chapter will then examine how the move from discourses of provision to learners and learning, and, as part of that, from inputs to outputs, has placed an emphasis: first, on the development of open and distance learning as a means of bridging boundaries between formal institutions and learners in a variety of settings; second, on credit frameworks as a means of 'embracing' learning wherever it takes place; and third, on initiatives to enable workplaces to become learning organisations. I shall also explore the ways in which these practices have themselves been reconfigured as they have become part of a discourse of lifelong learning.

Once again, the chapter will draw primarily on the experience of the United Kingdom. However, the processes governing change are also to be found elsewhere, including in European Commission policies to enhance the mobility of learners and workers as part of the Single European Market. The development of open and distance learning, outcomes-based assessment and accreditation – usually constructed within a discourse of competence – and concepts of the learning organisation also resonate with changes taking place in many parts of the contemporary globe.

PARTICIPATION AND NON-PARTICIPATION

While cultural restorationists tend to approach education and training as a form of selection based upon individual ability, standards and exclusion, in modernising and progressive discourses there is an encouragement for increasing and widening participation. However, the assumptions and purposes supporting lifelong learning differ. Within the modernising discourse, the need for a multi- and highly-skilled workforce for a competitive economy is the basis for policies to increase participation in vocationally relevant learning. Here it is the national and/or regional economic interest which is used to legitimise increasing participation. Without investment in human capital, it is argued that national economic interest will suffer. In the United Kingdom, comparisons with other countries in staying-on rates, levels of qualification, participation rates in technical, managerial and higher education and training are all drawn upon to support the case for greater participation as a response to lack of competitiveness. Such comparisons are used to insert a level of urgency into changing provision, often at the expense of a more considered view. Interestingly in this respect, a 1991 survey of 14–49 year olds in European Union countries found that the United Kingdom was only third in levels of participation behind Denmark and the Netherlands of the then twelve member states, with 21.5 per cent of this age group undertaking education and training in the previous four weeks (Employment Department Group 1993: 128). This suggests the spur of national comparisons is invested with particular meanings to create a climate into which particular agendas and changes can be inserted, when other issues of more relevance may be pertinent. Nor is this restricted to the United Kingdom – the competitive threat is one deployed in many of the most (over-)developed economies as a spur to change.

Meanwhile progressive discourses support the need for increased *and* wider participation to support greater equity and social mobility. Here the focus tends to be on the 'disadvantage' of those adults who did not 'benefit' from initial education and training in terms of qualifications, or the 'oppression' inscribed in social and economic exclusion and the need to transform the nature of education and training. Flexibility and the recognition of achievement provide the basis for practices aimed at promoting participation and inclusion. An interesting comparison here is that while modernising discourses often include a concern for equal opportunities, even if its implementation is more problematic, progressive discourses rarely if ever engage with issues of economic competitiveness. Central to both, however, are questions of participation and non-participation.

In general, there are three sets of inter-related discourses which can be said to frame debates around participation and non-participation. First, there are those which focus on providers of learning opportunities, on the need to transform the provision of learning opportunities to enable more adults to participate. Time-tabling, crèche facilities, physical accessibility, flexible delivery systems are encouraged to enable this to happen. Second, there are discourses which focus on the system of provision as a whole. These concentrate on the need for coherent frameworks of access and progression, not simply into and between institutions, but also, with increased student and labour market mobility, across the national boundaries. The focus shifts to credit frameworks, funding adults to learn and the need for a diverse range of learning opportunities. Third, there are the discourses which focus on culture and power. These address issues of participation not simply in terms of how learning is accessed, but also the content of that learning and its significance in the wider socio-economic and political context. This area is concerned with the politics of participation and non-participation. It is the institutional and systemic discourses which have tended to dominate the debates about participation and non-participation and govern changes in the provision of learning opportunities. These are framed largely within an instrumental and technical form of rationality. Institutional change itself has been to enable access and to support systemic change. All of which has resulted in the discussion of the politics of participation being marginalised from debate. Hence, even as we focus on the need for institutional change and increased flexibility, there is a politics implicit to this which is relatively silent and silenced.

In discourses of institutional change, providers of learning opportunities are critiqued for not adequately responding to adult learners and being unresponsiveness to the full range of such learners. They do not provide sufficient information and guidance on what they offer. Nor do they provide opportunities in settings or in ways which are appropriate to different adult groups. Staff attitudes do not help, as in many institutions staff feel 'intimidated' by working with adults, or with certain groups of adults. Provision needs to become more flexible and relevant and able to respond to the full range of adult requirements as a condition for increasing and widening participation – where the participation of adults in itself often widens the profile of learners. It is suggested that what is required is a combination of institutional change, curriculum change, changes in teaching and learning approaches and enhanced staff development. Here the normalising and seductive are deployed against those working in such institutions, appealing to them to become 'active subjects' in extending the availability of learning opportunities. Meanwhile, policies, managerial structures and funding formulas are deployed to support the necessary changes, as seduction is never sufficient or complete. It was to effect such changes that many exemplary initiatives and projects were undertaken during the 1980s, focusing on particular client groups, such as the unemployed (FEU REPLAN 1989), minority ethnic groups (FEU 1987b), adults with learning difficulties (Sutcliffe 1990). The aim was to highlight the parts of the adult population – target groups – that formal providers of learning opportunities were meant and needed to serve and how this was not and yet could be achieved by institutions. This was something which satisfied the market-making discourses of the modernisers and the access and equal opportunities discourses of progressives. In making more transparent the possibilities for institutions to provide for adults, the aim was to increase and widen participation.

Similar efforts were placed into encouraging and exhorting employers, and particularly private sector employers, to provide more training for their employees and have a greater involvement in the provision of learning opportunities generally (Briggs and Moseley 1986). Government-promoted initiatives, such as the United Kingdom Investors in People programme, encourage employers to take a systematic approach to the development of their employees. Employers have been brought in to play a more central role in the formal sector, sitting on the governing bodies of institutions, participating in the Lead Bodies for setting national standards of occupational competence, providing the backbone for Training and Enterprise Councils/Local Enterprise Companies. It would appear also that as some employers have become more involved, so certain concerns about participation and non-participation among specific groups in the workforce have been heightened. For instance, workers with literacy difficulties have been a constant concern for employers.

Conceptualising participation and non-participation within a discourse of institutional access and the consequent framing of practices has provided a basis for increasing the overall numbers of adults engaging in education and training. Whether this is because of increased institutional flexibility or would have occurred anyway to a greater or lesser extent is not clear. A position of increasing access certainly is embedded in the mission statements, policies and strategic plans of many institutions. However, the extent to which institutional changes alone can impact on the profile of participation is less certain as systemic features are also crucial to the possibilities for adult learners. The role of education and training institutions in social and economic selection through inclusion and exclusion is central here, with questions about the accessibility of the system of opportunities as a whole – incorporating issues of access, progression and outcomes to opportunity structures and not simply to specific institutional provision.

There are two broad strands in approaches to increasing and widening systemic participation that I wish to outline. First, there are policies based in welfare state social frameworks. Second, there are approaches which promote a market in learning opportunities and particularly in qualifications. While this distinction is never pure in specific policies, it is useful in highlighting different approaches to systemic change. Critics of the market-led approach (Tett 1993) to reforming the system argue that concern for consumer choice marginalises concerns for equity and accessibility – flexibility services those with already existing economic and cultural capital. Targeting of non-participant groups is suggested as a necessary alternative. However, Rinne and Kivinen's conclusion on Finland as an example of a country with a reasonably systematic provision of learning opportunities for adults, and where policies have been focused on providing a 'second chance' for non-participant adults, is stark:

> Today it is still the case that education selects people in the context of societal status, and contributes to cultural differentiation in their ways of lives. . . . Conventional educational policies seem to be almost powerless to change these fundamental conditions of social and cultural existence.
>
> (Rinne and Kivinen 1993: 126–127)

This view is supported by research elsewhere (Nordhaug 1989). Even where opportunities have been targeted, therefore, their perceived 'failure' to fundamentally alter forms of cultural differentiation and 'success' in promoting individual mobility raise questions about it as an approach to addressing questions of equity. The binaries of welfare state and market, equity and inequity, in which the former are put forward as the positive alternative to the latter, offer an overly simplistic, if powerful, perspective on the provision of learning opportunities for adults. This is not to say that changes in provision are unimportant to questions of equity. Nor that they are unaffected by the particular discourses of participation within which they are framed. Issues of childcare, ramps, appropriate time-tabling, staff attitudes, all have an impact upon who can or cannot participate.

Overall numbers of adults participating in formal institutions have increased in recent years in the United Kingdom (McGivney 1990, 1994). Similar trends are found elsewhere (Rubenson and Willms 1993). This in itself may be considered an advance. However, only certain forms of change are possible within a discourse focused on how provision is to be more flexible with specific impact on participation and non-participation. Systemic changes are contained within a certain cultural paradigm in which a specific construction of change is presented as neutral, with practical and technical difficulties to be overcome. This attempts to remove the powerful effects and the power embedded within that process from the discourses of those involved – including workers with adults who are 'encouraged' and 'developed' to implement changes decided elsewhere.

This leads into the third strand to the discourse of participation and non-participation – the marginal and marginalised discourse of culture and power. Within this discourse, the calls for flexible institutions and systems construct restricted senses of access, marginalising, in particular, the exercises of power embedded within the curriculum itself. Questions of participation and non-participation are thereby restricted to access to provision. The substantive content of the curriculum is left largely unchallenged, even as the delivery mechanisms become ever more diverse (Griffin 1983). As Connelly (1991: 140) suggests of contemporary trends, 'the institutional priority of numbers and the government strategy of manpower [sic] planning clearly can be placed within the narrower definition of access which is primarily concerned with provision and has a market-led ideological orientation'. It is important, therefore, to recognise that a discourse of access to provision may well increase and widen participation, but this will be within certain cultural boundaries, signifying specific exercises of power. Indeed, part of that power is precisely in constructing questions of participation and non-participation as non-cultural – that participation can be extended through the technical alteration to the delivery of the curriculum alone. This combines technical and practical rationality, thereby limiting the challenge to established practices and dominant norms. For example, commenting on two reports on the education of adults and adult basic education in Scotland in the early 1990s, Alexander states:

> Questions of value are reduced to questions of efficiency and the requirements of industry and the economy. The reports, while attempting politically to defend the field, encourage a view of adult education and curricula as commodities to which access should be created and of programmes of learning which are instrumental and centrally determined rather than responsive to the purposes of individuals.
>
> (Alexander 1994: 44)

Here learner choice is restricted to those who can finance their learning, as the market is regulated in relation to that in which the state will and will not invest. It is a market guided through administrative means by a particular vision of what that market should be providing.

The cultural perspective on participation and non-participation is overtly political in the sense that it constructs education and training as continually subject to struggle and negotiation. It is part of a discourse of socio-economic and cultural change. Adults' participation or non-participation is part of the wider cultural struggles and negotiations in which, for instance, many working-class people see educational institutions as 'not for people like them' (McGivney 1990). Here it is not just the way in which provision is organised which is at stake, but the content of learning and pedagogy, what in parts of the nineteenth-century English working-class movement was termed a struggle for 'really useful knowledge' – that which served the interests of the working class (Johnson 1993). State-supported provision, although presented as a neutral canon of knowledge necessary for the 'educated' individual, was held to reflect and serve the interests of the ruling capitalist class, to be a form of 'merely useful knowledge' to maintain the subordination of the working class. What constituted 'really useful knowledge' was largely derived from the marxist and socialist texts of the period.

A more recent example is the challenge by women that much education and training is inscribed with and inscribes masculinist norms. Here women are not simply gaining access to an established curriculum, but have also sought to construct a curriculum on feminist lines (Parsons 1993). This is not without its tensions and contradictions, particularly where feminism becomes a 'university subject' rather than altering the curriculum as a whole. Women's studies in universities is part of powerful institutions with certain cultural norms, raising tensions about feminist knowledge and practice. Inglis (1994: 64) describes the struggle by women for daytime provision in Ireland as 'a struggle for control of their own education. This struggle is a struggle for power. It is a struggle to redefine what is women's education and who controls it.' The limits placed by the discourse of and about providers and systems produces questions as to the cultural impact of increasing flexibility in widening participation, bringing to the fore questions of curriculum and pedagogy.

Similar arguments have been put forward in recent years by anti-racist and post-colonial writers against the ethnic, religious and nationalistic construction of knowledge (Joseph et al. 1990). In this, the institutional arrangements of learning opportunities are themselves held to be inscribed with a certain culture which positions certain groups unequally within and outside the cultures and canons of education and training. It is therefore the values, attitudes and practices inscribed in the provision of learning opportunities in relation to the values, attitudes and practices of the diverse groups within the social formation which are held to create the conditions for participation and non-participation. Part of this is itself the attitudes towards different types of culture, their meaning and significance.

The analysis of the cultural dimensions of participation and non-participation has become more complex as the range of groups and factors has increased and diversified. This exemplifies both postmodern diversity and the possibilities for a poststructural analysis of that diversity. As the cultural is foregrounded, it is therefore also transformed. An initial analysis based on a universal conception of the transformative power of education if it reflected the lives, interests, experiences and knowledge of the subordinated group that were identified – working class, women, minority ethnic groups, and so on – has been displaced by a notion of culture as diverse and dynamic, in which knowledge is located and provisional, resting in that which can be agreed among participants in particular space–time locations. Here knowledge is 'really useful' or 'transformative' not in a universal sense, but only in a provisional and pragmatic way. The cultural discourse has shifted therefore from a modernist framing, legitimised by the grand narratives of emancipation, to a postmodernist analysis of locatedness and contest. For some, this de-politicises the cultural. For others, it provides the grounds for a more inclusive politics.

The factors which affect the participation of adults in learning are many and complex. The very notion of 'learning' is problematic, as learning for some is constructed as training and/or leisure by others. Equally, the notion of participation is contested. Does it solely involve people entering formal institutions of education and training? If not, then how do we assess the many learning projects in which individuals engage? What makes a person's activity specifically a 'learning project'? Do we use enrolments on courses for statistical purposes? Or course completions? At what age do we start to term someone an 'adult'? Should we even seek to produce a unitary view of adult learning, given the structured heterogeneity of adults? It is clear that the debates about participation are not as straight forward as they are often presented in newspaper and other reports. The basis for the collection of statistics needs to be understood before it is possible to evaluate their significance. Even then, the explanations of differential rates of participation by different groups in the social formation may vary, tending to produce discourses which focus on specific issues and construct them in particular ways. Motivation, the cultural capital of individuals, the counter-culture of groups, physical and situational barriers to access, are all commonly found in the discussion of participation and non-participation. Yet even as apparently clear messages emerge from participation studies, their significance has to be evaluated in terms of investing a particular meaning in the information presented.

For example, McGivney's review of the literature (1990) tends to focus on participation in education and training rather than learning. By contrast, Sargant (1991) attempts to elicit the wider participation in learning by adults. Both studies provide evidence that older adults, those with limited initial educational experience and adults from poorer socio-economic backgrounds are all 'under-represented' in the take-up of learning opportunities. The link between social class and participation is marked in most studies. For instance, Sargant (1991: 12) found that in the United Kingdom 'the proportion of people studying now/recently are 42 per cent of ABs (upper and upper-middle classes), 37 per cent of C1s (lower-middle class), 29 per cent of C2s (skilled working class) and 17 per cent of DEs (unskilled working class)'. A later survey found the respective levels of participation to be 53 per cent, 52 per cent, 33 per cent and 26 per cent (Tuckett and Sargant 1996: 221). Thus, while overall levels of participation increased, these were still differentiated by class factors. If we focus on this factor, as well as current participation, class distinctions are also inscribed in the highest qualification obtained by individuals. Thus, in Britain in 1990–1, 35 per cent of the population were estimated to have no qualifications. For people from professional families the rate was 7 per cent. For those from unskilled manual families the proportion was 60 per cent (Central Statistical Office 1993).

More fundamentally, McGivney (1990) reports that the Organisation for Economic Co-operation and Development identifies economic and social deprivation as the main characteristic of non-participants. The provision of learning opportunities can only play a very small, perhaps insignificant, role in addressing this as an issue. However, it raises the question that resources should be pulled out of education and training to address more central issues of deprivation, such as poverty and poor housing, thereby providing a firmer base for lifelong learning in the future.

In keeping with the discursive approach adopted in this text, therefore, it is important to recognise that the identification of profiles of non-participation in the characteristics of individuals and groups and which characteristics are highlighted is not simply a neutral description. To identify non-participants on the basis of characteristics provides the focus for the issue or issues to be addressed in seeking to increase or widen participation. In this sense, the description of a characteristic becomes a causal explanation. Yet what is cause and what effect is open to question. For instance, can limited initial educational experience be attributed to socioeconomic background, or vice versa, or is there an inter-relatedness of factors which result in adult non-participation? If lack of initial education is a primary characteristic of non-participants, it may well be that resources should be allocated to initial rather than adult learning to enable future generations to become lifelong learners. If this was the case, it is likely that current cohorts of adults would have to fund a greater amount of their learning themselves. In itself, this would have an impact on participation as funding learning is currently another barrier to access. This was deemed to be the case in British Columbia, Canada, in 1992 (Rubenson and Willms 1993). However, a survey of adults for the 1994 Adult Learners' Week in the United Kingdom (Tuckett 1994) found the majority felt the individual and employer rather than the taxpayer should bear most of the funding. Only 16 per cent said cost was an inhibition to studying.

What this suggests is that although characteristics of non-participants can be identified, focusing on single factors as 'target groups' may not in itself overcome barriers to participation. And, as Butler (1996: 26) says of Australia, when it is estimated that 65 per cent of the population is encompassed by target groups, 'who is the system serving?' Barriers to participation may be reconfigured, but with advantages accruing to certain groups at the expense of others. Any notion of some simple technical rational 'fix' to enable participation by all groups based on identifying the characteristics of those groups seems misplaced. Indeed, as provision becomes more flexible, it can result in the pathologising and stigmatising of those groups as not being prepared to 'help themselves'. Difference can be turned into deficits.

As well as social class and age-related characteristics, studies in Britain demonstrate that those adults without a qualification vary according to gender and ethnic origin (Central Statistical Office 1993). If adults' participation in learning is restricted, it is unclear whether this is due to the issues related to gender, ethnic origin or lack of qualifications or a complex combination of a range of such factors which embraces all of the above and more. The picture is complicated further by statistics which illustrate that although a greater percentage of women overall lacked qualifications, in the period 1984–92 they have increased their participation in job-related training as a whole and in comparison with men (Employment Department Group 1993). In Australia, women were more likely to receive training than men, but this was likely to be unstructured learning within the workplace (Knox and Pickersgill 1993) and to be of less duration than training provided for men (Butler 1996). However, it is important also to note that it is women with higher qualifications who tend to have most of such training, suggesting important differentials among women. There are differences inscribed within genders as well as between them. Profiles of participation and non-participation may change also due to factors other than the characteristics of learners; in this case possibly due to the increasing participation of women in the labour market. These structural changes have meant that although part-time employment has increased at the expense of full-time employment, just over half the number of part-time employees were receiving training as full-time employees (Butler 1996) and fewer opportunities to train were provided. Women with higher qualifications are more likely to be in full-time employment and therefore have training opportunities available to them.

Participation is not necessarily a goal in itself – unless perhaps it is considered a way of 'warehousing' surplus labour and expectations through rational recreation and the normalising processes of education and training to engender governmentality. The outcomes of participation are perhaps more significant. For instance, adult employees' satisfaction with training paints a poor view of the effectiveness of participation: only 29 per cent of women were satisfied almost all or a lot of the time, while for men the proportion was 38 per cent (Butler 1996). This type of evidence has led McGivney (1994) to argue that the lack of opportunity for training among the mostly female part-time and temporary workers is an enormous waste of potential. Oglesby (1991) has examined how certain European Union programmes have enabled more women to engage in vocationally relevant learning. However, the focus on women's participation has also led others to argue that the vigorous targeting of unemployed men has become an important priority in the provision of learning opportunities (Neville 1994). We are in complex territory and therefore the significance of 'return to learn' and 'return to work' programmes for women also needs to be assessed. If the outcome is largely to enable women to participate in the low-paid, low-skills sector of the labour market, how does this sit with the equity and progressive intentions of many of those working with that group (*Adults Learning* 1991a)? Providing opportunities for women to participate may not contribute to equity goals in any straightforward sense. Thus, the changes in the provision of learning opportunities to enable increased and wider participation need to be situated in the wider changes in the economy and social formation and their particular discursive constructions need to be examined to evaluate their significance.

The very typologies and descriptors used to examine participation and non-participation, therefore, already tie us to certain boundaries of debate and discussion. A certain set of discourses are produced with consequences for practices developed. Generalisations about, for instance, 'social class and participation', 'women and participation' or 'minority ethnic groups and participation' may not give due account to issues such as the geographical location of learners, availability of opportunities, the field of learning in specific space–time contexts.

In other words, general characteristics about non-participants are not sufficient to tell us the reasons why particular groups do not participate in particular types of learning opportunities, why some people are situated as 'non-participants', as though participation in education and training or even learning is some contemporary road to 'salvation'. More contextualised studies are required for this information. It is also the case that what providers and policy-makers construct as a 'problem' of non-participation may not be a 'problem' for the non-participants themselves. Alternative forms of learning may be engaged in, which, as Sargant (1991) suggests, may simply be 'leisure' for those concerned. We therefore need to problematise the whole discourse of participation and non-participation, and in particular the notion of individual competitiveness for qualifications and skills as a condition of economic participation.

It is the characteristics of adults as individual learners which are constructed dominantly as the basis for change. This is part of the institutional and systemic discourses, constructing questions of participation as being about the characteristics of adult learners and developing an increasingly sophisticated monitoring of entrants into and through the system. These characteristics are treated as 'facts of life' to which providers of learning opportunities must respond to extend participation. A familiar range of discourses about adults come to be told. For instance, individual adults have a range of experiences that they draw upon, many of which may include bad or negative experiences of schooling. They lack confidence in entering education and training establishments and do not necessarily have the motivation to learn. They also have complex life circumstances in making time to engage in learning, which can be problematic, as can be the costs of learning. To enable participation, adults need to be able to fit their learning in with other areas of their life circumstances, and to be supported to build confidence and motivation. This notion of adults-as-learners and learners-as-adults has had a powerful effect in marshalling change in the provision of learning opportunities.

However, what happens when we examine the assumptions embedded within and consequences of such discourses and what they exclude from consideration? First, there is the 'norm' of adult life as it is constructed in such discourses. Certain norms exist within a historical, geographical and cultural context. However, in dominant discourses of participation and non-participation, these contexts and their significance tend to become ascribed to individuals, characteristics which they possess. Such characteristics are not pre-givens or unchanging. Indeed, they may not even be characteristics, but rather ascribed and self-ascribed aspects of identity and governmentality. However, in constructing adult learners within these norms, certain things are already assumed as unchangeable which are in fact capable of change. For instance, if we take the question of childcare. The lack of childcare is a major barrier to participation for women. However, there are multiple ways in which that issue can be addressed. In the discourse of provision, this is largely constructed as an issue of providing crèches and/or flexible time-tabling and/or open and distance learning. In this way, women are given the possibility to juggle ever more demands upon them. The possibility of addressing the issue of childcare at a wider social and political level, for example, through the provision of comprehensive nursery education, or, where there are two parents, for both to play a more equitable role in childcare, is thereby excluded from the boundaries of debate. This would rely on different norms for adult life being constructed, part of a wider cultural and political struggle.

Similarly, if we take the issue of the 'problem' of time to learn (Morrison 1992; Rubenson and Willms 1993; Blaxter and Tight 1994). Modularisation of the curriculum is often put forward as both increasing choice and enabling learners to move in and out of formal learning when it is convenient for them. This normalises a view of adults as not having the time to commit themselves to long periods of study. This is certainly true within current circumstance and modularisation is helpful within that specific context and regime of truth. However, modularisation can also be seen to play a strategic role in reinforcing rather than simply responding to that norm, as greater emphasis is placed on the individual to fund their own learning. It is less likely that adults will be able to fund a full programme of study themselves in one go, but individual modules can be chosen when they can be afforded. In other words, moving in and out of provision is as much about when an individual can afford it as whether they necessarily 'choose' it. Alternative ways of funding learners and learning would produce different discourses around which choices could be framed. What is suggested by these examples is that while adult life is marshalled as a series of challenges to be addressed by providers of learning opportunities, there are in fact wider issues that can be addressed in a variety of ways. One aspect of the focus on providers is precisely to undermine the possibilities of such debates. In this way, the changes in provision to extend participation contribute to constructing a 'norm' of adult life in taking certain assumptions as their starting point.

Recent research on time has started to problematise it as a uniform concept experienced universally (Adam 1994). Time itself is classed and gendered. Morrison's (1992) study uncovered gender differences in finding the self-disciplined time to study part-time. In particular, the fragmented time experienced by women – part of the flexilives mentioned in chapter 2 – made self-disciplined time a difficult achievement. Here it is noticeable that Morrison suggests adaptative strategies to be adopted by providers of learning opportunities to enable the effective use of fragmented time, rather than a reconstruction of gendered time to challenge fragmentation. Thus, even 'lack of time' as a reason for non-participation and the experience of time has a specific cultural dimension insofar as its use may vary from group to group and within groups.

In the discourses which construct adult participatio an non-participation as about characteristics, the complex social, economic and cultural factors which affect individual's attitudes towards learning can be turned into attributes or pathologies of the individual, their personal history and biography. This has important consequences. For instance, if providers of learning opportunities or the system becomes more flexible and yet certain groups continue not to participate, that 'failure' – and constructing it as a failure already assumes a certain value in participating – can be laid at the door of the people concerned. In chapter 1, I indicated the significance of this form of pathologising in relation to unemployed adults and the focus on 'motivating' them to participate in learning opportunities. This already assumes that motivation is the 'problem' to be overcome. It could be argued that, given the lack of employment opportunities, not to participate in learning may be an entirely understandable choice, particularly for those groups who have largely been positioned at the margins of or outside the system. As Iverson found in a study of short-term unemployed adults in Denmark and their attitudes towards career and life planning,

> many unskilled workers are used to just living out their lives, rather than trying to make a better life for themselves through planning. . . . Subjects called attention to the conflict they felt between an educational planning culture and their own life culture.
>
> (Iverson 1993: 44)

The negative experiences and attitudes attributed to individuals therefore may make perfect 'common sense' to those concerned for no matter 'what use and exchange value is attributed to training and qualifications in broad terms, individuals' own perceptions of self and career [*sic*] will affect how they experience such opportunities and determine the meanings and values they attach to them' (Fuller *et al.*, quoted in Maguire *et al.* 1993: 8). In other words, even as providers institute practices to more readily meet the needs of individuals, they reinscribe fresh barriers to participation if there is a lack of a cultural perspective on issues of participation and non-participation. The extension of opportunity through greater institutional flexibility and responsiveness may belie the cultural rigidities and barriers already inscribed in the institutional culture, and form and content of provision. Culture, attitudes and the positioning of subjects are crucial in this respect, wherein inclusions and exclusions are integral to institutional practices. The cultural dimension enables the grounds of those practices to be foregrounded and openly contested, creating a politics of participation and non-participation rather than it resting in a reified discourse of individual ability.

However, as with the pathologising of individuals, it is also possible for cultures to be pathologised in explanations of participation and non-participation. Cultural rather than individual characteristics and deficiencies are constructed as reasons for people's practices (Dadzie 1989). For example, certain groups of minority ethnic women do not participate in the formal provision of learning opportunities for religious reasons. This provides the basis for a discourse in which the 'problem' of their non-participation is ascribed to 'their' culture. Similarly, certain research demonstrates that participants and non-participants engage equally in mass culture, but that participants are 'significantly more engaged in cultural practices such as reading, and visiting cinemas, theatres, museums and exhibitions' (McGivney 1993: 14). If that lack of participation in the differentiated 'high' cultural spheres can be ascribed to specific groups, then it is possible to position them as responsible for their perceived lack of cultural capital. However, the consequences of de-differentiation in culture that were discussed in chapter 2 and the growth of cultural activities as forms of popular leisure start to problematise a stance which locates cultural deficiency in different groups within the social formation. The distinction here is between constructing culture as somehow the cause of events rather than as an expression of the relational, contested and dynamic values and power in the social formation, including the nature of the content and delivery of education and training. In other words, culture does not cause non-participation, but the inter-relationships between and positioning of people within cultures result in specific forms of participation and non-participation in education, training and learning.

In commenting on research into provision for women in 1991–2, McGivney (1994: 119) argues that the lack of financial support for women is explained by two aspects of culture: 'the hostility to women that lies only a fraction beneath the surface of acceptable social attitudes, and the persisting (but unacknowledged) drive to restrict women to the private domain'. While more women participate, they largely remain positioned in a certain range of learning opportunities and occupational areas. However, as well as an outcome of the practices of the dominant culture, non-participation may be constructed also as an active sub- or counter-cultural response to that which is on offer, or forced upon groups by those dominant cultural norms. While this gives an active role to non-participants in shaping their practices, the discourse of 'resistance' which often frames such analysis has itself become subject to criticism, giving meaning to practices which are not those of the people involved. Whitson (1991: 82) argues that 'what students get out of the course depends upon what they themselves make of their experience: how they construe the meaning of the course in relation to the structure of their prior understandings and beliefs'. A positioning of non-participants as 'resisters' may therefore invest alternative meanings in the practices of those concerned to those they would ascribe to themselves.

This is not to deny the major changes in participation that have taken place in recent years. However, these changes need to be specifically identified and located within the context of culture and power. Institutional change is not simply practical and technical, but also entails a change of culture. The possibilities and limitations upon this signify the relative balances of power within institutions and in the wider social formation at any time. Rubenson (1993) demonstrates this in his analysis of the shifts in Swedish adult education policy under the influence of changing social forces, in particular, the power of trade unions. Feminist, post-colonial and environmental movements, to name a few, constantly attempt to insert themselves into the processes which shape the changes taking place in the structure, delivery and content of learning opportunities, and, with that, who participates and who does not. Governments and employers constitute perhaps the most powerful influences in these processes.

Debates about participation and non-participation are crucial in response to the question of who gets what, how, when and where. Learning and qualifications are central to the opportunities people access in education and training, the economy and social formation. However, there is also a restricted range of opportunities for people to attain within the current structures of power. In attempting to widen participation, the shift from a focus on participation in education and training – a certain form of provision – to participation in learning – a focus on what people achieve – has been significant. In focusing on the learning which can be demonstrated wherever it takes place and finding ways to support that learning in different settings, a discourse of the moorland of lifelong learning shifts the emphasis to providing forms of open and distance learning, assessment and accreditation and turning the (paid) workplace into a learning organisation. Having revealed the moorland of lifelong learning, institutional and systemic practices develop to spread the boundaries to 'embrace' as much of that moorland as is possible. This is a process of uneven development and there is a tension between these developments as extensions of bounded fields of practice with a focus on inputs and such systems framed within a discourse of learning with an emphasis on outputs. This signifies the play of differentiation and de-differentiation discussed in the previous chapter.

There can also be tensions between the strategies of open and distance learning and assessment and accreditation, the former remaining positioned within a discourse of provision (inputs) and the latter within a discourse of learning (outputs). Much higher education in the United Kingdom is still provision-led, even if it increasingly has become modularised to become more flexible. The shift toward a focus on learning guided by funding and policy results in an emphasis on outcomes as an organising principle in producing coherence within the system of learning opportunities available to adults. If lifelong learning has many settings, it is through the provision of assessment and accreditation that those boundaries can most readily be bridged. In this sense, open and distance learning may be an institutional strategy to bridge boundaries, but credit frameworks provide the systemic response to a discourse of lifelong learning. If the latter is not bounded by specific institutional provision of courses and programmes, one way of bridging the boundaries of the different sites of learning is to provide forms of assessment and accreditation, and forms of credit accumulation and transfer to enable adults to move within a system of opportunities based on achievement rather than attendance. In this way, the non-formal and informal learning in which adults participate can be recognised by the more formal providers of learning opportunities. Here adults will be accessing accreditation as much as they participate in learning opportunities. However, even as more flexible provision expands opportunities to partici- pate for some, new exclusions are inscribed.

OPENING DISTANCES – DISTANT OPENINGS

In order to be more flexible, to provide a wider range of opportunities for adults to participate in learning, institutions at all levels of post-school education and training have been encouraged to become more flexible through the adoption of what in some quarters is constructed as open and distance education and in others as open and distance learning. This has been framed largely within a discourse of access – of extending opportuni- ties to adults who would not be able to attend institutions on a regular basis. There is no doubting that in the potential to reconfigure space–time through the deployment of different technologies and pedagogies such practices have resulted in an extension of participation. Such strategies have also been introduced as a (questionably) cost-effective way to expand participation within certain policy and funding constraints (Commission of the European Communities 1993a). An Australian report (National Board of Employment, Education and Training 1992) identifies the constraints and pressures resulting in the development of these approaches: the pressure of increasing student numbers; the unmet demands for new buildings; a 'shortage' of academic staff (or, more likely, academic posts!); and the pres- sures to serve industry, to become more entrepreneurial and to export education. These factors are echoed elsewhere around the globe, resulting in a general shift towards technologically mediated and flexible forms of delivery to the extent where it is possible to argue that 'the boundary between "distance education" and "conventional education" is becoming blurred; indeed is likely to disappear' (National Board of Employment, Education and Training 1992: 1).

In the process, the strategies of flexible delivery can be argued to be contested on the basis of whether they are situated within a discourse of provision or one of lifelong learning. While distance education has a provider-led focus, its relationship to a discourse of adult education is ambiguous, as witnessed by the different professional, academic and research spaces they occupy. Despite occasional transgressions, discourses of distance education have had a closer relationship with those of 'higher education' than 'adult education'. Yet open and distance learning has become a central plank in supporting lifelong learning, in spreading, bridging and breaking down boundaries. The discourses of distance education and open and distance learning are therefore not simply discourses about boundaries, but also a form of boundary-breaking discourse – transgressing and transgressed. There are two sides to this I wish to discuss here. On the one hand, I will examine how distance education is part of wider processes which reconfigure space–time and questions of participation. On the other, I shall seek to resituate distance education in a different discourse of open and distance learning as part of the moorland of lifelong learning. In other words, to understand distance education differently is to understand it in a different way which in this text is as open and distance learning.

Most discussion of open and distance learning and distance education is of a technical and practical nature, focusing on how to implement certain strategies and offering evaluations of their successes and problems. Attempts to locate the significance of such developments within the wider processes of economic, social and political change have tended to be at the margins of debate. It is in this sense that we can situate the burgeoning interest in the discussion of fordism, neo- and post-fordism and its significance for distance education in recent years. A literature born out of industrial sociology and the attempt to delineate changes in the organisation of the workplace (Bagguley, 1991) has found its way into the discussion of distance education and open and distance learning. This has been manifested in two ways. First, there are the changing demands made upon providers of learning opportunities by changes in the economy and the organisation of the workplace more generally (Edwards 1991b; Campion and Renner 1992). If the workplace is to be increasingly governed by forms of flexibility, a greater emphasis is placed on lifelong learning, as suggested in chapter 2. The curriculum demands upon providers change in terms of both content and delivery, demands which cannot be met effectively and efficiently through more traditional means. Second, there is the discussion of the impact of neo- and post-fordism on the internal organisation of providers of learning opportunities and the extent to which they take on the organisational forms of the flexible firm found elsewhere in the economy (Farnes 1993; Raggatt 1993). These debates have been supplemented by an examination of the significance of globalisation to distance education and open and distance learning and the contribution of such practices to globalisation (Evans 1989; Evans and Nation 1992; Edwards 1994a, 1995a).

What role can distance education be said to have played in the reconfiguration of space–time associated with globalisation and space–time compression? It is possible to identify a number of features. First, it undermines the necessity for people to attend specific institutions for education and training and foregrounds their own place – home, workplace, and so on – as a learning setting. It therefore contributes to possibilities for geographical dispersal, as learners and providers no longer need to be in the same place, or nation state, but are available increasingly on a global scale to each other. This can of course have paradoxical effects, as it can result in people being kept 'in their place', while at the same time enabling people across great physical distances to be brought together through the use of information and communications technologies. Evans and Nation (1992: 10) have suggested that 'distance education and open learning have been key dispersal agents' in the movement towards a post-industrial order. Whether or not we frame the order as post-industrial or as a reorganisation of the industrial order, the dispersal made available through the deployment of information and communications technologies is undeniable. These in turn impact upon the practices of distance education. Thus, the very distance distance education covers brings places together, compresses space and time and engenders specific possibilities for flexibility. The degree of compression of space–time is dependent on the media through which the learning is made available. Thus, the sending of printed materials through the post brings about a specific spatial–temporal relationship, one which is transformed through, for instance, the use of computer networking. However, at least in the short run, the post probably reaches more people than do computer networks. Evans (1989: 181) suggests that 'distance education is partly about "choreographing" a myriad of personal and collective movements in time–space' and that this is part of the hidden curricula of distance education. The notion of choreographing is an attractive one, as, in general, it signifies the looser organisation of space–time within distance education rather than the more conventional notion of the structured timetable. In distance education, there is less control over where and when the person undertakes their learning. However, choreographing still suggests a locus of control, one which is largely located in the timetable of outputs – assessments – more than in the inputs in the traditional form of class attendance. This places greater responsibility on the adult-as-learner to learn to 'dance' –

to be self-disciplined – rather than simply be schooled into the 'steps' – disciplined.

Second, it is also important to examine the formal curricula of distance education in relation to globalisation. In the potential global reach of distance education there is the question of the extent to which this results in the universalising and homogenising of the curricula. To sit in South East Asia studying materials produced in the United Kingdom is certainly a feat of access and enterprise, but we need to examine the extent to which such globalising trends bring into the curricula alternative voices, information and perspectives, or further exclude and marginalise less powerful alternative knowledges. This may vary from subject area to subject area, but even in the field of management, whose reach does seem to be truly global, there is the question over what and whose view of management is being conveyed. Distance education may purvey a globalising and globalised view which denies heterogeneity or keeps it contained within a specific set of parameters – colonising the discursive spaces and life-worlds of the learners. The extent of this may well depend on the degree of inter-activity in the specific arrangements for flexible delivery – how far it is education as conceived in one part of the globe delivered at a distance and/or the extent to which the learning includes diverse texts and texts of diversity, and is open to multiple readings. Evans (1989: 177) argues that 'distance education, particularly though its curricula, is part of a range of social processes which reproduce and transform places and distances in society'. However, an assessment is necessary of whether this results in a universalising of particular perspectives, as occurred with the adoption of the clock to measure time across the globe, or an assertion of multiple perspectives. Distance education curricula may therefore be one of those actions at a distance, the '"indirect" mechanisms of aligning economic, social and personal conduct with socio-political objectives' (Miller and Rose 1993: 76) that are part of the strategies of governmentality in contemporary social formations. However, even at its most homogenising, this process can never be complete due to the symbolic spaces that operate between providers and learners, and the differing and differential meanings adopted by learners in their practices. Globalisation and space–time compression, therefore, can never produce uniformity entirely. There is the constant incitement to heterogeneity and alternative understandings and practices.

Third, there is a need to situate conceptions of 'the learner' within particular configurations of space–time and the forms of identity associated with them. Certain assumptions which transcend space–time often are made about learners which are not consistent with the forms and ways of experiencing with which they are familiar. In a period in which learners are themselves subject to great changes in their positions and subjectivities, there is a question as to whether the universal humanistic notion of learner-centredness provides the categories to 'make sense' of the processes at play.

Here it is possible to identify two contrasting discourses: that of the adult-as-student and that of the adult-as-learner, with assumptions resting in the extent to which flexible delivery is constructed as extending institutional boundaries for students – distance education – or is reconfigured as a practice to support lifelong learning and learners – open and distance learning (Edwards 1996).

If we consider the notion of the 'student' first. Here there is a clear role and identity. A student is part of an institution. This sense of belonging is important in establishing a sense of identity. It provides a certain status which can be important to us as individuals and in negotiating boundaries with others. This is partly dependent on the value given to education and training and different forms of education and training within a culture, but none the less being a student provides a boundary against which other demands can be defended. It is a 'serious' role which, although capable of being a challenge to our sense of self and relations with members of family and friends, none the less provides the grounds for affirming a particular identity. This has been important for adults whose participation in formal education and training is dependent partially upon their ability to organise their learning, to defend a space–time around other demands (Morrison 1992). However, as Wakefield (1994) found in her research of mature students entering higher education from Access courses, there can be discomfort with different forms of student identity – 'mature', 'proper' – and varying degrees of social risk – within the institution and outside – dependent on age and gender. Shah (1994: 263) talks of her feeling that she 'wasn't a *real* student but an imitation'. Within the boundary of student identity, therefore, there are multiple meanings, engendering and in turn constituted by the desires and anxieties of adult students.

It is arguable that the concept of the student is linked to the modern conception of education in which a canon of knowledge, skills and understanding is transmitted to the participants. It is a serious and disciplined process of development and deepening in which a relative institutional stability is reflected in a relative stability of the canon and its ordering and, with that, a certain stability in the identity of the student. In many ways, therefore, modern education continues and extends the monastic tradition of initiation, order and stability, replacing the religious elite and vocation with the secular elite of the modern nation state, also with a sense of vocation, although overlaid by investments in professionalism. This notion largely depends on a full-time period of study in which there is a close proximity between the teacher and learner. With the shift towards distance education, however, that sense of boundedness and belonging increasingly becomes problematic.

As the range of opportunities for learning has grown, at least partly through the development of distance education, the configuration of space–time and the notion of 'an education' are reconfigured. Similarly, as more adults have begun to participate across the range of post-school provision, so the capacity of education in its modern guise to meet the requirements of constituencies with multiple roles and positions has been challenged. In the process, the notion of a canon to be imparted has itself been undermined as flexible delivery mechanisms become more significant. The result is that the range of learning opportunities available to people and the ways in which those are presented increase. The sense of trust invested in educational institutions to impart the canon to students is undermined as individuals are given greater opportunity to negotiate their own ways through the range of learning opportunities available to them, invest their own meanings within the learning process and negotiate the relationship between learning and other activities. As a result, the bounded sense of identity associated with being a student is challenged. The focus shifts from being a member of an institution to being an individualised and/or group learner packaging and processing learning in particular forms. The choices available and the conditions under which they are exercised by adults thereby create the conditions for less certainty and more unstable bodies of knowledge, subjectivities and senses of identity – a demise of the disciplines if not necessarily of discipline (Nicoll and Edwards, 1997). Adults 'are all "kaleidoscope" people, our shape constantly changing in accordance with how we are positioned and position ourselves' (Shah 1994: 266). The development of flexible learning opportunities thereby becomes ambiguously associated with changes in what it means to be a participant, with a shift from discourses of the student to ones of the learner, wherein learning becomes integral to lifestyle practices.

There is no clear boundary to the notion of the 'learner'. Consistent with a discourse of lifelong learning, it foregrounds the fact that people learn not only from institutions, but in various and diverse life settings and can adopt a learning approach to life. It also suggests a certain diffuseness about what constitutes learning. As learners, we are not part of something, we are individuals or members of groups negotiating the complexity and ambivalence of the contemporary period. In other words, inscribed in the very notion of the learner is the shift in emphasis wherein greater responsibility is being placed back upon individuals, identified as part of the cultural changes in chapter 2. The identity of being a learner becomes an ongoing process rather than a thing, part of the reflexive project of self-identity. The sense of being as a thing, of being a student, is displaced and overlaid by a sense of being as activity, of becoming, of learning and being a learner. Placing boundaries around that learning, creating spaces against other demands, becomes far more problematic. For some (Brown 1995), this can be partially achieved by reconstituting student identity around the activities of studentship. The notion of the student as a stage in life associated with youth and immaturity is overlaid and displaced by a notion of student life based on the activity of studying (Earwaker 1992) and a process of production of the self (Wakefield 1994). This is an attempt to place a boundary around studying which may be breached by other concerns and indeed by the more unbounded notion of the learner. Thus, as new forms of flexible learning are developed, so are different forms of participant identity, and these need to be foregrounded and examined rather than assumed and excluded.

This indicates the need for a shift in the discourses surrounding the development of more flexible approaches. The notion of the student is constructed within a discourse of provision, of a bounded field, while that of a learner can be situated within a discourse of lifelong learning. In compressing space–time and crossing boundaries in the ways it does, distance education therefore finds itself in the paradoxical situation of undermining the grounds for its own discursive construction, or at least making them more ambivalent and troubling. It is unsurprising, therefore, that flexible strategies themselves start to be reframed within a discourse of open and distance learning. Within this shift, it is possible to distinguish between distance education's emphasis on the transmission of a subject and open and distance learning's concern with the learners and learning. The former is positioned within a modernist discourse of education extended and modified by its provision at a distance. The latter expands the terrain to be encompassed and introduces the learners as active subjects in their own learning. In this shift, the discourses of providers are displaced and overlaid by discourses which place greater emphasis on the learner. In the process, the argument surrounding the extension of access through distance education becomes reconfigured, as what it is that is to be learnt and how that is organised becomes opened up for consideration under a discourse of open and distance learning.

Here there are resonances between the discourses of distance education and open and distance learning and those of fordism and neo- and post-fordism. Although fordism tends to be positioned as a discourse of the organisation of production, implicit to it are also forms of distribution and consumption. Mass-produced items for the mass market are emblematic of fordism and it is the organisation of production and the role of the producer which are given primacy in such discourses. Similarly, although there is a concern for access within discourses of distance education, the very fact such discourses focus on education – the provision of certain sorts of learning opportunities – results in and from a particular focus in which the availability of education is extended to different groups. However, it remains primarily a mass market that is accessed. Access is to the products already constituted as valuable within and by educational systems. Here openness and even distance are subservient to education as the latter extends its reach across the globe. The delivery mechanism may change and be extended, but the education to be carried at a distance overwhelmingly is invested with the cultural messages of modernity – of mastery, progress and moral superiority through the development of reason. For Seidler (1994: 27), this arises because modernity – and therefore education in the services of modernity – claims 'to embody a universal conception of human action and a conception of morality within which all can equally participate as rational agents . . . it has assumed itself to be superior to other traditions of thought and feeling'. Education at a distance extends the reach of that project, extending the boundaries of a specific field of practice.

Within a discourse of lifelong learning, it is possible to see flexible learning reconstituted as open and distance learning, foregrounding the possibilities for diverse forms of learning in diverse settings. This in itself can take a variety of forms. For Lyotard (1984), the development of open and distance learning is part of the postmodern condition of knowledge in which performativity or systemic efficiency is based not upon the cultural ideals of modernity, but on the diversity of the individual in the marketplace for learning opportunities. Performativity depends upon answering the question positively that there is a market for some learning opportunity, whether it be job-related training offered by formal providers of learning opportunities, or forms of info-tainment or edu-tainment provided by commercial organisations. Here distance is subservient to the discourse of open learning and 'educative' processes are displaced and reconstituted as relationships between producers and learners-as-consumers in which knowledge is exchanged on the basis of the 'usefulness' it has to the learner in maximising their contribution within the system. In a discourse of open and distance learning, therefore, mass markets fragment and become more volatile across the globe, giving rise to a wider range of learning and foregrounding the learner.

The focus on learning and with that the learner takes us into areas of opportunity beyond formally provided education and training and those areas of learning defined as valuable by and for educators. Distance educators who espouse open and distance learning therefore find themselves in something of a paradox as the two discourses do not necessarily sit comfortably with each other. If learners engage in and value learning which is not valued by distance educators, is it the openness of learning which is subordinated or the cultural values of the educator? Also open and distance learning may take place beyond the ambit of educators and providers of education altogether, involving alternative providers of learning opportunities mediated by the market. They may also exist outside the ambit of the market in forms of mutual learning as affirmations of identity in which there is a 'perpetual struggle to voice ideas, opinions or injustices systematically excluded from the universe of phrases: a continuous incitement to speech' (Barron 1992: 36).

Here there are resonances with discourses of neo- and post-fordism. This is not so much surrounding the organisation of work – although providers may indeed be reconstituted along such lines – as in the relationship between the consumer and producer. While neo- and post-fordism are primarily used as a way of analysing the organisation of work, more significantly for this discussion they signify a change in the conditions under which work is organised. Through the mediation of information and communications technologies learners-as-consumers have a greater say in what is to be produced through their purchase and use of goods and services. Consumption thereby displaces production as of prime significance as diverse market niches are satisfied through production based on more imme-diate market information. Discourses of open and distance learning also place greater emphasis on the articulated requirements of diverse learners in diverse settings to which providers of learning opportunities need to respond. Insofar as discourses of distance education are overlaid and displaced by those of open and distance learning, the organisation of learning opportunities at a distance sets up a number of possibilities within a wider notion of openness which may or may not involve distance providers or providers of learning opportunities at all.

In situating flexible forms of delivery within the contrasting discourses of providers and lifelong learning, it is possible to see both the ways in which institutions are able to extend the boundaries of their practices and the ways in which those practices are reconfigured. The inter-relationship of such shifts with those of neo- and post-fordism go further than servicing different working practices or the organisation of education and training itself. They are part of that increasingly influential wider 'regime of truth' governing the changing practices of the moorland of lifelong learning. In this producers/educators are placed in different positions to those many have come to expect, with consequences for practice and conceptions of self. However, even as such discourses displace the emphasis on production and the producer, they may also undermine themselves. For instance, to construct open and distance learning simply within a discourse of the marketplace entails placing a boundary around what can or cannot be construed as learning – those learning opportunities for which there is a market. However, as suggested, a lot of learning can be open in the sense that it is not mediated by the marketplace – mutual learning from each other – or even when mediated in these terms may not be approached simply as a relationship of consumption (Field 1994). Even as open and distance learning develops to bridge and open the boundaries on the moorland of lifelong learning, it is therefore possible for new boundaries to be inscribed.

WHO TAKES (THE) CREDIT?

A discourse of lifelong learning highlights the many settings in which adults learn. If the settings for learning are extended, then a question emerges over how the learning within them is to be encompassed, if at all. The result has been an increased attention to the provision and forms of assessment and accreditation and, in particular, assessment in the workplace. In this process, the notion of credit has itself been reconfigured with less attention to 'notional study time' and more focus on achievement and outcomes. Thus, even as credit, and the gaining of credit, is given greater priority in providing systemic support for the provision of learning opportunities for adults, it is itself subject to discursive reconstruction, decreasing the emphasis on the provider as the place to which one has to be attached for a certain period of time in order for credit to be obtained, and introducing the notion of outcomes divorced from the time it takes to achieve them and particular institutional arrangements within which they are to be gained. The tight space–time constraints of a bounded field of practice loosen to enable differing configurations of space–time in support of lifelong learning. At its most profound, the amounts of time to achieve certain learning and the specific spaces in which that learning occurs become irrelevant to the award of outcomes-based credit.

In a study of credit accumulation and transfer practices in higher education in the United Kingdom, Davidson (1992) identified five reasons for their development. First, they break down boundaries to access as adults are able to move more easily into and within the 'system'. Second, they enable people who wish to study part-time and at differential rates to do so. Third, for individuals, programmes can be altered if personal circumstances change, for instance, through a move from one part of the country to another. Fourth, they encourage lifelong learning in expanding opportunity structures and enhancing motivation. Fifth, learning from a variety of settings can be integrated into assessed and accredited programmes of study. The latter has been particularly influential in challenging the formal sectors of education and training and including other settings as sites of learning. In particular, and in line with modernising discourses, such settings have increasingly included those of the workplace, within which the achievement of a wide range of qualifications is now possible. Reviewing the motivations underpinning the development of different credit frameworks in the United Kingdom, Robertson concludes they emerge when there is a need to

> manage the diversity of learning opportunities between different institutions, different countries and different learning modes; manage or promote wider access to post-secondary learning opportunities; encourage student flexibility and mobility within and between different learning experiences; eliminate barriers to progression between different levels of learning, and between academic and vocational learning.
>
> (Robertson 1993a: 2)

Credit frameworks in themselves do not do away with issues of status and value. However, they do make possible a more explicit and open debate about what is valued through the processes of assessment and accreditation. Here the institutions invested with the power to award credit remain powerful, in terms of both the differential values and statuses ascribed to those institutions and the selective valuing of different forms of learning inscribed in different credit frameworks. Even as it is reconfigured, therefore, the significance of institutions and stakeholders in arbitrating what constitutes worthwhile knowledge, skills and understanding is still apparent. Perhaps more transparent would be a better way of terming this, as greater explicitness is demanded of providers in their assessment processes enabling greater scrutiny – some would argue 'accountability', others 'policing' – of what is occurring. The authority of such institutions is raised as something to be questioned, as forms of market and other pressure to deliver credit are exerted upon them. There is, however, no single meaning to such trends. Even as the award of outcomes-based credit foregrounds the criteria of selection, inclusion and exclusion which are central to the practices of education and training, it also provides new and varied forms of assessment and accreditation, including those of prior learning (Butterworth 1992), providing opportunities for access and progression which would not otherwise exist. Portfolio-based assessment, peer assessment, self-assessment and learning contracts have all developed significantly in support of accrediting learning across the lifespan and in different settings.

In principle, the foregrounding of different learning settings and the requirement for increased (and widened) participation in discourses of lifelong learning necessitate a credit system which is sufficiently flexible to provide for the mutual recognition of different types of achievements wherever and however they occur. In other words, a currency system is necessary which enables learners to aggregate learning achieved in different settings and through different modes of learning. Whether that system relies on a single currency or an accepted exchange rate mechanism will depend on the location and intent in its introduction and its implementation by those in institutions who make decisions. However, Pocock (1992) suggests that multiple pathways to entry-level training reproduce rather than help to address inequity, indicating the need for an approach based on a single currency. The extent and directions of mobility of adult learners usually remain in the control of institutions and departments who will decide the type and amount of credit they are prepared to recognise. This is particularly true in the higher education context. This can be affected by subject-specific concerns, such as the dating of knowledge and skills, or by judgements about where the credit was earned and therefore the quality of learning (Davidson 1992). However, the fact that such decisions are foregrounded means that institutions have to be able to justify their decisions more transparently than in the past. They may also find themselves excluding themselves from 'market niches' or opportunities if they take too restrictive a view of credit. However such a stance may be adopted deliberately by certain institutions in order that they may enhance their prestige by creating a 'market image' of quality and excellence, or, more pertinently, selection and exclusion.

The ambiguities of credit frameworks and systems within an increasingly consumer-orientated provision of learning opportunities may well result, therefore, in differential consequences, with certain providers adopting a 'pile it high, sell it cheap' approach and others an approach of 'excellence, quality and value-added'. In other words, trends operating in the wider economic sphere can be seen also at work in relation to the approaches to credit adopted by providers of learning opportunities, themselves reconstituted increasingly as part of the service sector of the economy. In theory, credit frameworks allow individuals to move easily into and within the plurality of learning opportunities available to them. This contributes to the de-differentiation of the notion of full- and part-time study. Individuals build portfolios of credit or records of achievement as they move in and out of and through the system. The system itself is not tightly bounded by attachment to specific institutional contexts, but involves a looser arrangement between the learner and the institution governed by the award of credit as people develop their learning 'careers'. There is still a structure, but the structuring takes place through the credit system rather than through institutional allegiances; more flexible and different power relations operate within it.

The growth and development of credit frameworks and systems has occurred not only in the United Kingdom, but also within the European Union, between its member states and elsewhere, such as in Australia, South Africa and New Zealand. Often such arrangements remain framed within a discourse of education and training, with credit awarded for a bounded period of dedicated learning – the notional study time mentioned above. However, the discourse of outcomes has come to the fore to challenge this concept of credit, particularly in the reforms of vocational qualifications and moves towards competence-based assessment in many parts of the globe. Credit agreements also often remain restricted within certain sectoral boundaries, allowing for only limited forms of progression. Credit frameworks do not necessarily result in a credit system. There may or may not be a formal coherence, but the values ascribed to different forms of credit have a powerful impact on participation and non-participation. I shall return to these two issues shortly when I discuss the question of 'parity of esteem' between different types of credit awards, an issue which has important consequences for differential consequences in the shifts towards supporting lifelong learning.

The question of what learning is valued and awarded credit and who decides what is to be valued and in what ways is fraught with difficulties. In many ways, it is central to the debate about education and training – what it means to be 'educated' and/or 'trained' – and its power and purposes within the social formation. According to the Unit for the Development of Adult Continuing Education (UDACE) in the United Kingdom (1989), there are a range of stakeholders in any credit system, including providers, learners and customers, that is, those who pay for learning opportunities. Each will have their own, not necessarily consistent, views on what should be valued in what ways. Frequently, learners will have a wider range of objectives than providers. Customers, for instance, the state or employers, may have different views on what is to be funded to those of learners. There are complex negotiations at play in decisions about what constitutes credit and what is constituted as credit. Within the differing discursive influences introduced in chapter 2, we can broadly identify three strands of learning to be valued. Cultural restorationists tend to value learning associated with a canon of usually university-generated knowledge and a 'high culture' of national identity and nationhood. Modernisers value learning associated with skills, knowledge and attitudes relevant to the world of work, increasingly articulated within a discourse of competence. Progressives value learning associated with citizenship and the knowledges of groups excluded and marginalised by the dominant culture, and practices to challenge that subordination. The differing strengths of influence in differing sectors of the education and training system can be seen in their relative influence upon differing credit frameworks.

There are currently three credit frameworks within England and Wales (Robertson 1993b, 1996) and I wish to use the discussion of them to illustrate the shift from a provider-led discourse to a discourse of lifelong learning. However, I also want to suggest that the process has been complicated by the continuing play of differential value to learning associated with powerful cultural norms. Thus, even as there is the attempt to value learning in its various settings – to provide 'parity of esteem' to a fuller range of learning and credit – the discourses framing that shift are actually already subordinated to certain binaries in which privilege remains with specific forms of learning. Here the very notion of 'parity of esteem' assumes a binary of the academic and vocational, with an inevitable privileging process of the former over the latter, despite calls for this not to be the case. Parity of esteem works with and within that binary rather than problematising it as a way of structuring what is to be valued in learning.

The first credit framework is associated with the assessment of academic knowledge. Conventional assessment of academic programmes is norm-referenced using traditional examination techniques and possibly including continuous assessment. This is framed within a discourse of education in which the provider initiates and encultures individuals into certain subjects and subjectivities. The second credit framework is associated with the assessment of vocational competence. Assessment is criterion-referenced with an over-arching criterion being whether the person with the qualification can perform in their job. Here it is the discourse of lifelong learning which has come to the fore with an emphasis on outcomes. The third credit framework is in many ways a hybrid of the other two, attempting to provide adults with opportunities to span different types of learning and incorporating notional time and personal referenced outcomes into the assessment process.

The binaries that can be seen to be operating here are education–training, academic–vocational, knowledge–skills, norms–criteria, providers–learners, inputs–outcomes. While neither static nor holding a single meaning, these are none the less powerful in shaping responses to change. Even as discourses of lifelong learning challenge those of education and training – and here it becomes clear why they have been formulated in relation to the vocational area, given its subordinate position in the play of dominant meanings – they are constantly subject to re-subordination. Here the unreflexive defence of educational institutions against the vocational – the 'other' to be subordinated – can be seen as part of a strategy to maintain the exclusive and excluding patterns of participation and non-participation associated with institutions conveying a dominant culture of academic knowledge. Both cultural restorationists and progressives are found defending the academic over the vocational, a position with a long history in the United Kingdom.

The roots of this notion of education lie in the practices of aristocracy and the notion of the cultivated 'gentleman' of leisure (and here it is important to note the gender and class connotations of this term) whose social position, although not a function of educational background, involved the cultivation of certain broad 'educated' qualities associated with disciplinary knowledge and academic forms of study. Williams (1962) pointed out that the particular way in which education developed in the nineteenth century in the United Kingdom can be understood in terms of the conflict between 'old humanists' and 'public educators'. The former were (white male) members of the leisured class for whom aristocratic cultural values were paramount and for whom the possibility of being educated could be open only to an elite. They were opposed, therefore, to mass schooling. The latter, by contrast, were committed to individual and social development through education available to all. Hence they were ardent proponents of mass schooling. It was largely through their influence that the notion of a modern meritocratic society and of individual mobility through education was inscribed in the discourses of the emerging education profession.

However, in a twist which helps us to understand some of our contemporary paradoxes, 'public educators' drew on the arguments of the 'old humanists' in their conflict with the 'industrial trainers', who saw education as preparation for work. Both the 'public educators' and the 'industrial trainers' wanted universal education, but the former were profoundly opposed to the latter's vocationalism. There was, therefore, a coming together of the 'old humanists' and the 'public educators', with the latter adopting the former's notions of liberal education, the cultivation of the intellect and learning grounded in academic scholarship. This coming together helped to define a specific terrain for the development of a particular form of universal education which has dogged the United Kingdom with its constant reinscribing of value in institutions and curricula which exclude the achievements of the less powerful from due recognition. This is played out as much today in the disputes over credit frameworks as it was in the nineteenth century over what constituted 'education'.

The development of credit frameworks ambivalently traverses and is traversed by a series of binaries and the play of power within and between them. This illustrates both the impossibility of 'parity of esteem' as an approach to valuing different forms of learning and the need for a single credit system – the single currency rather than the exchange rate mechanism – which recognises achievement in all domains. In other words, differentiated credit frameworks need to be de-differentiated so that differences in learning can be valued more equitably. Here de-differentiation helps to engender systemic coherence, but may also be said to extend the network of governmentality ever further. This is both part of and entails a discourse of lifelong learning, with certain uncomfortable consequences for certain practitioners, such as the notion of valuing the vocational. One possibility is for a credit system which values learning outcomes.

It is worth examining briefly the similarities and differences in a learning outcomes-based approach to assessment and accreditation and a competence-based approach. Both are concerned with recognising achievements within the wider moorland of learning and it is the discourse of lifelong learning which governs the emergence of them as credit systems. Each is concerned to construct explicit criteria against which learning can be assessed, rather than relying on implicit norms which assess people in relation to one another. In other words, rather than credit being awarded on the basis of a competition between individuals, public criteria are established against which individuals can be assessed and over which there can be open debate and contest. Outcomes and competence differ, however, over who decides what is to be valued. Even within a discourse of lifelong learning it is necessary, therefore, to establish what learning is worthwhile.

Vocational competences in the United Kingdom establish a highly detailed set of standards and performance criteria for the assessment process against which the learner can be appraised. The criteria are in principle derived from what is necessary to undertake a role in the workforce through a process of functional analysis. The learning outcomes are therefore already set, inscribed in the standards of competence. Any negotiation with the learner is over how and when they achieve those outcomes, not what the latter are. This leads some to suggest that competences offer a Taylorist inflexible approach to assessment, while for others its modular form signifies a post-fordist consumer-orientated credit framework. In this way, the competence-based framework would appear to sit most readily within a neo-fordist analysis.

With competences, it is performance within the job which is valued. Knowledge and attitudes necessary to successful performance are constructed as secondary, 'underpinning', and are thereby marginalised in the assessment process. Competence-based assessment has been attacked by many as narrow and behaviouristic (Ashworth 1992; Hodgkinson 1992). This has tended to result in a rejection of the principles of competence-based assessment rather than the specific form in which competence was constructed within its early development in the United Kingdom. Drawing on their experience in Australia, Chappell *et al.* (1995) and Hager and Gonczi (1996) suggest that different models of competence are possible, the behaviouristic being the most well-known, but least satisfactory. Hager and Gonczi identify two further notions of competence. One is associated with the general attributes of the practitioner. The second, preferred option relates general attributes to the context in which they will be employed, what they term an 'integrated model' of competence. Despite problems, for Hager and Gonczi, the advantages of competence-based approaches to credit are many, including issues of access and social equity.

While early developments of standards of competence in the United Kingdom were highly behaviouristic, they were none the less framed within a humanistic discourse of learner-centredness (Edwards and Usher 1994a). Also there has been much development of the notion more recently, partly taking account of the criticisms and difficulties of implementing the standards specified. However, more interestingly, developments in the notion of competence may reflect the different levels within the division of labour at which the specification of standards began in the United Kingdom by comparison with Australia. In the former, the development began with less skilled areas of work. In the latter, competences were developed for the professions at an earlier stage. The United Kingdom approach inscribed certain cultural assumptions in the ascription of competence with less skilled jobs within a binary of skills and knowledge in which the latter is privileged. Competence was primarily about the skills to do 'practical' work, rather than jobs associated with that work being reconstructed as particular forms of 'knowledgeable practice'. Knowledge was excluded not because it was not valued, but because it was valued in a way – as academic knowledge – which marginalised it in the early considerations of competence. With the development of competences for the professions, knowledge has been fore-grounded inevitably as a central component of competent practice, and thus the dilemmas and reassessments of recent years.

By contrast with the development of vocational competences, a learning outcomes approach is not confined to a set of externally established criteria solely related to performance in the workplace. It can embrace a wider terrain of learning and may also involve negotiation with the learners over the outcomes to be achieved. While this has been a common if informal approach in much non-accredited adult education practice, the shift towards assessment and accreditation has resulted in more systematic attempts to establish what such outcomes may look like and the differing levels at which they can be awarded. In higher education this has taken the form of asking the question of what it means to be a graduate (Otter 1992). In the process, what it is that is to be assessed is itself being redefined, with subject-specific outcomes being overlaid by concern for more generic outcomes, in particular, the attributes to be flexible and respond to change. In a learning outcomes approach, the notion emerges that one is learning to be a particular type of subject with a range of capabilities as well as learning a subject. This brings out the role of education and training in identity formation. Implicit notions of subjectification in the enculturing processes within a field of study become explicit when constructed within a discourse of lifelong learning and therefore more open to contest. The politics of identity thereby directly enters the discussion of credit frameworks on the moorland of lifelong learning.

It is unsurprising, therefore, that in the development of both competences and learning outcomes, the specification of a range of personal practices has come to the fore. In his study of the retail sector, for instance, du Gay (1996: 141) found that 'the emphasis shifted away from a primary concern with technical skills . . . towards a more concerted focus on the development of interpersonal skills and self-learning'. What these personal practices are and the ways in which they are discursively inscribed then becomes the terrain of contest. Harrison (1996) outlines some of the different ways in which these have been constructed as 'core skills', 'personal skills', 'common learning outcomes', 'generic competences', 'transferable skills'. The preoccupations of different stakeholders shape the precise nature of the discourses developed. Thus, even as those stakeholders move towards a common stance they inscribe differences. These stakeholders include governments (Commission of the European Communities 1993b), employers (CBI 1989, 1993) and educators and trainers (UDACE 1989).

Harrison identifies a major tension in these positions between those who ascribe the development of these personal practices to increased effectiveness in work – the 'enterprising' worker – and those who ascribe them to increased effectiveness in learning – the 'enterprising' learner. However, the example from the retail sector above suggests an attempt to make them reinforcing of a more general 'enterprising personality'. For instance, the former Employment Department in the United Kingdom (1991: 4) identified 'transferable personal skills' as including 'effective communication, negotiation skills, problem solving ability, and ability to work in teams. They are characterised by a resourceful approach to tasks . . . .' The National Curriculum Council (1990) identified cross-curricula skills of 'communication, numeracy, study, problem-solving, personal and social, information technology' as applicable across a variety of domains. There are thus important differences in the personal practices to be valued. Further, the fact that such practices tend to be constructed as skills and/or competences suggests an increased emphasis on the assessment of the type of person one is, linked to increasing deployment of practices or 'technologies of the self' in the construction of identity. In other words, the move towards the assessment and accreditation of personal practices is part of the exercise of governmentality as much as an extension of access and progression within the social formation.

This is a developing situation. Credit frameworks help to make visible the moorland of lifelong learning. Through them, adults are able to gain access to assessment and accreditations without attendance at formal institutions. In this, equity may well be enhanced, although questions of relative status of qualifications still come in. The development of learning outcomes approaches to assessment and accreditation can bring greater transparency to the encounter between providers and those they provide for in terms of what they are providing, and give a certain power to those previously excluded to demonstrate they are capable of those outcomes and to challenge what outcomes are valued. However, this does not stop the processes of selection and exclusion, even if, importantly, it does bring a greater transparency to such processes. We therefore have a messy picture. We also need to bring into this picture the perspective that although not all learners may be accessing formal or non-formal provision, they may still be accessing learning and creating opportunities to learn for themselves. Further, not all want or seek accreditation. If policy and funding are tied solely to the latter, then there will be the need for increased voluntary and self-organised activities by those for whom assessment is not a goal – as with organisations such as the University of the Third Age. The net of credit, like that of governmentality itself, is never complete or monolithic.

LEARNING ORGANISATIONS – A REFLEXIVE PROJECT?

It is not only providers of learning opportunities which have had to become more flexible. The same is true for employers. As the workplace has become recognised as an increasingly important setting for learning and employees constructed as a, or even the, key resource – despite the displacement of employment by technology! – so the capacity of employers to support lifelong learning to meet organisational goals has come to the fore. This shift in the conception of the workplace and employment relations is governed by the notion of the 'learning organisation'.

If individual identity is a reflexive project in contemporary times, this is also promulgated as a way of governing the workplace and of governing within the workplace. The capacity for organisations to reflect on and learn from their practices in order to be more flexible, efficient and/or profitable and/or effective has become a central feature of organisational and management theory. To enable organisations to change, the workforce has to have networks of communication within which to channel information and views, the opportunities to learn associated with facilitating flexibility and change, and ways of participating in decisions about these processes. This has been particularly marked in those organisations involved in employee development schemes, action learning sets, quality circles and the like (Metcalfe 1992a, 1992b). Learning organisations need to support lifelong learning and require it as an aspect of sustaining and developing themselves (Field 1995). Flexible organisations may not be necessarily learning organisations, but to be a learning organisation flexibility is required from structures, managers and employees.

The notion of learning organisations is not new (Pedler *et al.* 1991). It is most often associated with private sector employers and commercial environments. However, it has come to have a wider applicability, partly as a result of changes in the public and voluntary sectors, wherein organisations have had to restructure to become flexible and entrepreneurial like commercial workplaces. The workplace is subject to the discourse of the learning organisation wherein lifelong learning contributes to the overall performance of the organisation by 'encouraging each individual to apply the idea of continuous improvement to themselves' (Yates 1994). The downside of this is an intensification of work for those in employment.

It is not simply the provision of learning opportunities that distinguishes learning organisations from other types of workplace, but also the form and content that provision takes. Solving a problem, introducing a new product, scrapping an old one, reaching a different market, have been constructed as requiring participants to see the future in a new way. Whether the organisation is a company, an educational institution or a training provider, success in this rapidly changing environment is held to involve continuous learning and changes of behaviour. Organisations change only if the people within them change. Increasingly, learning is focused around how it helps the organisation to achieve its goals. Even those organisations which trade in learning have seen learning among their staff as a tool for the continuous improvement of performance.

What this means varies. Some organisations perceive it narrowly in terms of learning necessary new technical skills. Others take a broader view, that enhancing individual potential and performance and stimulating stronger identification within the workplace will improve the effectiveness of workers. Contrasting positions on the importance and significance of learning in the workplace are also found over the links between learning, skills and pay:

> The employers' associations may take a strategic view of training as a mechanism to support job restructuring through promoting multi-skilling and functional flexibility. The trade unions may see training as a route to increasing employee autonomy and control over the job, as well as maintaining pay rates. . . . Skill is a potentially contentious area because it forms a link between the consensual issue of training and the conflictual question of pay.
>
> (Winterton and Winterton 1994: 7)

Important attempts at restructuring the relationships between skills, jobs and pay are at work. When discussing workplaces in the high-technology industries in the United States, Waterman *et al.* (1996) talk of a new 'covenant' between employers and employees. In an earlier more stable and predictable period, the covenant was largely characterised by lifetime employment. These conditions no longer prevail and the covenant is being redefined in terms of much enhanced opportunities for employees to develop their potential. While in employment with the organisation, their enhanced skills and increased productivity will benefit the employer. If/when they are made redundant, they are held to be better placed to get another job. Such a covenant involves reciprocal responsibilities. In exchange for skills development, employees are expected to identify with the goals of the organisation – which they help to define – and share in its success. To do this, they need to be knowledgeable about market trends, the skills required, and to engage in continuous learning and improvement. Here employees can be seen as either in a win-win or no-win situation. Insofar as they are positioned by the employer to have the skills to overcome unemployment – a threat that underpins the impetus to continually improve – the employment relationship is one of gratitude for the provision of learning opportunities in the eventuality of this occurring, rather than a struggle over the availability and insecurity of employment. Jobs, salaries and conditions are displaced by learning opportunities as a locus of negotiation. In this scenario, how long might it be before employees are asked to pay for their learning opportunities in the workplace as an individualised responsibility in order to sustain their employability? We also need to question the extent of this new covenant, as continuous improvement and loyalty may result still in lifetime employment for some, as is suggested to be the case in Japan (Brown and Lauder 1996).

Burgoyne (1992: 327) identifies a number of characteristics for a learning organisation. These can be found to varying degrees within individual workplaces and may operate differentially within the gendered division of labour within organisations (Butler 1996). Learning organisations require: a learning approach to strategy; participative policy-making; open information systems; formative accounting and control; mutual adjustment between departments; reward flexibility; adaptable structures; boundary workers as environment scanners; inter-organisational learning; a learning culture and climate; and self-development opportunities for all. These enable the maintenance of excellence over time in changing circumstances. In her survey of employers providing non-work-related employee development schemes, Metcalfe (1992a) found a number of factors resulted in attempts to create a learning culture within the organisation: expectations about future business developments and change; increasing emphasis on the quality of service and product; the desire to reduce any dependence on external labour markets; the desire to improve staff morale and motivation; and the desire to improve industrial relations. Even though the learning opportunities provided in such schemes are not necessarily related to the jobs of individuals or even the employment area of the workplace, the expectation is none the less one of increased organisational effectiveness and efficiency.

Metcalfe (1992b) provides a number of examples of such schemes. For instance, Baxi Partnership Ltd is a manufacturer of heating equipment in the north-west of England. As its name suggests, the company is a partnership in which the employees are partners with shares. In the restructuring of the company, team-working was introduced as the basis for improving quality. Prompted by the company's trade unions, this gave rise to the recognition of the need for improved communication skills – 'within their teams employees have much wider decision making powers, they have to digest far more information and also make presentations' (Metcalfe 1992b: 1). A 'Learning at Work' scheme was developed in conjunction with a local further education college and an educational consultancy specialising in basic skills. The result was a roughly 18 per cent take-up of courses, the benefits of which were seen in greater participation in team meetings and increasing market share. As well as the benefits for team-working, the Learning at Work initiative also 'improved morale and support for the company' (Metcalfe 1992b: 4). Without this initiative, a survey of the employees suggested, industrial relations might have deteriorated.

A second example is the Ford Motor Company UK's Employee Development Assistance Programme (EDAP). Here management was interested in increasing 'the effectiveness of its workforce and had been seeking greater involvement and identification with the company by their employees' (Metcalfe 1992b: 7). The trade unions were interested in obtaining more non-pay benefits for Ford workers. EDAP provides the opportunity for employees to engage in non-job-related learning and the scheme is run jointly by the management and unions. In 1989–90, 45 per cent of Ford's workforce participated in EDAP; a survey of participants found that 70 per cent had not participated previously in continuing education (Metcalfe 1992b: 9). EDAP has been successful, therefore, from within certain discourses of access and participation. Ford itself has benefited through the attitudinal change it has brought about – 'management/worker/union relations have undergone an amazing transformation, with co-operation increasingly replacing the past adversarial approach' (Metcalfe 1992b: 11).

For some, such developments open up opportunities for employees and provide the basis for more interesting forms of work and ways of working. Employees are given more say and responsibility in their places of work. There is the possibility for mobility in the workplace. For others, such developments signify an intensification of labour, increasing productivity to increase competitiveness, and an undermining of notions of the workforce having separate interests from those of their employers. In this sense, the discourse of learning organisations can be argued to govern practices of securing consent in line with the objectives or mission of the organisation (Marchington 1992), and of producing new workplace subjectivities more closely aligned to organisational imperatives (Miller and Rose 1993; du Gay 1996). In attempting to answer the question, 'who benefits?', therefore, ambiguity and ambivalence govern the practices of learning organisations (Payne 1996).

The Baxi and Ford examples are capable, therefore, of being 'read' in contrasting ways. For instance, they improve the opportunities available to adults and enhance work. Organisational and individual flexibility are developed in response to the need to continuously change and develop. However, they can also be argued to align the subjectivities and interests of employees ever more closely into the goals of the organisation. As the market and competition have intensified in governing the workings of organisations, so conflicts previously internal to the workplace are externalised onto other organisations as a condition for 'survival'. Competition between organisations displaces conflict within them. The learning organisation becomes a more homogeneous unit in which employment relationships are reconfigured as forms of partnership rather than based on conflict. This can be part of an explicitly anti-trade union stance, or in partnership with trade unions. In a survey of four industrial sector organisations and seven enterprises, Winterton and Winterton (1994: 44) found that 'management in all the enterprises expressed a wish to involve employees closely in the arrangements for training, but the extent to which this entailed the union differed'.

In some workplaces, notions of 'employee involvement', 'job enrichment' and 'empowerment' have become powerful forces in governing the approaches to training and human resource development as a dimension of developing a learning organisation (Yates 1994). However, the substantive changes taking place in workplaces suggest a far more ambiguous and contradictory set of processes and interests. For instance, the replacement of hierarchical line management by team-working can be constructed as a more 'democratic' form of working practice. However, it has also been argued that it acts as a form of self-discipline replacing the discipline previously maintained by managers and supervisors (Mumby and Stohl 1991). Employees 'police' themselves and each other. Speaking of Japan, McCormick (1989: 142) observes, 'patterns of group working offer a further safeguard against "free riders" in this system; but a negative side has been the long hours of work accompanied by long hours or after-hours socialising'. Similarly, Townley (1994) argues that the practices of human resource management, including appraisal and development, are part of a range of disciplinary practices aimed at making the employees' behaviour predictable and manageable.

The workplace as a setting thereby contributes to lifelong learning and vice versa. This requires and supports both the development of flexibility within the workplace and the flexible provision of learning opportunities. The significance of these trends and the governing discourses of the learning organisation, however, are far more ambiguous.

OUT OF BOUNDS?

We therefore see how even in extending and de-differentiating boundaries on the moorland of lifelong learning through the development of open and distance learning and credit frameworks, and developing workplaces as learning organisations, different boundaries are inscribed. Even as such changes attempt to address institutional and situational barriers to access in the hope that these will overcome cultural barriers, different cultures of inclusion and exclusion are configured. This suggests the need for a pedagogy of location and dislocation as a way of 'making sense' of the ways in which people are positioned and position themselves on the moorland of lifelong learning. A central component in such positioning is the provision of guidance, for if the options available for learning expand and become more complex, how are adults to make appropriate choices for themselves? Here, however, it is necessary to examine the ways in which guidance as a 'client-centred' and 'impartial' service has powerful consequences as a form of socio-cultural practice of governmentality consistent with trends towards the self as a reflexive project (Usher and Edwards 1995; Connelly *et al.* 1996; Payne and Edwards 1996). Guidance develops to enable adults to plot their routes across the moorland, but this spreads the networks of governmentality in the very processes of 'empowering' individuals.

The discourse of lifelong learning and the practices it supports therefore can be seen as reshaping equity and inequity even as it seeks to give greater status to learning in a diverse range of settings. This suggests that while lifelong learning is ongoing, there are also no settled practices to support it. It is therefore itself a constantly changing discourse and terrain. Flexibility is an endless project open to constant rereadings. This seems like a tiring process for all concerned and it is to an examination of the implications for workers in the moorland of lifelong learning that I now turn.

Chapter 5

Professionals, activists, entrepreneurs

I have suggested that there are significant shifts in the discourses within and around the terrain of those concerned with lifelong learning and the education and training of adults. Those shifts signify changes in the construction of lifelong learning and the practices necessary to support it. They are reflected in the shifting and de-differentiation of boundaries discussed in chapter 3 and developments outlined in chapter 4. What, then, does this mean for workers in this terrain, the heterogeneous group working with adults in diverse ways in diverse settings who support and enable lifelong learning? If change, uncertainty and ambivalence are part of a general contemporary condition, what impact does this have on workers? Are the shifts towards neo- and post-fordist forms of work organisation to be found also in providers of learning opportunities? If the field has become a moorland, then the range of practitioners who may consider themselves as workers with adults will have expanded and diversified, raising questions about who considers themselves to be an 'adult educator' and whether the identity is, in fact, becoming many identities, or is even redundant. What forms of education, training and development, therefore, become necessary for this heterogeneous group of workers? In what ways are workers able to be a part of change as well as subject to it? These are the sorts of questions to be addressed in this chapter. These are interesting times for those working with adults, but in what ways they are interesting is not always clear, as we respond to the pressures of the intensification of work also experienced elsewhere in the social formation.

The chapter will be in four sections. First, I shall discuss the notion of the professional as 'reflective practitioner'. Derived from the work of Schön (1983, 1987), this notion has become a central feature of programmes of professional development for those working with adults. This has, in turn, raised questions about the very professionalisation of this terrain of work and the implications of that for the vocation of a strand of the field of adult education committed to radical social change (Collins 1991). This will be discussed in the second section. Third, I shall explore the relationship between workers with adults and the changes taking place in the provision of learning opportunities which are associated with multi-skilling and neo- and post-fordist forms of organisation. Here I shall explore how the worker is being reconstructed as an 'enterprising worker' (du Gay 1996).

The notions of the worker with adults as professional, activist or entrepreneur positions them in specific ways in relation to their roles, purposes, practices and identities. It might also be considered that each is part of one of the strands of influential discourse identified in chapter 2. A tidy typology might suggest that: the worker as professional is part of a cultural restorationist discourse attempting to bring some order and stability to a changing world; the worker as activist is part of a progressive discourse identifying with the interests of those with less power in the social forma- tion; and the worker as entrepreneur is part of a modernising discourse associated with supporting organisational change. While each of these strands of influence exists, it is also possible, for instance, for both modernisers and progressives to attempt to inscribe their own meanings into the identity of the professional. Similarly, a modernising discourse may well view the worker as an activist, if of a different sort to that within a progres- sive discourse. Multiple meanings can be and are read into the many constructions of the identities of workers with adults.

Finally in this chapter, therefore, I shall draw on recent work on self- identity among workers in this terrain to illustrate how the above trends are being played out in the narratives, metaphors and images of those concerned with supporting lifelong learning. The suggestion will be that the trends affecting people elsewhere in the social formation are also impacting upon those involved in the provision of learning opportunities as they adopt different roles to support lifelong learning. These changes in roles, practices and identities both bring forth the need for and emerge from the different discourses of what it is to be a worker with adults. In this sense, the very notion of the 'adult educator' – itself invested with a variety of meanings in the discourses of the field – is itself problematised in the moorland of life- long learning.

REFLECTIVE PRACTITIONERS

The notion of 'reflection' and the 'reflective practitioner' has become central to the processes of professional development in many areas of activity in recent years. This is also the case for those concerned with the preparation and ongoing development of workers with adults. Discourses of the educator and/or trainer as 'technical expert' have been challenged and displaced by that of the reflective practitioner, thereby de-differentiating the boundaries between different groups of workers engaged in providing learning opportunities for adults. In the process, different subject matter and subjectivities have been introduced into both the discussion of and courses for workers.

Simply put, Schön's view (1983) is that, unlike working on a Taylorised production line in which routine tasks are undertaken on a repetitive basis, a professional's working environment is far less predictable. Professional workers have to be able to analyse particular circumstances in order to assess how best to respond to them. They have a certain degree of autonomy open to them in their work which is not the case for those engaged in repetitive tasks. Schön also suggests that owing to their contextualised use of knowledge, professionals cannot be considered to be using scientific knowledge which is applied on the basis of technical rationality to the situations of others. The latter assumes that there is scientific knowledge which is applied to situations in neutral ways on the basis of an analysis of the situation. While this adoption of a technical rational stance is often assumed to be the case in the process of an occupation becoming a profession (Wilson 1993; Briton 1996), for Schön the work of the professional is unpredictable. Interpretation and judgement are necessary. As Usher comments,

> most skilled activity does not involve the conscious application of principles ... the skill consists ... in such things as attending and being sensitive to the situation, anticipating, making ad hoc decisions, none of which would be possible if we had to stop and find the appropriate theory before we acted.
>
> (Usher 1989: 72)

Disciplinary knowledge as the foundation of professional expertise is displaced to include a wide variety of interpretative practices. Professionals require, therefore, a practical, contextualised form of rationality in which scientific knowledge is a resource to be utilised rather than applied on a simple means/ends basis in addressing the situations of others. 'The question for the practitioner is not "what rules should I apply?" but "how ought I to act in this particular situation?"' (Usher and Bryant 1989: 82). This involves an interpretative process, on the basis of which professionals need to be considered artists or craftspeople rather than simply technical experts. Here reflection-in-action is held to displace technical rationality.

The process of reflecting on and analysing particular circumstances gives rise to the conception of the 'reflective practitioner', someone who is able to cope with and shape change and uncertainty by interpreting and responding to the particularities of the circumstances they find. It is not surprising, therefore, that the notion of the reflective practitioner has grown in significance in a period wherein the notion of change itself has been given greater prominence. If the contemporary condition is more complex and less predictable, rule-bound behaviour and technical rationality can be said to be of decreasing relevance. Complexity and uncertainty require creative participation and responses. Reflection and personal responsibility for one's actions displace the application of externally available scientific knowledge. The professional is repositioned away from being a technical expert above

the social formation to become an accountable member of the social formation in which their knowledge and judgements are open to contest. In this
way, the emergence of the notion of the professional as a reflective practitioner in particular locations can be seen to be part of wider discursive shifts
in which bureaucratic elites have been subject to challenge over their
patronage and patriarchal governance of the social formation. This is not, of
course, to say that such traces do not still exist nor have a powerful influence
upon social formations, but rather they are traversed by ambivalence. This
ambivalence can work in different directions, as Schön's persistent use of the
male pronoun to signify reflective practitioners attests – the reflective practitioner is gendered in particular ways.

The notion of the reflective practitioner has proved particularly influential in education and training circles. A strong strand of thinking in these
circles is that workers are not technical experts. There is none the less a
desire to establish the basis for the professional status of those working with
adults. Positioning these workers within a discourse of the reflective practitioner – a discourse of professional practice – thereby provides a basis for
establishing them as professionals. This interest in reflective practice has
become attenuated in certain situations since the 1980s by a not altogether
successful desire to differentiate professional practice from certain notions
of competence. However, attempts to inscribe reflective practice in and as a
dimension of competent practice have challenged such attempts at differentiation. For a range of reasons, therefore, the notion of the reflective
practitioner has proved particularly influential in recent years in the
discourses traversing the moorland of lifelong learning.

However, Schön's views are not without their problems. First, while he
confines the notion of the reflective practitioner to professional workers, it
would seem to have a wider relevance. For instance, in the context of the reorganisation of certain areas of work away from the routinised tasks of fordism
towards the multi-skilled, problem-solving workforce of post-fordism, it
would appear that autonomous, non-routine work tasks may not be confined
to professionals. There may be degrees of difference in the attributes required,
but they are not necessarily differences in kind. In research on competent
professionals, for instance, Scott (1996) identifies a number of characteristics
they need to possess in order they can 'manage the challenges of continuous
change effectively'. These are: a distinctive stance; a distinctive way of
thinking; a comprehensive set of job-specific diagnostic maps; relevant
generic skills and knowledge; and job-specific skills and knowledge which are
up-to-date. Yet diagnostic maps can be seen as similar to the 'chunking' which
is argued to be characteristic of all skilled activity (Sloboda 1993). Similarly,
the distinctive way of thinking by professionals is described as 'a "creative"
intelligence, as being able to "think on their feet", as being people who can
anticipate problems and who can consistently "read" what lies behind a tricky
situation and "match" an appropriate course of action' (Scott 1996: 22).

These are ways of thinking which are applicable also to the non-professional in post-fordist work organisations.

It is significant, therefore, that the notion of reflection has become important in many areas and forms of learning and work. Downs (1993), for instance, has demonstrated how work-related learning can be enhanced by providing people with the opportunity to reflect on and develop the extent and range of their learning strategies. In different ways, Kolb (1984) and Boud *et al.* (1985, 1993) have outlined the centrality of reflection to learning from experience and learning to learn, central principles in discourses of lifelong learning.

> The activity of reflection is so familiar, that as teachers or trainers, we often overlook it in formal learning settings ... reflection is a vital element in any form of learning and teachers and trainers need to consider how they can incorporate some forms of reflection in their courses.
>
> (Boud *et al.* 1985: 8)

It also plays an important role in the practices of a learning organisation where the workforce can be brought together in groups, such as quality circles and learning sets, to reflect on the quality of service and product they are providing and how this can be improved.

The growth in interest in the conception of reflection has been felt in a wide range of literature and practices across the whole field of lifelong learning. Reflective logs and journals, portfolios of learning and the integration of different forms of learning have become common features of not only professional development, but also a range of learning opportunities in adult, further and higher education, community-based learning, workplace learning, and so on. It is a feature also of much feminist and critical pedagogy aimed at producing personal and social emancipation. Although reflection has become a major feature of many programmes of lifelong learning, it is still found to be time-consuming and difficult, challenging many adults' previous experience of what learning involves (Dewar *et al.* 1994). The discourses of reflective practice, therefore, are far more diverse than conceived by Schön and it cannot be assumed that reflection has the same significance in each setting and process.

Thus, while Schön situates reflection within a discourse of practical rationality, it is capable of being articulated in a range of discourses with consequences for its meaning and significance. In other words, reflection is not a neutral process in professional practice – reduced to a form of instrumentalism to which it is meant to provide an alternative – but can serve a range of interests and have a variety of ambivalent and contradictory consequences. For instance, we can situate reflection within Habermas' typology of different forms of rationality. For Habermas (1978), there are three forms of rationality – technical, dialogic and emancipatory – each of which serves particular ends. Reflection can be conceived in different ways and plays a different role in each of those forms of rationality, with different consequences. Thus, reflection can be viewed as a neutral process, a cognitive activity of inputs, processing and problem-solving. In this form, as suggested, it contributes to the very form of means/ends technical rationality that Schön is critiquing. Second, it can be constructed as working in the interests of communication and understanding, of dialogic rationality, enhancing communicative competence. Third, reflection can be in the interests of action and change, part of an emancipatory rationality, an assumption which is often asserted despite evidence that this is not always or so clearly the case (Gore 1993). Thus, while reflection is perceived to be central to lifelong learning, its meaning and significance are themselves subject to interpretation and contest. Reflective practitioners are themselves capable of being situated within a range of discourses with differing assumptions and consequences. In this sense, reflective practice cannot be taken simply as a universal description of professional practice and professional identity.

A further apparent difficulty with Schön's position for workers with adults is the sense in which the prospects for professional judgement and autonomy are seen to be diminished by the changes taking place in the arrangements for the provision of learning opportunities. For instance, the introduction of prescribed learning outcomes – such as occupational competences – the pressures to increase productivity – of trying to do more with less – and the use of appraisal to monitor performance are held to decrease professional autonomy (Ball 1990b; Metcalfe 1991). If workers with adults are increasingly subject to neo-fordist Taylorism, managerial power and an intensification of work, in what ways can they be said to be a profession and able to act professionally? For some, therefore, professional autonomy is held to be diminishing and there is no need, or time, or requirement to reflect on practice. Is reflection less relevant, therefore, as the contextualised rationality of the professional is reduced to the technical rationality of the implementer of decisions taken elsewhere? Do instrumentalism and humanistic psychology guide practice rather than a critical and interpretative form of reflection (Foley 1992)? If so, why has growth in interest in reflection developed in a period when its relevance for 'professional' workers in the field of lifelong learning may be questioned? Does a more pragmatic form of reflection displace one that is more critical? A more intense working environment may require the artistry of a reflective practitioner able to respond 'on their feet' rather than the more bureaucratic procedures of the technical expert. Here self-management within organisational frameworks displaces autonomous activity. In this sense, reflective practice may be part of the 'moral technology' and forms of governmentality through which professional work is intensified and indeed regulated/made accountable.

Associated and as part of the trend towards the increasing focus on the reflective practitioner as a model for professional development and form of identity, and the intensification of work for those in employment, has been an increasing emphasis on 'practice'. As well as being 'reflective', the professional worker is also constructed as a 'practitioner'. Like much else discussed in this text, the significance of this is much debated and ambivalent. On the one hand, 'practice', and the knowledge generated by practitioners reflecting on and in practice, has been seen to have an important role in valuing their experience and views in relation to knowledge generated through the formal methods of academic disciplines. Practitioner knowledge is thereby given greater value in relation to academic knowledge. For some, this is a beneficial corrective to abstract disciplinary knowledge. This would certainly be the case within certain modernising and progressive discourses. For others, particularly in discourses of cultural restoration, it signifies a dilution of legitimate bodies of knowledge and the culture and standards of conduct associated with them. Similar shifts and discussions of their significance can be seen in the increased value given to the practical experiences of learners in student-centred approaches, whereby knowledge generated from experience is given greater value in relation to learning formal bodies of knowledge. The discourses of 'practice' alongside those of 'practitioners' and 'reflective practitioners', therefore, have given greater status to knowledge generated in the wider moorland of lifelong learning and, in particular, to the knowledge of workers with adults (Bright 1989; Usher and Bryant 1989).

However, the turn to 'practice' has been based to a large extent on a polarisation against 'theory'. Here we can see a set of binaries in operation – of theory and practice; knowledge and competence; the academic and vocational – over which there is much contemporary contest. The formally dominant side of the binaries – of academic knowledge constructed as 'theory' – is being challenged as to its relevance to the contemporary condition and the requirement for vocational competence in 'practice'. 'Getting on with the job' has become the primary criterion of professionalism, where the 'job' is increasingly conceived as what goes on in the immediate setting. Noses are to the grindstone. Academic knowledge is constructed pejoratively as 'theory', as out of touch with the 'realities' of practice and devalued accordingly. This position is not restricted to the United Kingdom, as Welton's discussion (1987) of similar trends in Canada makes clear. Writing in the United States, Aronowitz and Giroux (1991: 92) argue in somewhat strident terms that 'privileging practice without due consideration of the complex interactions that mark the totality of theory/practice and language/meaning relationships is not simply reductionist; it is a form of theoretical tyranny'.

Here, however, it is important to explore the extent to which particular discourses of 'reflection', 'practice' and 'theory' are themselves culturally specific. It may well be that European countries other than the United

Kingdom have different perspectives, with the academic disciplines having a more significant role in learning and not inscribed so directly in a theory–practice binary. Certainly the notion of *technik* mentioned earlier suggests alternative formulations. Other parts of the globe may have very different ways of examining the area of professional learning and work. An evaluation of the extent to which the specific discourses of reflection on practice which hold such sway in the United Kingdom may not be shared elsewhere only enhances the need for culturally specific and contextualised understandings of the discourses of the role and purposes of workers with adults.

At one level, the discourses which construct the relationship between 'theory' and 'practice' as problematic are the outcome of certain ways in which the issue is framed as a 'problem' within the binary logic governing the terrain. It is a terrain of constant contest with differing strands of influence seen to be operative in different parts of the provision of learning opportunities. For instance, in the mid-1990s in the United Kingdom, there is a greater emphasis being placed on learning in schools for trainee teachers, of learning to be competent practitioners through greater emphasis on the practical dimensions of teaching. Academic knowledge about teaching and education is displaced as lacking 'relevance'. Meanwhile, trainee nurses now spend more time in academic institutions rather than learning within the hospital environment, with greater emphasis being placed on the learning of formal, disciplinary knowledge. This suggests a strengthening of the scientific paradigm, as this group of workers moves towards professional status, even as the professional status of teachers is questioned. As these issues play out, so what constitutes the curriculum and learning and what is to be valued through assessment and accreditation are themselves reshaped, with the possibility, at least in principle, of moving beyond current binaries, such as might be inscribed in a notion of 'knowledgeable practice'.

Within a binary logic, however, the assertion of the primacy of 'practice' can be argued to undermine the possibility of 'practitioners' – a term which itself becomes a problematic construct – being able to critically review and evaluate the significance of the practices in which they are engaged. Certain notions of reflecting on practice, such as anecdotal descriptions of experience, undermine the possibility of people being able to critically interpret the situations in which they find themselves, as 'practice' is already informed by overt or covert discursive understandings and exercises of power. Unless these are made explicit, reflection can result in ill-informed or misguided interpretations. In other words, locating the already existing discursive understandings traversing 'practice' is integral to the process of critically reflecting on and interpreting practice. 'Knowledgeable practice' requires more than 'practical knowledge', and the processes of reflection can be deployed to enhance critical interpretation and/or a rationality bounded by the immediacy of practice. If knowledgeable practice and critical interpretation are the meanings to be inscribed in the notion of the reflective practitioner, the issue becomes one of how this is to be effected (Usher 1993b). This requires us to locate discourses of 'reflection', 'theory' and 'practice' within the arena of culture and power, without which practice remains 'directed to the instrumental purposes of professional practitioners' (Griffin 1987: 138) within the parameters of technical rationality.

In the process, it may be that the notion of the reflective practitioner as the model for professional development and identity in the moorland of life-long learning itself starts to be displaced by that of the 'reflexive worker' located and locating themselves within a range of discourses, able to translate discourses into one another and constantly renegotiating the meanings and significance of their work across domains. This requires 'theory' and 'practice' to be reread as discourses, which is not without its difficulties, as

> the notion of practice as discourse offends commonsense thinking. Neither theory nor practice is delivered in recognisable form: there are no foundation courses to be presented and there are no teaching skills to be acquired. Instead, there is a strangely structured conversation about language that all students are expected to participate in.
>
> (Millar 1991: 22)

In other words, 'theory' and 'practice' as constructs are problematised and, with that, the notion of professional work as a form of either technical rationality or reflective practice. Those working with adults, therefore, may need to be resituated as reflexive workers capable of knowledgeable practice, if they are to not only adapt to change, but also participate in and be able to challenge it, both for themselves and for the adults with whom they engage. Does this mean also that they should not be considered professionals? This is a question to which I now wish to turn.

PROFESSIONALISM AND VOCATION

In chapter 3, I reviewed the position that the development of adult education as an academic field of study has been associated with the development of a profession of adult educators – the two being mutually supportive processes. The university subject, 'adult education', has been constituted as that specialist or expert knowledge necessary for a person to be able to be and act as a professional adult educator. However, it is that very process of professionalisation which is, for some, at the least problematic, or, more stridently, positively harmful to what are constructed as being the values, purposes and sense of mission of adult education – or at least those values, purposes and mission as specified by particular writers (Alexander 1991; Wilson 1993; Briton 1996). An irony is that this position is mostly argued by university-based academics whose very position implicates them in the ambivalent processes of professionalisation they criticise.

In much of this literature, it is the increased professionalisation of what was and, for some, still is considered to be adult education as part of a movement for progressive social change which is constructed as problematic. Historically, the 'adult education movement' aligned itself with working-class emancipation, supporting the learning and activities of working people and their institutions, such as the trade unions. It is argued that this work enabled both individual mobility and a more effective articulation of working-class interests in relation to employers and the capitalist state (Simon 1992). In the last twenty-five years, working-class movements have been challenged by: the resurgence and globalisation of capitalism; the rise of the new right and the collapse of communism; and feminist and post-colonial challenges to the largely white male construction of working-class interests. Working-class movements in many parts of the world have sought to redefine their position, purposes and practices in response to these challenges. In particular, many trade unions have sought to improve their institutional efficiency and services to members – in this way almost reconstituting themselves as 'business-like' – at the expense of more overt political goals. For those linking the provision of learning opportunities to working-class interests, the changes in the labour movement, the largely white middle-class profile of participants in adult education and the increased policy interest by the state in learning opportunities for adults has placed increased doubt over its efficacy to effect change and constraints on what is or is not to be funded. This is not to deny the continuing tradition of work with different parts of the labour movement, including the trade unions (McIlroy 1993; Newman 1993).

Some have sought to reposition their contribution to equity and emancipation through support for lifelong learning in the activities of 'new social movements' (Finger 1989; Welton 1993a). By contrast with the universal aspirations of the working-class movement to emancipate humanity, new social movements, such as the environmental movement, the peace movement, land rights for native groups and parts of the women's movement, tend to have a more specific focus to their activities. Local effort and local struggles – themselves a dimension of the postmodern marginalised by the dominant modern binary of capital–labour – create patchworks of social action which aim to transform forms of emancipation–oppression. Many feminists have sought to create their own settings and pedagogic practices uncolonised by the patriarchal power inscribed in much adult education discourse (Thompson 1983; Weiler 1991). Others again suggest that learning linked to social activism is not restricted to new social movements, but encompasses all those settings in which people seek participation in decision-making, such as tenants' groups – a process through which democracy can be revitalised (Croft and Beresford 1992). As the field of adult education has de-differentiated into the moorland of lifelong learning, so the boundaries of the adult education movement itself have been subject to challenge with diverse forms of learning related to diverse forms of social action traversing the terrain. However, as Newman (1995: 255) observes, 'localised sites of power may proliferate, but considerable power continues to reside in state apparatuses that have extensive bureaucracies and surveillance technologies, in huge enterprises that have the wealth and expertise to do what they want . . .'.

Different forms of adult education, community education, community development and community action have been one way in which the relationship between the professional worker and social movements has been mediated. However, for some writers, such as Cowburn (1986), 'community' is simply another way of displacing the working class from their privileged position as bearers of social change, a view which itself marginalises the concerns of other groups, such as women and minority ethnic groups. Questions also remain about the 'newness' of new social movements – each has a history – and the assumption of a 'progressive' nature to all such movements. For instance, the environmental movement has conservationist parts which may hinder 'progressive' social and economic change. Similarly, change is not simply 'progressive', as it entails different forms of exclusion and oppression. Further, while the emphasis has been on supporting particular 'progressive' social movements, less attention has been paid to the strategies and practices of those movements and forms of social actions which have shaped the dominant processes of change in contemporary social formations – the new right as a social movement. The possibilities of learning from such activities and deploying them in relation to alternative agendas have not been a strength of the adult education movement, tied as it largely is to modern (romanticised?) views of specific forms of collective and community 'struggle'. All of which suggests that the notion of a bounded adult education movement working for progressive social change – always a small, if discursively powerful, part of the moorland of lifelong learning – is increasingly problematic. However, rather than simply the result of increased professionalisation, it may be also that the increased complexity of what constitutes 'progressive' social change and the class-based traditions of much of the adult education movement contribute to a sense of the displacement and/or demise of this as a particular discursive tradition in the contemporary period.

What, then, is the significance of this for workers with adults? Part of the historical trend certainly has been that greater prominence is given to questions of professionalisation. Rather than a role of movement participant – 'social activist', 'community activist', 'organic intellectual' – the worker with adults has faced increased pressure for greater professionalism and accountability to funders and managers rather than to themselves or interests linked to social action. It should also be noted that the pressure to be constructed as a profession also comes partly from those working within this terrain, as part of a strategy to gain increased status, recognition and, with that, better pay and conditions. However, increased accountability and professionalisation also engender closer governance of the moorland and of who is to be considered a legitimate, and now competent, worker.

In this way, as Arvidson (1993) suggests of Swedish adult education, the instruments for the creation of the welfare state have become the instruments of the welfare state. In other words, parts of the movement in opposition to the capitalist state, in this case adult education, have become a part of state-supported activities. They now defend parts of the state – the 'public services' – against marketisation and privatisation. Nordhaug (1986: 55) also comments 'while popular and political movements earlier regarded adult education as a weapon in the current struggle for power, people today tend to view it as a private consumption or investment good'. Struggles for the welfare state became struggles within the welfare state, which, in turn, have become struggles to defend the welfare state, as it has come under assault by governments pursuing agendas of economic competitiveness. In the process, collective activism and change through learning have been displaced by individual mobility through learning and accreditation. Concerns over a shift towards the worker as professional and away from the construction of movement activist, therefore, come at a time when it is possible to argue that the former already is being displaced by a notion of worker as entrepreneur, a point to which I shall return in the next section of this chapter. In this sense, the attack on professionalism from those concerned for an adult education movement may be uncomfortably aligned with the attack on professionals as welfare state bureaucrats by those pursuing neo-liberal agendas.

A recent influential attempt to critique the notion of the worker as professional has been provided by Collins (1991), who argues that contemporary trends in adult education displace vocation with utility. The vocation is that of emancipatory social change and adult education's role in participating and supporting such change. Utility signifies the increased emphasis on the development of skills relevant to the world of work. For Collins, the shift towards utility is also linked to a growing professionalisation in the field of adult education, in which the professional deploys a form of technical rationality devoid of concern for the politics of their practices. The potential for professionals to act in ways other than those inscribed with technical rationality would seem to be excluded by Collins. This may be, at least partly, to do with his location in North America, where the development of technique among adult educators is the dominant paradigm in programmes of professional formation (Brookfield 1989; Briton 1996). However, insofar as he constructs professional work as dominated by technical rationality, Collins is able to develop an argument for an alternative form of adult education work based on vocation – the commitment to certain values and stances. Rather than the professional adult educator, it is adult education as vocation that should act as a guide to activity.

Here we are in interesting territory, for a number of reasons, as both the historical and contemporary resonances of the concept of vocation are ambivalent for many of those working with adults. For some, the rejection of vocationalism within the contemporary field of adult education has become an article of faith in the affirmation of the non-vocational and, in some cases, emancipatory character of their work. If vocationalism is rejected as a dimension of work with adults, how then can adult education be a vocation? Here it might be argued that Collins is attempting to reclaim the notion of vocation from contemporary concerns for vocationalism, investing the former with a sense of values, purpose and cultural calling which is not to be found in the instrumentalism of the latter. On this reading, vocationalism can be seen to be a debased form of vocation, the calling of the latter displaced by the imposition of the former through narrowly conceived concerns for occupational competence. However, such an attempt is deeply ambivalent for the historical roots of vocation as a calling to God and the church suggests a form of missionary zeal inscribed in the work of adult educators, with disturbing associations with forms of patriarchal and colonial oppression. Newman (1995) comments how educators with a sense of mission can constitute an invasion. In this respect, it is notable that it is primarily, although not solely, white male university-based adult educators who have been loudest in their call for those working with adults to retain a sense of social emancipatory purpose in their practices – the secular mission of the academic 'priesthood'!

In contrast to Collins' position, Hammersley (1992) argues that the shift towards a utilitarian view of education and training signifies a shift not towards but away from a professional orientation. Here 'the professional orientation views the occupational task as a sacred calling requiring a cultural outlook rather than mere technical expertise' (Hammersley 1992: 172). In other words, it is in professional work itself that there is a form of cultural calling rather than the latter being an alternative to professional work. In this formulation, the inscription of the 'sacred calling' may signify the position of the professional as the secular priest of the modern bureaucratic state. For Hammersley, the focus on technical expertise is linked to the utilitarian notions of education and training and a market orientation to their provision. Rather than reclaiming vocation from the professional, it is a question of reclaiming the professional from technical expertise. Both Collins and Hammersley share the increased concern for technical expertise among workers in education and training, but have contrasting stances on the relationship between professionals and technical expertise based on a dichotomy between the latter and vocation or cultural calling.

This dichotomy itself has been problematised (Hunter 1993). It is argued that the vocation of intellectual cultivation and aesthetic sensibility was never purely an end in itself, but also a form of technical expertise, an intellectual and moral technology linked with certain political rationales and programmatic interventions by governments. In this sense, it may be the binary logic that is the problem, as certain forms of technical expertise and vocation are implicated with each other, even where they deny this to be the case. West (1994: 94) notes that 'the issue of vocation is a political and ideological one even though it surfaces in our time as a discourse about professionalism'. Particular discourses of the professional and vocation, therefore, have to be examined to foreground the assumptions and exclusions upon which they are constructed and the consequences of particular formulations. In this context, to act professionally, to have a vocation and to have expertise may not be mutually incompatible, although we may want to align the sense of vocation more with conceptions of liberation theology than with missionary zeal. However, even this is problematic and may involve reformulations which attempt to move beyond this particular binary towards a form of pragmatics which is not reducible to utility, wherein expertise and purpose is constantly negotiated between workers and those with whom they work, as is the case in much feminist practice (Lather 1991b). Herein working professionally may signify something different from being a professional in the senses conceived by either Collins or Hammersley.

The different ways in which the worker is constructed are not merely the result of the contestation of meaning among those working in the terrain. Public policy discourses also position workers in particular ways in relation to their work. In this sense, it is possible to conceive the notion of the professional, mediating the competing demands made upon them in order to meet needs as part of a welfare state model of provision (Armstrong 1982). By contrast, the activist involved in developing and promoting the partial interests of those whom and/or that which the movement encompasses could be seen as part of a social redistribution model of provision. However, while the debates have generally been centred on these two conceptions among those working in the terrain, public policy has tended to move on. In recent years, in many countries a market model of provision has become increasingly influential, displacing alternative conceptions or at least being strengthened in relation to those alternatives. Here the business of providing learning opportunities for adults is conducted by the 'enterprising worker' seeking to maximise the potential learners and sources of funding available to the organisation. It is to a discussion of enterprising workers supporting lifelong learning within the changing workplace that I now turn.

ENTERPRISING WORKERS?

As with other areas of the economy, the provision of learning opportunities for adults is being reconstructed as different settings, practices, curricula and learners are constituted as legitimate areas of concern. Policy and funding in many countries have sought to increase and widen participation in this new world. As I have suggested, provision is being reconstituted as more relevant to the world of work and more flexible in order primarily to be able better to support the agenda of economic competitiveness. In the process, contemporary trends in the wider economy and in the nature and organisation of work are to be found increasingly in the provision of learning opportunities for adults and the structures of provision. The multi-skilling and flexibility that increasingly characterise neo- and post-fordist work organisations are reflected also in the increasing range and diversity of providers of learning opportunities, their modes of operation and the roles and functions of those working in them (Edwards 1991b, 1993a). With these developments, many of the defining traditions of adult education as a field of practice, and the institutions maintaining and reproducing it, themselves are becoming reconstituted. Many providers of learning opportunities are constituting themselves as learning organisations (*sic*). In evaluating the changing role of workers in organisations supporting lifelong learning, therefore, it is important to examine the extent to which these workplaces are themselves increasingly subject to similar forms of governmentality as elsewhere in the economy. As increased flexibility is demanded of providers of learning opportunities, so debates about neo- and post-fordism within these organisations have emerged, particularly in relation to those involved in flexible delivery through forms of open and distance learning.

In relation to all providers of learning opportunities for adults, the context is one wherein increasing cost efficiency, effectiveness and accountability are highlighted (Power 1994) – where the latter is defined increasingly through the discourse of accountancy. More students are moved into and through the system at a lower cost to the state if not to the students. An integral part of this development is that staff are required to assume new roles and take on new responsibilities, in other words, they are required to become more flexible and multi-skilled. Teaching staff engage in innovatory approaches to teaching and learning, market their courses, manage budgets and staff, write open and distance learning materials, appraise themselves and others, research, provide guidance and counselling for learners. The notion of the teacher as the expert in a body of knowledge and/or skills, imparting that to students, is reconstituted as a manager of learning undertaking a range of roles to assure the quality of their work and that certain outcomes are achieved. Nor is this increased flexibility restricted to those engaged in teaching. For example, administrators are having to become familiar with budget management, secretarial and reception staff with providing initial information and guidance to learners. All are having to engage in becoming consumer-orientated and customer-friendly, wherein responding to learners-as-consumers – with rights embedded in charters – becomes a dimension of supporting learning. A flexible response to the consumers of learning opportunities is thereby reconstituting the roles, subjectivities and identities of those working to provide learning opportunities for adults, as elsewhere in the social formation.

Roles and demarcations within and between institutions are breaking down as tasks mutate across boundaries of status and salary. Here multiskilling and the blurring of job demarcations themselves signify a further dimension of de-differentiation. The individual teacher is increasingly subject to team-work, particularly with moves towards forms of flexible delivery through open and distance learning. As well as increased forms of functional flexibility, organisations are increasingly engaging in practices of numerical flexibility, with more people employed on a part-time and casual basis. Contractual relations are displacing employment relations, as services are bought in rather than being provided in-house. There is the development of a core and periphery workforce in this situation (Atkinson and Meager 1990) and the inscription of gender divisions within that workforce. In addition, through appraisal there is pressure for more performance-related pay, even when funding cuts mean that rather than rewarding performance such practices encourage workers to compete against each other and engage in 'conspicuous busyness' in the hope of some reward. These trends are both complex and ambivalent. On the one hand, the reconfiguration of what it means to be a worker in this terrain is 'empowering' in the sense that it constitutes active, skilled subjects and the work may become more diverse and interesting – post-fordist new artisans. On the other hand, it is also 'disempowering' as regulation and surveillance intensify through the spread of accountability and self-monitoring procedures – the spread of neo-fordist Taylorism. The flexibility found in organisations supporting lifelong learning is increasingly grounded in the insecurity of employment experienced elsewhere in the workplace. The recognition of the transferability of skill, which workers with adults rightly celebrate, is deployed against them as part of the reinforcement of a labour market discipline associated with flexibility and insecurity.

Here it is useful to return briefly to Schön's conception of the reflective practitioner, as it is possible to situate this notion as a key signifier in the professional development of those working with adults in relation to changes associated with the neo- and post-fordist organisation of the provision of learning opportunities. In Schön's work, reflection-in-action is constructed as a response to the epistemological limits of technical rationality in the sphere of professional practice. However, it is its relationship to the changing patterns of employment and working practices which in many ways is more illuminating. In an era of flexibility and multi-skilling, predictable and standardised working practices are being undermined and, with that, the rationale for technical rationality as a way of structuring and organising knowledge. The lack of predictability in educational and training employment is an increasing aspect of the organisation of work per se. Being a reflective practitioner, bringing together thought and action, reflecting whilst you are doing, is a key condition of flexibility. Hence, the significance of reflective practice becomes clearer when it is situated within socio-economic changes. It is not simply the nature of professional practice that necessitates reflection-in-action. It is also a part and an outcome of a particular division of labour within which flexibility is a key component. The reflective practitioner signifies the worker in neo- and post-fordist organisations par excellence. However, there are still likely to be divisions between those still subject to neo-fordist Taylorism and those governed by post-fordist artisanship.

Nor is this link perhaps surprising when we bear in mind du Gay's (1996) argument that the contemporary workplace is increasingly characterised by forms of governmentality associated with 'an ethos of enterprise'. As I suggested in chapter 2, this ethos is crucial to the development of discourses of flexibility among nations, organisations and individuals in support of economic competitiveness. As business and market models increasingly come to govern the provision of learning opportunities for adults, workers in those organisations are themselves subject to practices of management, appraisal and development which position them as enterprising, engaged in an 'enterprise of the self'. In this position,

> no matter what hand circumstances may have dealt a person, he or she remains always continuously engaged . . . in that one enterprise. . . . In this sense the character of the entrepreneur can no longer be seen as just one among a plurality of ethical personalities *but must rather be seen as assuming an ontological priority*.
>
> (du Gay 1996: 181; emphasis in original)

This is the case both for the curriculum and pedagogies available to adults and also for the workers providing such learning opportunities. For the latter, the exposure to the risks and costs of their activities is constructed as enabling them to better create opportunities, signifying a form of 'empowerment' and 'success' within the organisation. Nor is this restricted to careers alone, as the whole of life – individual, group, organisational – becomes inscribed with the ethos of enterprise.

For du Gay, this contemporary form of governance of the self as an enterprise is related to the increased role of contractualism in social relations. As Yeatman (1994b: 9) argues, 'marketisation, privatisation, devolution, and contractualisation . . . fit the modern regime of regulation, namely one where government works by means of the self-regulating capacities of citizens as these are informed by the normalising effects of professional expertise among other things'. Enterprising identity and the self as an enterprise for workers emerge as organisations become subject to measures of performance in the delivery of services and goods through a contract. Rather than being governed simply by bureaucratic and hierarchic procedures wherein decisions are taken elsewhere and handed down to be implemented, workers are given 'responsibility' for achieving certain outcomes efficiently and effectively, for instance, budgets, delivering learning opportunities, managing and training staff. 'In keeping with the principles of enterprise, performance management and related techniques function as forms of responsibilisation which are held to be both economically desirable and personally "empowering"' (du Gay 1996: 182). The precise forms and levels of responsibility ascribed will obviously vary according to the type of organisation, its practices and the person's position within the division of labour.

The nature and extent of such processes and this form of governance would need to be examined both in relation to the economy as a whole and in relation to practices within organisations providing learning opportunities for adults. There is also the need to address the ambivalent consequences of such approaches – the extent to which they enable more creative forms of work and/or contribute to increased exploitation of the self in response to the insecurity engendered by such practices. In different organisations and different parts of the organisation, the enterprise of the self for workers may well signify different things. However, the analysis of worker-as-entrepreneur suggests that this form of governance should not simply be dismissed as impacting negatively upon the provision of learning opportunities and the workforce therein. New possibilities are opened up by the adoption of norms of enterprise. In this sense, it may be no accident that there has been a massive expansion of opportunities for adults, if a less successful widening of access to formal provision, in a period in which these norms have become increasingly influential. Here also the potential for enterprise to signify meanings other than those espoused in certain strands of narrowly conceived economistic thinking needs to be considered. Active, creative, risk-taking workers – change agents – with certain degrees of autonomy in how they define and achieve their work goals, engaging in practices of social entrepreneurship, would suggest an 'empowering' dimension to work which Taylorist principles deny. In some ways, a conception of an enterprising worker can be used to contest the continuation of Taylorised forms of work. As with enterprise, so with contractualism. While at one level it closes down options by making explicit the outcomes to be achieved, it can actually bring forth issues for political contest and debate which were previously passed over in silence by powerful discourses (Yeatman 1994a, 1994b).

To suggest that workers with adults may well be positioned and position themselves as entrepreneurs within neo- and post-fordist work organisations and that this might have some positive aspects is not a popular or easy position to adopt for those involved in education and training. It is traversed by ambivalence as to the consequences and can all too easily be read as a 'sell out' to new right agendas and discourses of modernisation. However, if, as suggested, organisational changes within providers of learning opportunities are those associated with neo- and post-fordism, contractualism and enterprise, it becomes necessary to engage with these discourses, in terms of how they impact upon workers and their identities, the forms of professional development associated with them, and the possibilities they offer for forms of work and reformulated programmes of development to enable workers to maximise the opportunities for diverse groups of learners to learn, including themselves.

However, such notions may not be comfortable to many working in this terrain, particularly those dominantly positioned within welfarist and social redistribution discourses. This is an issue which can be examined by exploring the narratives and metaphors through which workers with adults position themselves and their identities in their current work situations (Edwards and Usher 1996).

IDENTITY, MULTIPLE SELVES AND BORDER-CROSSING

Typologies are a common feature of all educational discourse and lifelong learning is no exception. One well-known typology (Darkenwald and Merriam 1982) classifies 'adult educators' by using the metaphor of 'tribes'. This typology presents five tribes of adult education, each with its own distinct aims, concerns and pedagogic style. In the language of narrative, each tribe has its own plot, characters and (usually) 'heroes'. The tribes are summarised in Table 5.1.

On the face of it, this typology appears to be simply a classification device for systematically describing a pre-existing world. In other words, it represents that world. However, adopting the stance outlined in chapter 1, a different reading is possible. This highlights the presentational features of the typology, the ways in which it constructs a particular perspective. First, the typology is itself a narrative about work with adults as 'adult education'. Second, it is about adult education as 'tribal'. Third, it suggests that workers locate themselves as 'adult educators' and that, within that field, they locate themselves and are located in particular tribal stories which define worlds, influence practice and shape identity.

Narratives are lived and through membership of a tribe workers accept and tell a narrative with which they feel comfortable, which feels like a 'good' story that makes sense of the world for them. Thus, a worker with adults identifies with a particular story and equally is identified by it. To become a member of a particular tribe is to be provided with clear and secure definitions (a way of knowing) and bounded ways of practising (a way of doing). It is to be provided with a set of signifiers by means of which allegiance becomes a matter of emotional investment (a way of feeling) rather than merely rational calculation or mere convenience. To be a member of a tribe involves commitment, a belief in the value and worth of what one is doing. It is this combination of ways of knowing, doing and feeling that produces a bounded and unambiguous identity (a way of being).

Table 5.1 'Tribes' of workers with adults

Tribe	Aim	Focus	Content	Relationship with learners	Teaching/ learning metaphors
Traditionalists	Discipline of the mind. Pass on 'worthwhile' knowledge, skills and attitudes.	Individual.	Classics – perennially valuable knowledge.	Teacher superior to learner.	Empty vessels, conduit, doctor–patient.
Self-actualisers	Full personal happiness.	Individual.	Feelings, personal experience.	Teacher inferior to learner.	Social director, garmenter.
Progressives	Growth of all individuals (especially disadvantaged) to benefit society.	Individual in a social context.	Immediate problems and life needs of the learners.	Teacher and learner equals.	Coach.
Guerillas	Creation of a new and better social order.	Individual in a struggle to transform societal structures and priorities.	Sources of oppression.	Teacher and learner equals.	Guide, leader, joint venturer.
Organisational maintainer	Better organisational effectiveness.	Organisation's needs.	Determined by organisational needs assessment and broken down into objectives and performance indicators.	Teacher superior to learner.	Manufacturer, shaper, builder.

Source: Adapted from Scott 1992

Adult education and lifelong learning have always been characterised by more than one narrative. Some narratives have declined in their impact since each has to be told and retold to maintain its significatory and creative power. In the literature, the identities of workers are described and constructed in a multiplicity of ways in addition to the five tribes outlined above. Miller (1993: 76) recounts her fears of being discovered as an 'impostor' in the academic world of university adult education, a view Brookfield (1993c: 69) feels to be relevant to many students of adult education. Miller (1994: 82) says of her initiation into work in adult education that she initially identified herself as a 'sociologist' because of her background discipline. Mezirow *et al.* (1990: 360) construct the adult educator involved in social action as an 'empathetic provocateur'. In his discussion of metaphors as shorthand encapsulations of reality, Brookfield (1993c: 75) uses the examples of 'midwives', 'gatekeepers' and 'enablers' as ways of framing practices. Specific identities are adopted according to the perceived roles of workers.

Here, while there may be different narratives, the difference is constructed largely as playing out between individuals rather than within individuals. This suggests a grounded and bounded concept of identity. Similarly, in their research on identity among Canadian adult educators, Fenwick and Parsons (1996: 242) suggest that the use of metaphors 'provided an identifiable and coherent picture that synthesised fragments of practice and belief into something concrete and communicable'. Participants in their research produced metaphors such as 'fire-starter', 'safari guide', 'hiking leader', 'adventure outfitter' and 'museum curator' to describe their practices. While these vary from the tribal stories of adult education, once again the individual metaphors suggest a bounded if complex identity. However, this would appear to be in part an outcome of the methodology and focus of the research, which asked workers to choose a single metaphor for themselves to describe their practices of teaching and learning. While displaying a certain metaphorical richness, this research would appear to both assume and produce an individualised and bounded sense of identity for the worker with adults. It may also be the case that despite or even because of ambivalence over questions of identity – what Bauman (1991) refers to as a sense of 'homelessness' – workers may continue to strive for a bounded metaphor to anchor themselves.

However, under contemporary conditions of change and ambivalence a question emerges as to the continued adequacy of the narratives of identity and their construction as either tribal stories or individualised metaphorical narratives. These issues have been explored in a number of recent pieces (Edwards and Usher 1994b, 1996; Edwards and Miller 1996; Miller and Edwards 1996). As has been argued throughout this text, the social, political, economic and institutional contexts in which work with adults takes place have changed and continue to change significantly. The terrain of lifelong learning is characterised by diversity, with the result that there is a sense of uncertainty about what constitutes 'adult education' and what it means to be an 'adult educator'. Rather than a single bounded identity, it is suggested that workers with adults are increasingly having to adopt multiple identities and be part of many narratives as a way of negotiating the complexity of their working lives. Here the ambivalence within the social formation becomes inscribed and embodied in the identities of those working with adults.

This resonates with a wider literature on 'neo-tribalism' in contemporary social formations which is concerned with the forms of sociality, of shared sentiment, collective bonds and customs through which groups constitute themselves (Maffesoli 1996). Here the contractualist, individualised selves in certain contemporary social formations – itself a form of social relationship (Yeatman 1994b) – position themselves into a range of tribal-like allegiances with others. In contrast to the classical tribalism of ethnographic studies, with its tightly controlled membership which shapes all aspects of the individual's existence, and in line with contemporary forms of individualisation, these neo-tribes '"exist" solely by individual decisions to sport the symbolic traits of tribal allegiance' (Bauman 1991: 249). As with Giddens' notion of the self as a reflexive project, it is self-identification which establishes the neo-tribe. Rather than occupying a position within a single narrative or tribe – a bounded identity – 'neo-tribalism is characterised by fluidity, occasional gatherings and dispersal' (Maffesoli, 1996: 76). Accordingly, people belong to many and various neo-tribes within which they play diverse roles as expressions of their sociality. Within this perspective, the moorland of lifelong learning becomes a terrain in which to investigate heterogeneous and transient neo-tribal groupings as expressed in the narratives, images and metaphors which workers tell and that are told about them. The identities of workers become multiple, ambivalent and shifting, signifying the complexity of the worlds within and between which they operate. Singular, bounded tribal narratives of identity lose their power to give meaning in relation to this complexity. Here stories, narratives and metaphors are 'mediators and filters through which we not only live our lives with others in our environment but understand and symbolise that life and ourselves' (Adam 1994: 157).

In reporting on an action research workshop with workers in different organisations – although primarily based in higher education – from the United Kingdom, North America and Australia – primarily the former – Miller and Edwards (1996) note the extensive range of labels and metaphors produced by participants. Noticeable is the lack of those labels associated with the traditional academic disciplines of adult education, such as sociologist, psychologist or historian. This suggests that notions of disciplinary and disciplined identities in adult education are not currently strong, a view consistent with the diversity of the moorland of lifelong learning. The labels and metaphors can be placed within a range of differing inter-related discourses and thereby aspects of identity. There are those which are part of an instrumental discourse which situates workers within their role and relates to activities in which they need to engage in order to fulfil the functions of that role. There are two strands within the instrumental: that associated with a professional discourse and that with a market-orientated discourse. Aspirational discourses express the wishes of workers to achieve certain goals through their activities and signify their values and beliefs. This also has two strands: a liberal discourse and a radical discourse. Affective discourses are those which express feelings about the person's identity and their practices. The meanings invested in particular narratives vary according to place, time and the social and cultural location of the subject.

In an earlier paper, Edwards and Miller (1996) note that the most popular labels and metaphors chosen by participants were those which formed part of the instrumental discourse, with those that could be seen as part of a traditional professional identity, such as facilitator and learner, predominant. Fenwick and Parsons (1996) note a similar trend in their research. However, instrumental labels associated with market-orientated identities, such as 'accountant' or 'entrepreneur', or those associated with assessment, such as 'judge', were eschewed by workers. This suggests tensions between the practices in which they engage, the forms of governance to which workers are subject, and their own self-identities. In particular, the 'ethos of enterprise' would appear to be constructed as 'other' to the ethos of working with adults. Edwards and Miller (1996) also note a great diversity both in the range of metaphors and labels adopted and in the differing combinations of these which were compiled by groups within the workshop to represent their members' self-identities. Fenwick and Parsons (1996: 243–244) draw out a number of overlapping themes from their own research. They argue that the metaphors in use portray the adult educator as: one who shows the way; catalyst; one who knows how; care-giver; dispenser of provisions, and good host. 'People use patterns already developed to define their new "self" and to understand the concrete relations between, self, objects, and systems of the material world' (Fenwick and Parsons 1996: 242). This illustrates the inter-textuality and cultural locatedness of self-identity, image and metaphor. It also signifies a world of work which contrasts strongly with that which existed in the context of discipline-based interest groups such as sociology, psychology and history, or tribal identities. It suggests that workers in this terrain need to be able to construct themselves not as a uniform community, but as a community of differences, inclusive rather than exclusive.

It seems, therefore, that the changes, uncertainties and ambivalences faced by workers with adults are to be found in the narratives, metaphors and images through which they construct their self-identity. Ambivalence is illustrated by the fact that no single metaphor or image adequately embraces their sense of identity and the lack of affiliation to single, bounded tribes and tribal narratives put forward by Darkenwald and Merriam (1982). With the proliferation and diversification of forms of lifelong learning and with confusion as to its direction, the roles, values and feelings expressed in the self-identities of workers within this moorland are themselves increasingly ambivalent. Attempts to place boundaries around the field of adult education and the identity of the adult educator, therefore, appear increasingly misplaced, if still powerful.

For some, all this is a disturbing pleasure, opening up the possibility of rewriting the moorland of lifelong learning to encompass and encourage a greater heterogeneity of practices and workers and a multiplicity of narratives. Freed from the master signifiers and universal messages of modernity's grand narratives, such practices can provide a space for subjugated and marginalised groups whose actions assist in opening such spaces. Here the loss of bounded tribal allegiances and identities throws up new possibilities, wherein the ambivalence of multiple, perhaps disjunctive, identities – of being part of many neo-tribes – can be stimulating, if uncertain. For many, however, this breaking down of a single tribal boundary and the sense of uncertainty this gives rise to is a painful experience, a form of tribulation. The result can be personal breakdown, a need for counselling and/or the ever more strident assertion of single bounded tribal affiliation, the clinging to a single, confirmatory and liveable narrative. A relevant question here, which perhaps can only be answered speculatively, is the extent to which such responses are gender-specific, given that occupying many subject positions is argued to have been part of women's flexilives, but less familiar to men occupying full-time work in the fordist division of labour (Hart 1992).

The grounding and fixing of identity in and through membership of a single, bounded tribe seems to be undermined and displaced by multiple and shifting identities in which what it means to be a worker is constantly reconfigured. The very discourse of multiple identities itself helps to foreground those aspects of identity which are marginalised and silenced by a notion of a bounded identity. We now live and contribute to many narratives. However, this does not stop the desire for a single bounded tribal affiliation. For many, a need to tell a simple and universal story continues. Indeed this may be the only strategy available to deal with those other contemporary tribulations of individualised responsibility, reflexivity and ambivalence.

The implications of this for the diverse groupings who work with adults remain uncertain. While the loss of a single, bounded tribal identity may be personally troubling, in occupying the space of many narratives and multiple identities – including those which at first glance may appear discomforting, like 'professional' or 'entrepreneur' – a different range of practices and possibilities is correspondingly opened up. Some may see this as a lack of clarity of purpose, a failure to define a ground on which to stand as an 'adult educator', with corresponding concerns about what is displaced by the different. However, rather than being planted simply and firmly in the ground of modernity, workers with adults may need now to construct themselves more as 'postmodern travellers', treading the ground lightly as they pass, taking themselves less seriously and making more modest claims for their practices. This, in fact, seems to be very much the case when we examine the shifting discourses of workers in this terrain. Different narratives and metaphors are being put forward for new times.

In this way, and in the context of debates over and within feminist and critical pedagogy, Giroux (1992) has argued that 'educators' need to reposition themselves as cultural workers with an identity of 'border-crossers' engaging in border pedagogy. This points to the need to 'understand otherness in its own terms, and to further create borderlands in which diverse cultural resources allow for the fashioning of new identities within existing configurations of power' (Giroux 1992: 28). It is the possibilities of creating and occupying these borderlands or 'in-between spaces' (Bhabha 1994) and 'speaking from the margins' which open up different possibilities for identity and practice.

Notions of border-crossing, postmodern travelling, in-between spaces and speaking from the margins open up the spaces of troubled and troubling identity. These are spaces in which many women and minority ethnic groups feel they have been positioned and have already occupied, where it is the very spaces themselves which have increased significance in the formation and re-formation of identity and possibilities for future practices. How powerful such narratives and metaphors are or can be and, how, by telling different and multiple narratives, workers can move to different positions and produce different practices, remains to be seen. The research reported above suggests that the multiple identities are dominantly governed by instrumental discourses of the professional. However, the complexity of the self-identities constructed also suggests a greater degree of ambivalence and negotiation of positions than this at first might indicate.

Chapter 6

The/a learning society?

We have travelled a long way in this text, traversing many borders and boundaries – institutional, geographical, disciplinary, textual – in order to examine some of the major trends reshaping the field of adult education into what I have suggested from a United Kingdom location may be constructed as a moorland of lifelong learning. In this sense, the text attempts to illustrate reflexively the forms of writing and analysis I am suggesting may be necessary to be able to engage with and participate in the processes governing changes in this terrain in the contemporary period. This is not to say that any one person will occupy all the possible locations available to them on this moorland. While positioning oneself and being positioned in many discourses may be a feature of the times, many discourses are not all discourses and certain discourses have more powerful effects than others. A sense, even if an ambivalent sense, of location is therefore part of the meaning inscribed in this text and the readings and rereadings to which it will be subject.

As a final chapter, therefore, rather than attempt a conclusion to what is a contribution to an ongoing dialogue about the present and future, I wish to suggest ways in which one of the concepts most associated with lifelong learning has been rewritten over time and in which different meanings have been inscribed. This is the notion of 'a learning society', or, as it is more problematically constructed at times, 'the learning society'. In itself, this starts to differentiate what I will suggest to be a postmodern stance on a learning society from a modern stance on the learning society. The former indicates a variety of forms for such social formations and diversity within them, while the latter suggests a universal model of what such a society should be. I also want to demonstrate how the notion of a learning society is invested with particular meanings which themselves have been subject to change with the emergence of discourses of lifelong learning. The latter may be said to reflect the diverse moorland of practices and settings in which adults learn, but part of the argument in this text is that the shift in discourse is partly about investing the terrain with different meanings. As such, it immediately becomes itself a site of contest and we can examine this though an exploration of the different meanings embedded in discourses of a learning society, which is both a condition for and an outcome of the emergence of the practices of lifelong learning.

Since the economic crises of the mid-1970s, there has been a growing interest in the development of lifelong learning opportunities among policy-formers and policy-makers in many of the industrialised countries. This has developed from and to a certain extent displaced earlier discourses of lifelong learning as a condition of and for equal opportunities and (usually liberal) forms of democratic politics and citizenship. It has become a governing principle of much discourse that lifelong learning is necessary for 'successful' – competitive – economies as we move towards the twenty-first century. The European Commission, national governments, employers and trade unions, as well as those involved in working with adults, articulate support for the development of lifelong learning. This discourse is no longer restricted to those who have used the notion to support the provision of education and training for adults. As we have seen, this increased visibility and importance given to lifelong learning is marked by shifts in its conceptualisation and increased contestation.

Implicit to much of this debate, and an increasingly explicit governing concept, has been and is the notion of a learning society. This is by no means a new notion (Faure *et al.* 1972; Hesburgh *et al.* 1974; Husen 1986). Central to a learning society is the proposition that the economic, social and cultural challenges confronting individuals and social formations in the late twentieth century and into the twenty-first century make reliance on initial education as a preparation for the full extent of adult life unsustainable. The capacity to meet those challenges requires continuing learning and recurrent opportunities to learn. As with individuals and organisations, the notion of a learning society signifies a reflexivity to processes of change which is characteristic of contemporary times.

The notion of a learning society is, of course, as prone to hype as any other. While that hype might enable influence to be brought to bear, as has happened in the 1990s in the United Kingdom (Ball 1992), its significance may be less than might be apparent. An analysis of the 1992 United Kingdom general election found little evidence of notions of a learning society impacting upon the debates over and policies aimed at increasing the levels of participation in learning opportunities by adults (Small 1992). However, it is also notable that in 1995 the Economic and Social Research Council in the United Kingdom, the principal funding body for academic research in the social sciences, funded for the first time a programme to examine dimensions of a learning society. Also in 1995, in the European Union a White Paper was published sub-titled *Towards a Learning Society* (Commission of the European Communities 1995). This indicates the increased importance given to the notion as a means of governing an increased emphasis on lifelong learning.

While there is much rhetorical support for a conception of a learning society, little detailed analysis of the precise formulations supported and by whom has been undertaken. There appears to be a widely shared assumption that a learning society and its goals are inherently worthwhile. The emphasis seems to be on establishing it as a governing principle and focusing on the implementation of changes in the provision of education and training to support lifelong learning, particularly in raising levels of participation post-school. The assumptions underpinning and the significance of these changes and their consequences for learners and social formations have been largely left unexamined. The general notion of a learning society, therefore, provides a large banner behind which a range of differing bodies can walk, apparently in some form of solidarity (Edwards 1995b). This in itself may not be a bad thing, as upon such ambivalence gains for adults can be made. However, those differing bodies have differing agendas which need to be examined to establish the extent to which they can or do all walk in the same direction. In other words, multiple discourses invest different meanings in the terrain of a learning society. In this chapter I identify three such senses: the learning society as an educated society; a learning society as a learning market; and a learning society as learning networks. In exploring these three, I also wish to illustrate the ways in which the/a learning society can be located within the modern and postmodern and the different discourses of cultural restorationists, modernisers and progressives. Having outlined the three, I shall then provide an analysis of the ways in which they may be said to be played out in the contemporary period. The final section of the chapter will involve a reflexive comment before closing the writing of the text and opening it to readings and rereadings.

AN EDUCATED SOCIETY

Early notions of a learning society developed alongside those of lifelong learning and recurrent education (Husen 1986; Wain 1987). In such discourses, lifelong learning was to be achieved through strategies aimed at providing opportunities for adults to learn what, when and how they wished. These were to result from national policies and plans to maximise the learning opportunities and potential of the population as a whole. Strategies were particularly needed for those adults 'disadvantaged' by lack of success in initial education. Thus, the notion of a learning society was tied to a discourse of provision and, as such, might more accurately be termed an 'educated society', 'an education-centred society', 'an educative society' or, as Abrahamsson (1993) refers to it when discussing post-Second World War Sweden, a 'lifelong educated society'. 'We propose lifelong education as the master concept for educational policies in the years to come' (Faure *et al.* 1972: 182), a proposal which continued the modernist, gendered claim for mastery and mastering in the construction of learning practices.

In such discourses, the role of education – and note the exclusion of training – is to provide opportunities for adults to be educated to enable them to be active as citizens in the social formation. In other words, a learning society is constructed and legitimised within a modernist meta-narrative of emancipatory progress, aimed at creating the conditions for self-realisation and citizenship within a liberal democracy (Sutton 1991). Herein the reflexivity of individuals and organisations is inscribed in the social formation itself within a teleology of development and democracy.

> The 'learning society' is therefore one that is exceedingly self-conscious about education in its total sense; that is conscious of the educational relevance and potential of its own institutions and of the general environment that is its own way of life, and is determined to maximize its resources in these respects, to the utmost.
>
> (Wain 1987: 202–203)

A seamless web of personal and social development is the goals within the institutional and value frameworks of liberal democracy.

The perceived success of the Swedish example of a learning society was for a long period marked by favourable reporting and dissemination through such bodies as the Organisation for Economic Co-operation and Development and the European Commission. However, it was also built upon relatively secure economic prosperity, a dimension which seemed to be assumed as an ongoing rather than contingent condition. A learning society, in this sense, would seem to assume and produce a certain stability and order, which contemporary globalisation and space–time compression fundamentally challenge. In this discourse, the economic and training are not primarily the concerns of those providing learning opportunities for an educated society. The location of this discourse within the wealthy first world welfare states of the 1950s and 1960s is important as the assumptions upon which this construct of a learning society was articulated were largely passed over in silence.

A learning society as an educated society was articulated largely within a strategy of recurrent education (OECD 1973). Unlike adult education and continuing education, which can be argued to take a stage of life or a sector of provision as their organising principles, recurrent education 'is a strategy to underpin all education from the cradle to the grave' (Chadwick 1993: 21). This strategy aimed to support a socio-cultural environment in which, as well as having a developmental need due to changing circumstance, it was also perceived that individuals had a moral duty to learn, a duty 'one owed to the collective by virtue of one's participation in its collaborative forms of life' (Wain 1991: 277). In other words, the right to be part of the collectivity, to be included and participate as a citizen within a learning society, resulted in a duty to learn to be a responsible citizen. Lifelong education becomes a form of socialisation into the norms and practices of the collectivity, part of the social order and ordering of the social, reflecting the advent of education in the 'non-democratic domains of bureaucractic government and spiritual discipline' (Hunter 1994: 176). An educated society is, therefore, both a condition for and an outcome of participation in liberal democratic social formations – a specific form of governmentality.

What is left unspecified is the precise nature of the forms of participation and by whom. Lifelong recurrent education supports learning and participation. The emphasis is highly normative, apparently divorced from an analysis of power in the social formation and, with an emphasis on provision, very much situated within a view of the assumed inherent worth of liberal education. Little is done to explain the contemporary paradox that, in social formations which are experiencing greater levels of education and training than previous generations, participation in formal politics has not been revitalised and there has been the election of governments which institute market-based policies which progressive supporters of an educated society largely view as opposing the teleological goals of reason and emancipation. Contemporary educated societies would not appear to be operating within the modernist teleology prescribed within this discourse of a learning society. The latter is part of the modernist project of education to enlighten and emancipate, to humanise those who might otherwise upset the social order. We, therefore, see how this notion of a learning society can be part of a discourse of cultural restoration in which education is about producing order and an educated society is one which is ordered and orderly – disciplined.

However, it also possible for a progressive modernist reading of an educated society. Here lifelong education supports the participation of the 'disenfranchised', to have their voices heard in the decision-making bodies that affect their lives. An educated society is one in which power struggles are resolved through reasoned debate in which everyone has a role to play. The order is not imposed through education as discipline, but invoked in the seduction of individuals to self-discipline as a condition for their collective well-being – a revival or continuation of liberal contractualism. For both, however, it is a liberal democratic order which governs the limits of a learning society, even when the latter is argued to be oppressive, ignoring the class, gender and 'race' inequalities embedded in its practices.

This view of a learning society as a modernist educated society governed – if not mastered – by reason is still influential. It can be found in a recent work by Ranson (1994). This provides a critique of current trends in education, in particular the forms of governance associated with the administered market. Ranson argues for the renewal of the comprehensive ideal as the foundation for democratic citizenship and a learning society. However, in a somewhat backward-looking way, this work grounds 'the learning society' in initial education with little or no mention of the lifelong challenges of the contemporary moment. We are left, therefore, with a somewhat truncated

view of a learning society and a number of normative claims for the need for
an 'educated public'. This masks the contested nature of the teleology of the
notion of citizenship espoused, what form and content are necessary in the
education of the public and who constitutes the public in conditions of globalisation, including large-scale migrations of populations across national
boundaries.

Indeed the use of 'the learning society' by Ranson is indicative of a
universalising modernist view of the goal to be achieved, as though the
notion can be clarified in advance of its making and sit comfortably with all
members of a social formation. An educated society is bounded and ordered
and concerned with the transmission of a canon of worthwhile knowledge.
By contrast, this text has suggested there is a contested and unending
unfolding of an uncertain future to be made. The difference signifies a view
that the future is something to be made rather than something towards
which we are heading.

Two significant and inter-related challenges to such discourses of a
learning society as a society educated towards the 'progressive' goals of
liberal democratic citizenship or more conservative goals of social order can
be identified. These arise from the forms of economic, social and cultural
changes identified in chapter 2. Each gives rise to and invests a different
meaning in the notion of a learning society. The first constructs a learning
society as a learning market, the second as learning networks.

A LEARNING MARKET

As the economic security and certainties underpinning early discourses of a
learning society have been challenged, the substance of the notion and who
articulates it have changed in three significant ways. First, as in discourses of
lifelong learning more generally, a greater emphasis is placed on the
economic relevance of learning; certain forms of lifelong learning are
constructed as conditions for economic competitiveness in a globalised
economy. Second, greater emphasis is placed on the learner to secure their
lifelong learning in a marketplace of opportunities throughout their life.
Third, it is not simply educators and particularly adult educators who
engage in debates, but policy-makers, employers, trade unionists, and so on.
Thus, the notion of the educated society embedded in early discourses of a
learning society, which largely lacked influence, has been displaced by more
powerful discourses of a learning market in which individuals are
constructed as having to take responsibility for their own learning. This shift
is one from the *polis*, in which members of a community decide their collective fate, to the market, in which individuals pursue self-interest as
consumers. For some, this is liberating, as it 'frees' them from the 'deadening
hand' of the collective and the bureaucratic management of the state-funded
and state-administered institutions. However, this is largely at the expense of

a conception of the collective, of society, as having the possibility for being a shared condition and one of mutual interests and responsibilities. This indicates a notion of a learning society which embeds market principles, economic relevance and individualism. A learning market, servicing the market economy and acting in market-like ways, both reflects and contributes to processes of social differentiation within the contemporary globe. In contrast to Wain's view on the interdependence of individuals in communities, individualism, in this sense, is based on and inscribes self-interest in which individuals compete in a revitalised form of 'possessive individualism' (Macpherson 1975).

The nation state in a range of countries has redrawn and continues to redraw its responsibilities and with that the boundaries between the public and private, the collective and individual. It has engendered market-like solutions to many of the challenges of contemporary economic, social and cultural change. In the process, it has contributed to undermining some of the structuring processes and forms of sociality which have been a condition for social formations bounded by nation states. Alongside this, a conception of lifelong education, based on a discourse of provision with a goal of supporting the infra-structure of 'society', has been overlaid and displaced by one in which the discourse of lifelong learning is put forward in which self-reliance and economic competitiveness are the goals. As Abrahamsson (1993: 67) concludes on developments in Sweden, 'with some oversimplification, it is possible to conclude that Sweden is taking a big step from recurrent education to recurrent learning'. Many contemporary discourses of a learning society, therefore, more readily signify a learning market. A 1995 United Kingdom government consultation document made this clear: 'the learning market should be driven by customers and their choices, not by providers or other organisations' (Department for Education and Employment 1995: 10).

A market is supported through providers of learning opportunities being reconstituted as businesses and becoming more open and flexible. In the United Kingdom, targets – outcomes or performance indicators – have been set to be achieved by a learning market. The National Targets for Education and Training act as a measure of what needs to be achieved to produce a skilled, flexible and motivated workforce to compete in world markets. These targets provide the framework against which the success of practice can be evaluated. However, they also provide the basis to evaluate the success of policies based primarily on a learning market. The targets are split between those for Foundation Learning and those for Lifetime Learning. The latter were originally specified as:

1. By 1996, all employees should take part in training or development programmes.

2. By 1996, 50 per cent of the workforce aiming for NVQs or units towards them.
3. By 2000, 50 per cent of the workforce qualified to at least NVQ three (or equivalent).
4. By 1996, 50 per cent of medium to larger organisations to be 'Investors in People'.

(NACETT 1995: 11)

By 1993, progress towards these targets suggested that: Target 1 – around one in five of all employers provided no off-the-job training; Target 2 – only 3 per cent of the workforce held or were working towards NVQs; Target 3 – this was achievable as 38 per cent of the workforce were already qualified to this level; Target 4 – only 2.4 per cent of companies had gained this kitemark (*Adults Learning* 1994; Murray 1994). Gender and regional differences were also found in progress towards targets. In the light of this assessment, it was the targets rather than the policies to achieve targets which were reviewed. In 1995, the Lifetime Learning targets were set for 2000 and became:

1. 60 per cent of the workforce to be qualified to NVQ level three, Advanced GNVQ or two GCE A level standard.
2. 30 per cent of the workforce to have a vocational, professional, management or academic qualification at NVQ level four or above.
3. 70 per cent of all organisations employing 200 or more employees and 35 per cent of those employing 50 or more, to be recognised as 'Investors in People'.

(NACETT 1995: 10)

Within a learning market, initiatives are introduced to give individuals 'choice' and 'consumer power'. For instance, in a range of European countries: the notion of the individual credit/voucher/loan to buy one's own learning has been adopted (Van der Zee 1991; Abrahamsson 1993; Commission on Social Justice 1994). In the United Kingdom, vouchers both for learning and for guidance have been introduced as a basis for increasing the market responsiveness of providers of services. In this way, individuals are said to have been 'empowered' in relation to the 'bureaucratic' and 'unfriendly' providing institutions (Hand *et al.* 1994). However, as with all forms of 'empowerment' it is fraught with contradictions, as it is only those with the necessary cultural and other capital who are likely to benefit from such developments. As Watts (1994: 9), for instance, suggests, 'the notion of a market in guidance may limit the take-up of guidance to those who can see its benefits and can afford it, or be given vouchers for access to it'.

The individualisation produced by the construction of a learning market may thereby contribute to increasing opportunities available to some while reinforcing and reproducing inequalities within the social formation as a

whole. These trends both result from and in a fragmentation of social relations in which 'society' is reconfigured as the contractual and consumer
relations of individuals. Here new right approaches coalesce with some of the
wider process of cultural change and conceptions of a consumer society. This
reinscribes inequalities even as it puts forward the requirement for lifelong
learning and lifelong learners. For some, there is greater choice and freedom
in a market, but not for all, as within 'the marketplace all are free and equal,
only differentiated by the capacity to calculate their self-interest. Yet of
course the market masks its social bias. It elides but also reproduces the
inequalities which consumers bring to the marketplace' (Ranson 1992: 72).

This notion of a learning society can be seen to be part of a modernising
discourse and to be located within a postmodern condition of performativity in which knowledge is valued on the basis of its usefulness to the
functioning of the social formation (Lyotard 1984). Learners-as-consumers
are constituted as the active agents within a learning market through which
individual, organisational and social efficiency, effectiveness and quality are
optimised. Meanwhile, within a cultural restorationist discourse, a learning
market is welcomed insofar as it contributes to individual freedom, but
becomes problematic as the institutions of social and cultural order are
subject increasingly to marketisation, which, in turn, undermines the canon
of worthwhile knowledge. In other words the disorder of the market can
work against the order of individual freedom and responsibility, when
desires are incited which cannot be met within the confines of pre-existing
traditions. This ambiguity is not apparent in most progressive discourse, as
the individualisation and inequitable consequences of a learning market are
held to be in contradiction to collective and emancipatory goals. However,
as I have suggested, this simplistic rejection of the market signifies an
inability to engage with the ambivalence of the contemporary period, a
reflexive silence on the fact that it was primarily white, middle-class families
who benefited from welfare state policies and the fact that it is under conditions of marketisation that there has been a massive expansion of the
learning opportunities available to adults. In addition, as suggested in
chapter 2, there is complexity inscribed in processes of consumption. All of
which suggests that markets are not inherently detrimental to progressive
discourses of lifelong learning, even if certain forms of market may be.

LEARNING NETWORKS

The second challenge to the discourse of the educated society has been social
and cultural, in which the bounded homogeneity of the notion of society has
been found wanting in explaining the increasingly de-differentiated
conditions within the contemporary globe. The study of societies has largely
been conducted on the basis of nation states. In other words, societies have
been considered to be a correlate of the boundaries of the nation state, itself

historically a very recent arrival. National education systems have played a central role in providing cohesion and cultural hegemony within nation states (Green 1994). However, as with other boundaries, those of the nation state have been breached by globalising trends in the economy, communications, migration, tourism, and so on. Alternative identities to those of the nation have been asserted, for example, around gender, religion, ethnicity. The notion of society, therefore, has come to be seen as problematic in itself, with concerns for cross-cultural and inter-cultural understanding as people migrate for the purposes of work, learning and leisure and the media bring the globe to people's homes (Arthur 1994).

> There are no fixed boundaries to cultures, and cultures are always changing. Any individual lives in and between many different cultures: the culture of the workplace; the culture of educational institutions; culture as ethnic background; culture as aspiration, interest or inclination. In this sense, all our cultures have multiple layers, each layer in a complex and dynamic relation to the others.
>
> (Queensland Department of Education,
> quoted in Brosnan *et al.* 1995: 192)

In this situation of less bounded sociality, what are the boundaries of collective self-interest to which 'we' belong that 'we' can call 'our' society? Given the heterogeneity and differences of those living within the boundaries of a nation state, who is the 'we' that is referred to in discourses of 'social and/or national interest'? A sense of 'bounded place' is displaced by a notion of 'spaces of interaction' (Massey 1991). Rather than being members of a single society, it is suggested we are part of a heterogeneous series of overlapping and inter-related local, regional, national, international, global societies. The challenge to society here is grounded not in self-interested individualism, but in the recognition and mediation of communities of difference (Frazer and Lacey 1993) and neo-tribes (Maffesoli 1996). Here it is not individuals as consumers in markets who signify the challenge to traditional notions of a learning society, but persons participating in a range of neo-tribal networks with which they identify and through which that identity is constituted. Society is not a bounded entity, but an interactive space of multiple shared sentiments, collective bonds and customs, of sociality.

Globalisation, with its paradoxical consequences of increased integration (the supra-national) and increased emphasis on place and the local (the sub-national), challenges and problematises the notion of an educated society as a unifying and unified body of self and social development. The possibilities of the state providing a coherent national policy – to put a boundary around 'its' society – are undermined by the very globalised conditions within which it is seeking to formulate policy. Some continue to construct a learning society as a way of binding the heterogeneity into a 'learning nation' (NIACE 1993), or helping to overcome tendencies for society to 'fall apart'

(Labour Party 1993). However, the forces which are undermining conceptions of society built upon nation statehood may well be stronger than those which are seeking to sustain their viability. Education may bind 'us', while learning fragments, but not necessarily to the level of the individual, but perhaps to the level of the neo-tribal network. The consequences of this are contradictory, as that fragmentation may provide the possibility for and result from a celebration of diversity, or it can be a condition of and lead to conflict.

The discourse of learning networks is one that locates a learning society within the postmodern and in so doing problematises the notion of society. It foregrounds the local and micro-narratives which Lyotard (1984) suggests are a response to performativity and are suggestive of the diversity of knowledges produced in a range of settings. These networks are not simply those of immediate face-to-face forms of sociality, but are also constituted and mediated through the emerging forms of information and communications technology. Different forms of sociality and learning networks are developing, therefore, in which the notion of the person as cyborg – part human and part technology – starts to emerge as a metaphor. Here it is the potential of information and communications technologies and networks which link people into different networks and different forms of sociality that is highlighted. It is argued that this provides the possibility for a greater 'openness' (Mulgan 1994).

While this stance is one that for many is part of a progressive discourse, learning networks may be situated within a wide range of such discourses, including modernist ones, and also within the discourses of modernisation and cultural restorationism. Here they are more normally constituted as forms of community learning, of active citizenship and self-help through which the state is able either to divest itself of certain of its responsibilities (Rifkin 1995) or to proselytise over the benefits of 'standing on one's own two feet'.

A LEARNING SOCIETY?

A number of key themes have come to govern the contemporary moorland of lifelong learning: individualisation, the market and economic relevance. The significance of these themes is not confined to education and training, as they are having powerful effects throughout the social formation, nor restricted to the United Kingdom, as, to a greater or lesser extent, they are found elsewhere around the globe. As there has been a growth in the notion of a learning society, so these themes have become embedded in its discourses. Earlier conceptions, with their concerns for equity and citizenship (*Adults Learning* 1992), have been displaced.

To summarise some of the various meanings invested in the different discourses of a learning society outlined above:

1   The learning society is an educated society, committed to active citizen-ship, liberal democracy and equal opportunities. This supports lifelong learning within the social policy frameworks of post-Second World War social democracies. The aim is to provide learning opportunities to educate adults to meet the challenges of change and citizenship. Support for this conception was put forward largely by liberal educators in the metropolitan areas of the industrialised North in the 1960s and 1970s. This is part of a modernist discourse.

2   A learning society is a learning market, enabling institutions to provide services for individuals as a condition for supporting the competitiveness of the economy. This supports lifelong learning within the economic policy framework adopted by many governments since the middle of the 1970s. The aim is for a market in learning opportunities to be developed to meet the demands of individuals and employers for the updating of skills and competences. Support for this conception has come from employers' bodies and modernising policy think-tanks in the industri-alised North since the mid-1970s in response to economic uncertainty. The usefulness or performativity of education and training becomes a guiding criterion.

3   A learning society is one in which learners adopt a learning approach to life, drawing on a wide range of resources to enable them to support their lifestyle practices. This supports lifelong learning as a condition of indi-viduals in the contemporary period to which policy needs to respond. This conception of a learning society formulates the latter as a series of overlapping learning networks or neo-tribes, for example, local, national, regional, global, and is implicit to much of the writing on postmodernity with its emphasis on the contingent, the ephemeral and heterogeneity. The normative goals of a liberal democratic society – an educated society – and an economically competitive society – a learning market – are displaced by a conception of participation in learning as an activity in and through which individuals and groups pursue their heterogeneous goals.

In these three strands there is a shift from the focus on the provision of learning opportunities to one on learning. However, it is important to bear in mind that these discourses may be inscribed with a range of meanings and interweave with one another in any particular discourse of a learning society or lifelong learning. For instance, over twenty years ago it was propounded that 'the learning society is based in the concept of life-long learning and refers to the universe of purposeful learning opportunities found both within and outside the formal or core, academic systems' (Hesburgh et al. 1974: 5). This position resonates with certain contemporary discourses, but is also rooted in a notion of an educated society with its focus on 'citizens'. More recently:

The learning society is about recreating our democracy within and as part of its twenty-first century world, a world which includes European membership and also, no doubt, strong regional and local memberships and loyalties. We enjoy a plurality of such loyalties, memberships and responsibilities, including a central citizenship one.

(Duke 1995: 301)

Here Duke invests his notion of a learning society with meanings drawn from conceptions of an educated society and learning networks. By contrast, but also recently, a European Union White Paper (Commission of the European Communities 1995) combines a conception of a learning society which embraces a learning market, but has concerns over 'social exclusion' traversed by meanings more readily associated with discourses of an educated society and learning networks. The objectives set in this paper – encouraging the acquisition of new knowledge; promoting closer relations between schools (*sic*) and business; combating exclusion; developing proficiency in three Community languages; and treating investment in training on a par with capital investment – aim

to show that the future of Europe and its place in the world depend on its ability to give as much room for the personal fulfilment of its citizens, men and women alike, as it has up to now given to economic and monetary issues.

(Commission of the European Communities 1995: 54)

While the different strands may be found in specific discourses, it is the notion of a learning society which embeds a learning market that has become dominant in recent years. This may actually contribute to the fragmentation of 'society' as it was originally conceived, as the market responds to economic and individual rather than social and political imperatives. This has posed threats and created possibilities, both for lifelong learning and for participation in the wider social formation.

The disparities between the different discourses of a learning society and the impact of a learning market provide both the basis for some critical purchase on contemporary trends and the possibilities for foregrounding conceptions of an educated society and learning networks. Insofar as the learning market does not produce a learning society in which all are able to participate, then it is itself capable of contest and displacement. However, this displacement can itself be contested as notions of an educated society and learning networks, while not necessarily inconsistent, do not necessarily cohere.

For some, it is the moral and political dimension of the learning society which has been displaced in the shift from an educated society to a learning market (Ranson 1992, 1994). Here, as MacIntyre (quoted in Fryer 1992: 315) suggests, a notion of an 'educated public' is 'a ghost haunting our educational system', not totally displaced by the dominance of a learning market. However, who determines what the morality and politics of such a social formation may be is not itself problematised, leaving the liberal humanistic assumptions underpinning such critiques – of rationality, democracy, tolerance, pluralism – to be passed over in silence. The exclusions and oppressions embedded in such discourses, even when invoked as a failure of a learning market, are left unaddressed within this discourse. Further, the educated public may be more active in the public arena of consumption than is often suggested, particularly when mobilised through the media. Participation and citizenship may themselves need to be redefined away from the hegemony of Greek notions of the democratic *polis*, with its economic base in slavery and patriarchy. It is here that the language of stake-holding offers opportunities for reframing discourses of a learning society, with the ambiguity of the notion of a stake – a bet and a holding – seeming to be appropriate to the uncertainties of the contemporary moment.

It also has to be recognised that the trends away from 'society' as embodied in and by the nation state may be stronger than trends to reinforce it. In this sense, it may be necessary to develop alternative strategies to those which focus on the nation state and state policies as the cause of problems and capable of providing solutions to them – of providing the structures for an educated society. It is here that the discourse of learning networks enters. In other words, to compare the lack of support for the integral nature of provision for adults to that provided by the state for young people may misconstrue both the situation and the possibilities available. If the nation state redraws its boundaries of responsibilities, new gaps are created for action and these provide both possibilities and dangers. It is into such gaps that people fall, but it is also in such gaps that new forms of sociality and voluntary practices can be engendered (Elsey 1993; Rifkin 1995). In this conception, adults participate in a variety of learning networks rather than in an educated society as such. Learning networks signify the structured heterogeneity of contemporary social formations rather than the homogeneity of society and the individualisation of the market.

However, while these networks provide the basis for a notion of a vibrant social formation in which different and multiple forms of sociality are supported – and, as such, are part of a progressive discourse – such a notion also appears to be very close to the notion of active citizenship within a modernising discourse. For such networks can themselves be said to be a response to the failures of a learning market – a sticking plaster that will eventually fall away to expose the wound – rather than a vibrant alternative to a bureaucratised state and marketised social formation.

While discourses of lifelong learning and a learning society are intertwined and mutually supportive, their meanings and significance are multiple and contested. Generalised support for a conception of lifelong learning and a learning society by those working with adults will embody practices which work against the interests and worsen the circumstances of certain groups and the opportunities available to them. Universal provision for all is a chimera, as education, training and learning differentiate and are part of wider processes of differentiation in the social formation. The possibilities exist for various forms of adaptation and challenge to the currently dominant learning market and for many and multiple ambivalent positions. Such are the constant negotiations necessary for those working on the moorland of lifelong learning.

REFLEXIVITY: EXISTENTIAL ANXIETY AND TROUBLED PLEASURE

I have argued throughout this text that the emergence of an interest in and discourse of lifelong learning in the contemporary period both results in and reflects changes in the settings and practices in which adults learn and the forms of governmentality to which they are subject. In the de-differentiation of boundaries set in train by a discourse of lifelong learning, a different terrain or moorland is opened up for exploration, critical examination and practice. The terrain of practice, policy and study becomes inscribed with different forms of discourse. With that comes different ways of working and identities for those working with adults. The boundaries of the field of adult education become ragged, fuzzy and permeable. The many facets of this are signified in the notion of changing places.

In a sense, this text itself sits ambivalently in relation to that which is its content, not only charting the shifting discourses, the reasons behind such moves and their consequences, but also arguing that to engage with the contemporary scene it is necessary to locate oneself within this discursive location – different language is necessary for 'new times'. This ambivalence contributes to both existential anxiety and a form of troubled pleasure. For the modernist educator or trainer, some of the different settings, practices and identities that emerge with a discourse of lifelong learning challenge the foundations of their work. Indeed they challenge the very notion of foundations itself. For those who locate themselves more within the postmodern, anti-foundationalism opens up new possibilities, if, however, with more limited goals than might previously have been thought possible. In some ways, this text crosses the border between these two and, therefore, has an ambivalent stance towards the ambivalence, uncertainty and complexity it constructs as being part of the moorland of lifelong learning. Here, while it would be mistaken to 'wait for the post' and possible to get 'lost in the post', part of the process of engaging with this complexity is to enable us to at least have the possibility of 'catching the post', even if that involves 'playing the last post' over certain of the institutional arrangements and practices which have been part of a certain tradition and discourse of adult education. This is neither comfortable nor comforting.

As the author of this text, I am as troubled by the contemporary trends as I am excited about the possibilities they raise. In this sense, I return to the notion of the need to contest change, to which this text is both a reflexive contribution and an example of contesting change in a particular way. Boundary-crossing, de-differentiation and ambivalence may indeed be at least part of the contemporary condition governing learning opportunities and workers with adults. However, rather than being a basis for resignation, this itself opens up possibilities for inscribing many different meanings into practice and, with that, different practices into our work with adults. In this sense, 'waiting for the post' signifies the active anticipation of change, being 'lost in the post' signifies that we may not end up where we expect, 'catching the post' that we need to keep ourselves abreast of contemporary trends, and 'playing the last post' that, with every passing, there is still some form of continuation.

There are many narratives on the moorland of lifelong learning and this text is only one. Having introduced some of the many facets of changing places in chapter 1, it would also appear that this text has provided me with a place and space within which to change, as certain of the positions I have suggested are not ones I intended or expected. Changing places does indeed involve being placed in change and vice versa!

Bibliography

Abrahamsson, K. (1993) 'Concepts, organization and current trends of lifelong education in Sweden', *International Journal of University Adult Education* 32, 3: 47–69.

ACOSS (Australian Council of Social Service) (1996) *Training Linkages for Secure Jobs, Sydney*, ACOSS Paper No. 77, Sydney: ACOSS.

Adam, B. (1994) *Time and Social Theory*, Cambridge: Polity Press.

Adults Learning (1991a) 2, 7.

—— (1991b) 2, 10.

—— (1992) 3, 10.

—— (1994) 5, 6.

Alexander, A. (1991) 'Critiquing social theory: a perspective for critiquing professionalization in adult education', *Canadian Journal for the Study of Adult Education* 5: 120–132.

Alexander, D. (1994) 'The education of adults in Scotland: democracy and curriculum', *Studies in the Education of Adults* 26, 1: 31–49.

Allison, M. and Duncan, M. (1992) 'Women, work and flow', in M. Csikszentmihalyi and I. Csikszentmihalyi (eds) *Optimal Experience: Psychological Studies of Flow in Consciousness*, Cambridge: Cambridge University Press.

Arber, S. and Ginn, J. (1992) *Gender and Later Life*, London: Sage.

Archer, D. and Costello, P. (1990) *Literacy and Power: The Latin American Background*, London: Earthscan.

Armstrong, P. (1982) 'The myth of meeting needs in adult education and community development', *Critical Social Policy*: 24–37.

Aronowitz, S. and DiFazio, W. (1994) *The Jobless Future: Sci-Tech and the Dogma of Work*, Minneapolis: University of Minnesota Press.

Aronowitz, S. and Giroux, H. (1991) *Postmodern Education: Politics, Culture and Social Criticism*, Minneapolis: University of Minnesota Press.

Arthur, L. (1994) 'Cultural awareness and communication: a perspective on Europe', in R. Benn and R. Fieldhouse (eds) *Training and Professional development in Adult and Continuing Education*, Exeter: University of Exeter, Centre for Research in Continuing Education Occasional Paper Number 1.

Arvidson, L. (1993) 'Adult education and democracy: the role of the Swedish social movements', in Gam, P., Tøsse, S., Tuomisto, J., Klasson, M. and Wahlgren, B. (eds) *Social Change and Adult Education Research: Adult Education Research in Nordic Countries 1991/92*, Copenhagen: Royal Danish School of Educational Studies.

Ashworth, P. (1992) 'Being competent and having competencies', *Journal of Further and Higher Education* 16, 3: 8–17.

Atkinson, J. and Meager, N. (1990) 'Changing working patterns: how companies achieve flexibility to meet new needs', in G. Esland (ed.) *Education, Training and Employment, Volume 1: Educated Labour – The Changing Basis of Industrial Demand*, Wokingham: Addison-Wesley.

Australian Bureau of Statistics (1995) *Australian Social Trends 1995*, Canberra: Commonwealth of Australia.

Bagguley, P. (1991) 'Post-fordism and enterprise culture', in R. Keat and N. Abercrombie (eds) *Enterprise Culture*, London: Routledge.

Ball, C. (1992) *Towards a Learning Society*, London: RSA.

Ball, S. (1990a) *Politics and Policy Making in Education: Explorations in Policy Sociology*, London: Routledge.

—— (1990b) 'Management as moral technology: a luddite analysis', in S. Ball (ed.) *Foucault and Education: Disciplines and Knowledge*, London: Routledge.

—— (1990c) 'Introducing Monsieur Foucault', in S. Ball (ed.) *Foucault and Education: Disciplines and Knowledge*, London: Routledge.

—— (ed.) (1990d) *Foucault and Education: Disciplines and Knowledge*, London: Routledge.

Barron, A. (1992) 'Lyotard and the problem of justice', in A. Benjamin (ed.) *Judging Lyotard*, London: Routledge.

Baudrillard, J. (1981) *For a Critique of the Political Economy of the Sign*, St Louis: Telos Press.

—— (1988) *Selected Works*, Cambridge: Polity Press.

Bauman, Z. (1989) *Legislators and Interpreters*, Cambridge: Polity Press.

—— (1991) *Modernity and Ambivalence*, Cambridge: Polity Press.

—— (1992) *Intimations of Postmodernity*, London: Routledge.

BBC2 (British Broadcasting Corporation) (1994) *The Giant Awakes*, 12 March.

Beck, U. (1992) *Risk Society: Towards a New Modernity*, London: Sage.

Bell, B. (1996) 'The British adult education tradition: a reappraisal', in R. Edwards, A. Hanson and P. Raggatt (eds) *Boundaries of Adult Learning*, London: Routledge.

Benington, J. and Taylor, M. (1993) 'Changes and challenges facing the UK welfare state in the Europe of the 1990s', *Policy and Politics* 21, 2: 121–134.

Bhabha, H. (1994) *The Location of Culture*, London: Routledge.

Blaxter, L. and Tight, M. (1994) 'Juggling with time: how adults manage their time for lifelong education', *Studies in the Education of Adults* 26, 2: 162–179.

Boud, D., Keogh, R. and Walker, D. (1985) *Reflection: Turning Experience into Learning*, London: Kogan Page.

Boud, D., Cohen, R. and Walker, D. (eds) (1993) *Using Experience for Learning*, Buckingham: SRHE and Open University Press.

Bourdieu, P. (1984) *Distinction: A Social Critique of the Judgement of Taste*, London: Routledge.

Briggs, M. and Moseley, P. (1986) *Increasing College Responsiveness: An Analysis of Local Training Needs due to New Technologies*, York: FEU/Longman.

Bright, B. (ed.) (1989) *Theory and Practice in the Study of Adult Education: The Epistemological Debate*, London: Routledge.

Briton, D. (1996) *The Modern Practice of Adult Education: A Postmodern Critique*, New York: State University of New York Press.

Brookfield, S. (1989) 'The epistemology of adult education in the United States and Great Britain', in B. Bright (ed.) *Theory and Practice in the Study of Adult Education: The Epistemological Debate*, London: Routledge.

—— (1993a) 'Self-directed learning, political clarity and the critical practice of adult education', *Adult Education Quarterly* 43, 4: 227–242.

—— (1993b) 'Through the lens of learning: how the visceral experience of learning reframes teaching', in D. Boud, R. Cohen and D. Walker (eds) *Using Experience for Learning*, Buckingham: SRHE and Open University Press.

—— (1993c) 'Breaking the code: engaging practitioners in critical analysis of adult education literature', *Studies in the Education of Adults* 25, 1: 64–91.

Brosnan, D., Scheeres, H. and Slade, D. (1995) 'Cross-cultural training in the Australian context', in G. Foley (ed.) *Understanding Adult Education and Training*, St Leonards: Allen and Unwin.

Brown, J. (1995) 'The changing images of guidance', *Educational Guidance: News and Views*, Spring: 1-2, 24.

Brown, P. and Lauder, H. (1996) 'Education, globalisation and economic development', *Journal of Education Policy* 11, 1: 1–25.

Bulletin from the Foundation (1996) 48.

Burbules, N. (1995) 'Postmodern doubt and philosophy of education', *Philosophy of Education 1995*: 39–48.

Burgoyne, J. (1992) 'Creating a learning organisation', *RSA Journal*, April: 321–330.

Butler, E. (1996) 'Equity and workplace learning: emerging discourses and conditions of possibility', unpublished paper presented to National Colloquium on Workplace Learning, University of Technology, Sydney, July.

Butterworth, C. (1992) 'More than one bite at APEL – contrasting models of accrediting prior learning', *Journal of Further and Higher Education* 16, 3: 39–51.

Campanelli, P. and Channell, J., with contributions from McAulay, L., Renouf, A. and Thomas, R. (1994) *Training: An Exploration of the Word and the Concept with an Analysis of the Implications for Survey Design*, Sheffield: Employment Department.

Campion, M. and Renner, W. (1992) 'The supposed demise of fordism: implications for distance education and higher education', *Distance Education* 13, 1: 7–28.

Candy, P., Creber, G. and O'Leary, J. (1994) *Developing Lifelong Learners Through Undergraduate Education*, Commissioned Report No. 28, Canberra: AGPS.

Carnegie Inquiry (1993) *Life, Work and Livelihood in the Third Age*, Dunfermline: Carnegie UK Trust.

CBI (Confederation of British Industry) (1989) *Towards a Skills Revolution – A Youth Charter*, London: CBI.

—— (1993) *Routes to Success*, London: CBI.

Central Statistical Office (1993) *Social Trends 23*, London: HMSO.

Chadwick, G. (1993) 'Towards a vision of recurrent education', *Journal of Access Studies* 8: 8–26.

Chappell, C. and Melville, B. (1995) *Professional Competence and the Initial and Continuing Education of NSW TAFE Teachers*, Sydney, University of Technology.

Chappell, C., Gonczi, A. and Hager, P. (1995) 'Competency-based education', in G. Foley (ed.) *Understanding Adult Education and Training*, St Leonards: Allen and Unwin.

Chase, M. (1995) '"Mythmaking and mortmain": the uses of adult education history', *Studies in the Education of Adults* 27, 1: 52–65.

Clarke, A. (1996) 'Competitiveness, technological innovation and the challenge to Europe', in P. Raggatt, R. Edwards and N. Small (eds) *The Learning Society: Challenges and Trends*, London: Routledge.

Collard, S. and Law, M. (1989) 'The limits of perspective transformation: a critique of Mezirow's theory', *Adult Education Quarterly* 39, 2: 99–107.

Collins, M. (1991) *Adult Education as Vocation: A Critical Role for the Adult Educator*, London: Routlege.

Commission for the Future of Work (1996) *A Future that Works for All of Us: Goals and Strategies for Australia*, Sydney: ACOSS.

Commission of the European Communities (1993a) *The Outlook for Higher Education in the European Community: Responses to the Memorandum*, Luxembourg: Office for Official Publications of the European Communities.

—— (1993b) *Growth, Competitiveness, Employment: The Challenges and Ways Forward into the 21st Century*, Luxembourg: Office for Official Publications of the European Communities.

—— (1995) *Teaching and Learning: Towards a Learning Society*, Luxembourg: Office for Official Publications of the European Communities.

Commission on Social Justice (1993) *The Justice Gap*, London: Institute for Public Policy Research.

—— (1994) *Social Justice: Strategies for National Renewal*, London: Vintage.

Connelly, B. (1991) 'Access or access? A framework for interpretation', *Journal of Access Studies* 6, 2: 135–146.

Connelly, G., Milburn, T. and Thomson, S., with Edwards, R. (1996) *Impartiality in Guidance Provision for Adults: A Scottish Study*, Milton Keynes: Centre for Education Policy and Management, Open University.

Cooper, C. (1996) 'Guidance and coherence in flexible learning', in P. Raggatt, R. Edwards and N. Small (eds) *The Learning Society: Challenges and Trends*, London: Routledge.

Cowburn, W. (1986) *Class, Ideology and Community Education*, London: Croom Helm.

Cripps, F. and Ward, T. (1993) *Europe Can Afford to Work: Strategies for Growth and Employment in the European Community*, Nottingham: Spokesman.

Croft, S. and Beresford, P. (1992) 'The politics of participation', *Critical Social Policy* 35: 20–44.

Crook, S., Paluski, J. and Waters, M. (1992) *Postmodernization*, London: Sage.

Csikszentmihalyi, M. and Csikszentmihalyi, I. (eds) (1992) *Optimal Experience: Psychological Studies of Flow in Consciousness*, Cambridge: Cambridge University Press.

Cutler, T. (1992) 'Vocational training and British economic performance: a further instalment of the "British Labour Problem"?', *Work, Employment and Society* 6, 2: 161–83.

Dadzie, S. (1989) 'Guidance for a change', conference paper, in *Guidance for a Change: Providing a Quality Service for Black and Minority Ethnic Unemployed*, London: REPLAN.

—— (1993) *Older and Wiser: A Study of Educational Provision for Black and Ethnic Minority Elders*, Leicester: NIACE.

Darkenwald, G. and Merriam, S. (1982) *Adult Education: Foundations of Practice*, New York: Harper.

Davenport, J. (1993) 'Is there anyway out of the andragogy morass?', in M. Thorpe, R. Edwards and A. Hanson (eds) *Culture and Processes of Adult Learning*, London: Routledge.

Davenport, J. and Davenport, J. (1985) 'A chronology and analysis of the andragogy debate', *Adult Education Quarterly* 35: 152–159.

Davidson, G. (1992) 'Credit accumulation and transfer and the student', in R. Barnet (ed.) *Learning to Effect*, Buckingham: SRHE and Open University Press.

Davies, P. (1992) *The Mind of God: Science and the Search for Ultimate Meaning*, London: Penguin.

Day, C. and Baskett, H. (1982) 'Discrepancies between intentions and practice: re-examining some basic assumptions about adult and continuing professional education', *International Journal of Lifelong Education* 1: 143–155.

Dearden, R. (1984) 'Education and training', *Westminster Studies in Education* 7: 57–66.

Debord, G. (1983) *The Society of the Spectacle*, Detroit: Black and Red.

Deem, R. (1993) 'Popular education for women: a study of four organizations', in R. Edwards, S. Sieminski and D. Zeldin (eds) *Adult Learners, Education and Training*, London: Routledge.

Department for Education and Employment (DfEE) (1995) *Lifetime Learning: A Consultation Document*, London: HMSO.

Dewar, K., Hill, Y. and MacGregor, J. (1994) 'Continuing education for nurses: orientating practitioners towards learning', *Adults Learning* 5, 10: 253–254.

Downs, S. (1993) 'Developing learning skills in vocational learning', in M. Thorpe, R. Edwards and A. Hanson (eds) *Culture and Processes of Adult Learning*, London: Routledge.

Duke, C. (1995) 'Metaphors of learning', *Adults Learning* 6, 10: 300–302.

Earwaker, J. (1992) *Helping and Suporting Students*, Buckingham: SRHE and Open University Press.

Edwards, R. (1991a) 'The politics of meeting learners needs: power, subject, subjection', *Studies in the Education of Adults* 23, 1: 85–97.

—— (1991b) 'The inevitable future? Post-fordism in work and learning', *Open Learning* 6, 2: 36–42.

—— (1993a) 'Multi-skilling the flexible workforce in post-compulsory education and training', *Journal of Further and Higher Education* 17, 1: 44–53.

—— (1993b) '"Managing" adult unemployment in Canada and Britain: the lack of opportunity through education and training', *British Journal of Canadian Studies* 8, 1: 103–110.

—— (1994a) 'From a distance: globalisation, space–time compression and distance education', *Open Learning* 9, 3: 9–17.

—— (1994b) 'Are you experienced? Postmodernity and experiential learning', *International Journal of Lifelong Education* 13, 6: 423–439.

—— (1995a) 'Different discourse, discourses of difference: globalisation, distance education and open learning', *Distance Education* 16, 2: 241–255.

—— (1995b) 'Behind the banner: whither the learning society?', *Adult Learning* 6, 6: 187–189.

—— (1996) 'Troubled times? Personal identity, distance education and open learning', *Open Learning* 11, 1: 3–11.

Edwards, R. and Miller, N. (1996) 'Demystifiers, champions and pirates: how adult educators construct their identities', in *Proceedings of the 37th Annual Adult Education Research Conference*, Tampa: University of South Florida.

Edwards, R. and Usher, R. (1994a) 'Disciplining the subject: the power of competence', *Studies on the Education of Adults* 26, 1: 1–14.

—— (1994b) '"Tribes" and "tribulations": narratives and the multiple identities of adult educators', in P. Armstrong, B. Bright and M. Zukas (eds) *Reflecting on Changing Practices, Contexts and Identities*, Leeds: SCUTREA.

—— (1995) 'Postmodernity and the educating of educators', in M. Collins (ed.) *The Canmore Proceedings: International Conference on Educating the Adult Educator: Role of the University*, Saskatoon: University of Saskatchewan.

—— (1996) 'What stories do we tell now? Narrative and the multiple identities of adult educators', *International Journal of Lifelong Education* 15, 3: 216–229.

—— (1997a) 'All to play for? Adult education, leisure and consumer culture', *Studies in the Education of Adults* 29, 1.

—— (1997b) 'University adult education in the postmodern moment: trends and challenges', *Adult Education Quarterly*.

Edwards, R., Hanson, A. and Raggatt, P. (1996) 'Introduction: beyond the bounds', in R. Edwards, A. Hanson and P. Raggatt (eds) *Boundaries of Adult Learning*, London: Routledge.

Ellsworth, E. (1989) 'Why doesn't this feel empowering anymore? Working through the repressive myths of critical pedagogy', *Harvard Educational Review* 59, 3: 297–324.

Elsey, B. (1993) 'Voluntaryism and adult education as civil society and the "third way" for personal empowerment and social change', *International Journal of Lifelong Education* 12, 1: 3–16.

Employment Department (1991) *Enterprise in Higher Education: Key Features of Enterprise in Higher Education 1990–1*, London: Employment Department.

—— (1993) *Prosperity Through Skills: The National Development Agenda: Developing the National Vocational Education and Training Systems*, Sheffield: Employment Department.

Employment Department Group (1993) *Training Statistics 1993*, London: HMSO.

Employment and Immigration Canada (1989a) *Success in the Works: A Profile of Canada's Emerging Workforce*, Ottawa: EIC.

—— (1989b) *Success in the Works: A Policy Paper: A Labour Force Development Strategy for Canada*, Ottawa: EIC.

European Foundation for the Improvement of Living and Working Conditions (1990) *Roads to Participation in Technological Change: Attitudes and Experiences*, Luxembourg: Office for Official Publications of the European Communities.

Evans, T. (1989) 'Taking place: the social construction of place, time and space in the re-making of distances in distance education', *Distance Education* 10, 2: 170–183.

Evans, T. and Nation, D. (1992) 'Theorising open and distance learning', *Open Learning* 7, 2: 3–13.

Farnes, N. (1993) 'Modes of production: fordism and distance education', *Open Learning* 8, 1: 10–20.

Faure, E., Herrara, F., Kaddoura, A.-R., Lopes, H., Petrovsky, A., Rahnema, M. and Ward, F. (1972) *Learning To Be*, Paris: Harrap/UNESCO.

Featherstone, M. (1991) *Consumer Culture and Postmodernism*, London: Sage.

—— (1995) *Undoing Culture*, London: Sage.

Fennell, E. (1994) 'Education and training: a coherent system', *Competence and Assessment* 24: 3–5.

Fenwick, T. and Parsons, J. (1996) 'Metaphors of adult educators' identity and practice', in *Proceedings of the 37th Annual Adult Education Research Conference*, Tampa: University of South Florida.

FEU (Further Education Unit) (1987a) *Relevance, Flexibility and Competence*, London: FEU.

—— (1987b) *FE in Black and White: Staff Development Needs in a Multicultural Society*, London: FEU.

—— (1990) *Developing a Marketing Strategy for Adult and Continuing Education*, London: FEU.

—— (1992) *Vocational Education and Training in Europe: A Four-Country Study in Four Employment Sectors*, London: FEU.

—— (1993) *Paying Their Way: The Experiences of Adult Learners in Vocational Education and Training in FE Colleges*, London: FEU.

—— (1994) *Broadcasting and Further Education*, London: FEU.

FEU REPLAN (1989) *Developing Education and Training for the Adult Unemployed: A Checklist*, London: FEU.

Field, J. (1991) 'Out of the adult hut: institutionalization, individuality and new values in the education of adults', in P. Raggatt and L. Unwin (eds) *Change and Intervention: Vocational Education and Training*, London: Falmer Press.

—— (1994) 'Open learning and consumer culture', *Open Learning* 9, 2: 3–11.

Field, L. (1995) 'Organisational learning: basic concepts', in G. Foley (ed.) *Understanding Adult Education and Training*, St Leonards: Allen and Unwin.

Finger, M. (1989) 'New social movements and their implications for adult education', *Adult Education Quarterly* 40, 1: 15–22.

Foley, G. (1992) 'Going deeper: teaching and group work in adult education', *Studies in the Education of Adults* 24, 2: 143–161.

Foley, G. and Morris, R. (1995) 'The history and political economy of Australian adult education', in G. Foley (ed.) *Understanding Adult Education and Training*, St Leonards: Allen and Unwin.

Foucault, M. (1979a) *Discipline and Punish: The Birth of the Prison*, Harmondsworth: Penguin.

—— (1979b) 'On Governmentality', *Ideology and Consciousness* 6: 5–22.

—— (1980) *Power/Knowledge: Selected Interviews and Other Writings 1972–77*, Brighton: Harvester Press.

—— (1981) *The History of Sexuality, Volume 1: An Introduction*, Harmondsworth: Penguin.

—— (1986) 'What is enlightenment?', in P. Rabinow (ed.), *The Foucault Reader*, Harmondsworth: Peregrine.

—— (1987) *The Use of Pleasure: The History of Sexuality, Volume 2*, Harmondsworth: Penguin.

Frazer, E. and Lacey, N. (1993) *The Politics of Community: A Feminist Critique of the Liberal–Communitarian Debate*, Hemel Hempstead: Harvester Wheatsheaf.

Freire, P. (1978) *Pedagogy of the Oppressed*, Harmondsworth: Penguin.

Fryer, B. (1992) 'The challenge to working class education', in B. Simon (ed.) *The Search for Enlightenment: The Working Class and Adult Education in the Twentieth Century*, Leicester: NIACE.

Fullan, M. (1993) *Change Forces: Probing the Depths of Educational Reform*, London: Falmer Press.

Fullan, M., with Stiegelbauer, S. (1991) *The Meaning of Educational Change*, London: Cassell.

Gabriel, Y. and Lang, T. (1995) *The Unmanageable Consumer: Contemporary Consumption and its Fragmentation*, London: Sage.

Gaffikin, F. and Morrissey, M. (1992) *The New Unemployed: Joblessness and Poverty in the Market Economy*, London: Zed Books.

Galbraith, J. (1992) 'Culture of contentment', *New Statesman and Society* 5, 201: 14–15.

Gane, M. and Johnson, T. (eds) (1993) *Foucault's New Domains*, London: Routledge.

du Gay, P. (1996) *Consumption and Identity at Work*, London: Sage.

Gelphi, E. (1985) *Lifelong Education and International Relations*, London: Croom Helm.

George, S. (1992) *The Debt Boomerang: How Third World Debt Harms Us All*, London: Pluto Press

Giddens, A. (1990) *The Consequences of Modernity*, Cambridge: Polity Press.

—— (1991) *Modernity and Self-Identity: Self and Society in the Late Modern Age*, Cambridge: Polity Press.

Giroux, H. (1992) *Border Crossings: Cultural Workers and the Politics of Education*, New York: Routledge.

—— (1994) *Disturbing Pleasures: Learning Popular Culture*, London: Routledge.

Glyn, A. (1996) 'The assessment: unemployment and inequality', *Oxford Review of Economic Policy* 11, 1: 1–25.

Gore, J. (1993) *The Struggle of Pedagogies: Critical and Feminist Pedagogies as Regimes of Truth*, London: Routledge.

Gorz, A. (1989) *Critique of Economic Reason*, London: Verso.

Green, A. (1994) 'Postmodernism and state education', *Journal of Education Policy* 9, 1: 67–83.

Green, B. and Bigum, C. (1993) 'Aliens in the classroom', *Australian Journal of Education* 17, 3: 119–141.

Griffin, C. (1983) *Curriculum Theory in Adult and Lifelong Education*, London: Croom Helm.

—— (1987) *Adult Education as Social Policy*, London: Croom Helm.

Group for Collaborative Inquiry (1993) 'The democratisation of knowledge', *Adult Education Quarterly* 44, 1: 43–51.

Guardian, The (1992) November 18.

Habermas, J. (1978) *Knowledge and Human Interests*, London: Heineman.

Hager, P. and Gonczi, A. (1996) 'Professions and comeptencies', in R. Edwards, A. Hanson and P. Raggatt (eds) *Boundaries of Adult Learning*, London: Routledge.

Halal, W. and Liebowitz, J. (1994) 'Telelearning: the multimedia revolution in learning', *The Futurist*, Nov–Dec, 21–26.

Hall, B. (1994) 'Re-centring adult education research: whose world is first?', in R. Coreau, J. Dawson and B. Sigaty (eds) *Theory and Practice: Proceedings of the 13th Annual Conference of the Canadian Association for the Study of Adult Education*, Vancouver: Simon Fraser University at Harbour Centre.

Hall, S. and Jacques, M. (1989) 'Introduction', in S. Hall and M. Jacques (eds) *New Times: The Changing Face of Politics in the 1990s*, London: Lawrence and Wishart.

Hammersley, M. (1992) 'Reflections on the liberal university: truth, citizenship and the role of the academic', *International Studies in the Sociology of Education* 2, 2: 165–183.

Hand, A., Gambles, J. and Cooper, E. (1994) *Individual Commitment to Learning: Individuals' Decision-making about 'Lifetime Learning'*, Sheffield: Employment Department.

Handy, C. (1985) *The Future of Work: A Guide to a Changing Society*, Oxford: Basil Blackwell.

Hanson, A. (1996) 'The search for a separate theory of adult learning: does anyone really need andragogy?', in R. Edwards, A. Hanson and P. Raggatt (eds), *Boundaries of Adult Learning*, London: Routledge.

Harrison, R. (1996) 'Personal skills and transfer: meanings, agendas and possibilities', in R. Edwards, A. Hanson and P. Raggatt (eds) *Boundaries of Adult Learning*, London: Routledge.

Hart, M. (1990) 'Critical theory and beyond: further perspectives on emancipatory education', *Adult Education Quarterly* 40, 3: 125–138.

—— (1992) *Working and Educating for Life: Feminist and International Perspectives on Adult Education*, London: Routledge.

Harvey, D. (1991) *The Condition of Postmodernity*, Oxford: Basil Blackwell.

Haughton, G. (1993) 'Skills mismatch and policy response', in R. Edwards, S. Sieminski and D. Zeldin (eds) *Adult Learners, Education and Training*, London: Routledge.

Held, D. (1993) *Democracy and the New International Order*, London: IPPR.

Hesburgh, T., Miller, P. and Wharton, C. (1974) *Patterns for Lifelong Learning*, San Francisco: Jossey-Bass.

Himmelstrup, P., Robinson, J. and Fielden, D. (eds) (1981) *Strategies for Lifelong Learning 1: A Symposium of Views from Europe and the USA*, Esbjerg: University Centre of South Jutland.

HMSO (1991) *Social Trends 21*, London: HMSO.

Hodgkinson, P. (1992) 'Alternative models of competence in vocational education and training', *Journal of Further and Higher Education* 16, 2: 30–39.

hooks, b. (1994) *Teaching to Transgress: Education as the Practice of Freedom*, London: Routledge.

Hugo, J. (1990) 'Adult education history and the issue of gender: towards a different history of adult education in America', *Adult Education Quarterly* 41, 1: 1–16.

Hunter, I. (1992) 'Part-timers climb without safety net', *Independent on Sunday*, 13 September.

Hunter, I. (1993) 'Personality as a vocation: the political rationality of the humanities', in M. Gane and T. Johnson (eds) *Foucault's New Domains*, London: Routledge.

—— (1994) *Rethinking the School: Subjectivity, Bureaucracy, Criticism*, St Leonards: Allen and Unwin.

Husen, T. (1986) *The Learning Society Revisited*, Oxford: Pergamon Press.

Hutton, W. (1995) *The State We're In*, London: Jonathan Cape.

Inglis, T. (1994) 'Women and the struggle for daytime adult education in Ireland', *Studies in the Education of Adults* 26, 1: 50–66.

Iverson, M. (1993) 'The starting point in difference', in Gam P., Tøsse, S., Tuomisto, J., Klasson, M. and Wahlgen, B. (eds) *Social Change and Adult Education Research: Adult Education Research in Nordic Countries 1991/92*, Copenhagen: Royal Danish School of Educational Studies.

Jansen, T. and Van der Veen, R. (1992) 'Reflexive modernity, self-reflexive biographies: adult education in the light of the risk society', *International Journal of Lifelong Education* 11, 4: 275–286.

Jarvis, P. (1993) *Adult Education and the State: Towards a Politics of Adult Education*, London: Routledge.

Jenkins, C. and Sherman, B. (1979) *The Collapse of Work*, London: Eyre Methuen.

Johnson, R. (1993) '"Really useful knowledge", 1790–1850', in M. Thorpe, R. Edwards and A. Hanson (eds) *Culture and Processes of Adult Learning*, London: Routledge.

Johnston, R., MacWilliam, I. and Jacobs, M. (1989) *Negotiating the Curriculum with Unwaged Adults*, London: FEU.

Jordinson, R. (1990) 'Access to higher education in Scotland: an overview', *Journal of Access Studies* 5, 1: 72–88.

Joseph, G., Reddy, V. and Seare-Chatterjee, M. (1990) 'Eurocentrism in the social sciences', *Race and Class* 31, 4: 1–26.

Keane, P. (1988) 'The state, laissez-faire and the education of adults in Britain', *International Journal of Lifelong Education* 7, 1: 13–31.

Keddie, N. (1980) 'Adult education: an ideology of individualism', in J. Thompson (ed.) *Adult Education for a Change*, London: Hutchinson.

Kellner, D. (1993) 'Popular culture and the construction of postmodern identities', in S. Lash and J. Friedman (eds) *Modernity and Identity*, Oxford: Basil Blackwell.

Kenney, J. and Reid, M. (1986) *Training Interventions*, London: Institute of Personnel Management.

Kenway, J. (1990) 'Education and the right's discursive politics: private versus state schooling', in S. Ball (ed.) *Foucault and Education: Disciplines and Knowledge*, London: Routledge.

Kenway, J. with Bigum, C. and Fitzclarence, L. (1993a) 'Marketing education in the postmodern age', *Journal of Educational Policy* 8, 2: 105–122.

Kenway, J. in association with Bigum, C., Fitzclarence, L. and Collier, J. (1993b) 'New education in new Times', paper presented at the Australian Curriculum Studies Association Conference, Brisbane.

Kinneavy, T. (1989) *The Outreach College: Design and Implementation*, London: FEU.

Kirkup, G. and Jones, A. (1996) 'New technologies for open learning: the superhighway to the learning society?', in P. Raggatt, R. Edwards and N. Small (eds). *The Learning Society: Challenges and Trends*, London: Routledge.

Kivinen, O. and Rinne, R. (1993) 'Adult education in different regions of Finland', in Gam, P., Tøsse, S., Tuomisto, J., Klasson, M. and Wahlgen, B. (eds) *Social Change and Adult Education Research: Adult Education Research in Nordic Countries 1991/92*, Copenhagen: Royal Danish School of Educational Studies.

Knowles, M. (1970) *The Modern Practice of Adult Education: from Pedagogy to Andragogy*, Chicago: Follett Publishing Company.

—— (1979) 'Andragogy revisited, part II', *Adult Education* 30, 1: 52–53.

Knox, M. and Pickersgill, R. (1993) *Women and Training: Education in the Workplace Literature Review*, AGRRT Working Paper No. 29, Sydney: University of Sydney.

Kolb, D. (1984) *Experiential Learning: Turning Experience into Learning*, Englewood Cliffs, NJ: Prentice Hall.

Kumar, K. (1995) *From Post-industrial to Post-modern Society: New Theories of the Contemporary World*, Oxford: Basil Blackwell.

Labour Party (1993) *Opening Doors to a Learning Society: A Consultative Green Paper on Education*, London: Labour Party.

Lane, C. (1993) 'Vocational training and new production concepts in Germany: some lessons for Britain', in R. Edwards, S. Sieminski and D. Zeldin (eds) *Adult Learners, Education and Training*, London: Routledge.

Lash, S. (1990) *Sociology of Postmodernism*, London: Routledge.

Lash, S. and Urry, J. (1994) *Economies of Signs and Space*, London: Sage.

Lather, P. (1991a) 'Post-critical pedagogies: a feminist reading', *Education and Society* 9, 2: 100–111.

—— (1991b) *Getting Smart: Feminist Research and Pedagogy within/in the Postmodern*, London: Routledge.

Laurillard, D. (1993) *Rethinking University Teaching: A Framework for the Effective Use of Educational Technology*, London: Routledge.

Le Magazine for Education, Training and Youth in Europe (1996) 5.

Lee, A. (1996) *Gender, Literacy, Curriculum: Re-writing School Geography*, London: Taylor and Francis.

Lee, A. and Wickert, R. (1995) 'Reading the discourses of adult basic education teaching', in G. Foley (ed.) *Understanding Adult Education and Training*, St Leonards: Allen and Unwin.

Limage, L. (1993) 'Adult literacy and basic education in Europe and North America: from recognition to provision', in R. Edwards, S. Sieminski and D. Zeldin (eds) *Adult Learners, Education and Training*, London: Routledge.

Lovett, T. (ed.) (1988) *Radical Approaches to Adult Education: A Reader*, London: Routledge.

—— (1993) 'Adult education and community action', in R. Edwards, S. Sieminski and D. Zeldin (eds) *Adult Learners, Education and Training*, London: Routledge.

Lowe, J. (1991) 'Leisure: adult education', in *International Encyclopedia of Education*, Oxford: Elsevier Science Ltd.

Lyotard, J.-F. (1984) *The Postmodern Condition: A Report on Knowledge*, Manchester: Manchester University Press.
—— (1992) *The Postmodern Explained to Children*, Minneapolis: Minnesota University Press.
McCormick, K. (1989) 'Towards a lifelong learning society? The reform of continuing vocational education and training in Japan', *Comparative Education* 25, 2: 133–149.
Macdonell, D. (1991) *Theories of Discourse: An Introduction*, Oxford: Basil Blackwell.
Mace, J. (1992) 'Television and metaphors of literacy', *Studies in the Education of Adults* 24, 2: 162–175.
McGivney, V. (1990) *Education's for Other People: Access to Education for Non-participant Adults*, Leicester: NIACE.
—— (ed.) (1991) *Opening Colleges to Adult Learners*, Leicester: NIACE.
—— (1992) *Motivating Unemployed Adults*, Leicester: NIACE.
—— (1993) 'Participation and non-participation: a review of the literature', in R. Edwards, S. Sieminski and D. Zeldin (eds) *Adult Learners, Education and Training*, London: Routledge.
—— (1994) *Wasted Potential: Training and Career Progression for Part-Time and Temporary Workers*, Leicester: NIACE.
McIlroy, J. (1993) 'Tales form smoke-filled rooms', *Studies in the Education of Adults* 25, 1: 42–63.
MacIntyre, A. (1981) *After Virtue*, London: Duckworth.
Mackeracher, D. (1994) 'Working women as relational learners', in R. Coreau, J. Dawson and B. Sigaty (eds) *Theory and Practice: Proceedings of the 13th Annual Conference of the Canadian Association for the Study of Adult Education*, Vancouver: Simon Fraser University at Harbour Centre.
McLaren, P. and Leonard, P. (eds) (1993) *Paulo Freire: A Critical Encounter*, London: Routledge.
McNair, S. (1996) 'Learning autonomy in a changing world', in R. Edwards, A. Hanson and P. Raggatt (eds) *Boundaries of Adult Learning*, London: Routledge.
McNay, I. (1991) 'Co-operation, co-ordination and quality in employer and education partnerships: a role for the regions', in P. Raggatt and L. Unwin (eds) *Change and Intervention: Vocational Education and Training*, London: Falmer Press.
McNeil, M. (1991) 'The old and new worlds of information technology in Britain', in J. Corner and S. Harvey (eds) *Enterprise and Heritage: Crosscurrents of National Culture*, London: Routledge.
Macpherson, C. B. (1975) *The Political Theory of Possessive Individualism: Hobbes to Locke*, Oxford: Oxford University Press.
McRobbie, A. (1994) *Postmodernism and Popular Culture*, London: Routledge.
Maffesoli, M. (1996) *The Time of Tribes*, London: Sage.
Maguire, M., Maguire, S. and Felstead, A. (1993) *Factors Influencing Individual Commitment to Lifetime Learning: A Literature Review*, Sheffield: Employment Department.
Marchington, M. (1992) 'Managing labour relations in a competitive environment', in A. Sturdy, D. Knights and H. Willmott (eds) *Skill and Consent: Contemporary Studies in the Labour Process*, London: Routledge.
Marshall, J. (1989) 'Foucault and education', *Australian Journal of Education* 33, 2: 99–113.
Marsick, V. and Watkins, K. (1990) *Informal and Incidental Learning in the Workplace*, London: Routledge.

Martin, I. (1993) 'Community education: towards a theoretical analysis', in R. Edwards, S. Sieminski and D. Zeldin (eds) *Adult Learners, Education and Training*, London: Routledge.

Massey, D. (1991) 'A global sense of place', *Marxism Today*, June, 24–29.

Mayo, P. (1993) 'When does it work? Freire's pedagogy in context', *Studies in the Education of Adults* 25, 1: 11–30.

Metcalfe, A. (1991) 'The curriculum vitae: confessions of a wage-labourer', *Work, Employment and Society* 6, 4: 619–641.

Metcalfe, H. (1992a) *Releasing Potential: Company Initiatives to Develop People at Work, Volume One*, Sheffield: Employment Department.

—— (1992b) *Releasing Potential: Company Initiatives to Develop People at Work, Volume Two: The Case Studies*, Sheffield: Employment Department.

Mezirow, J. (1983) 'A critical theory of adult learning and education', in M. Tight (ed.) *Adult Learning and Education*, London: Croom Helm.

—— (1989) 'Transformation theory and social action: a response to Collard and Law', *Adult Education Quarterly* 39, 3: 169–175.

Mezirow, J. and Associates (eds) (1990) *Fostering Critical Reflection in Adulthood: A Guide to Transformative and Emancipatory Learning*, San Francisco: Jossey-Bass.

Millar, C. (1991) 'Critical reflection for educators of adults: getting a grip on the scripts for professional action', *Studies in Continuing Education* 13, 1: 15–23.

Miller, N. (1993) 'Auto/biography and life history', in N. Miller and D. Jones (eds) *Research Reflecting Practice*, Boston: SCUTREA.

—— (1994) 'Invisible colleges revealed: professional networks and personal interconnections among adult educators', in *Proceedings of the 35th Annual Adult Education Research Conference*, Knoxville: University of Tennessee.

Miller, N. and Edwards, R. (1996) 'Like an elephant on the high wire: songs of adult educators', in M. Zukas (ed.) *Diversity and Development: Futures in the Education of Adults, Proceedings of the 26th Annual Conference*, Leeds: SCUTREA.

Miller, P. and Rose, N. (1993) 'Governing economic life', in M. Gane and T. Johnson (eds) *Foucault's New Domains*, London: Routledge.

Minichiello, V. (1992) 'Meeting the educational needs of an ageing population: the Australian experience', *International Review of Education* 38, 4: 403–416.

Mitchell, R. (1992) "Sociological implications of the flow experience', in M. Csikszentmihalyi and I. Csikszentmihalyi (eds) *Optimal Experience: Psychological Studies of Flow in Consciousness*, Cambridge: Cambridge University Press.

Morley, D. and Robins, K. (1995) *Spaces of Identity: Global Media, Electronic Landscapes and Cultural Boundaries*, London: Routledge.

Morrison, M. (1992) 'Part-time: whose time? Women's lives and adult learning', *CEDAR Papers 3*, Coventry: University of Warwick.

Mulgan, G. (1994) 'Networks for an open society', *Demos* 4, 2–6.

Mumby, D. and Stohl, C. (1991) 'Power and discourse in organisation studies: absence and dialectic of control', *Discourse and Society* 2, 3: 313–332.

Murray, I. (1994) 'National Targets for Education and Training', Unemployment Unit and Youthaid, *Working Brief*, April.

Murray, R. (1989) 'Fordism and post-fordism', in S. Hall and M. Jacques (eds) *New Times: The Changing Face of Politics in the 1990s*, London: Lawrence and Wishart.

NACETT (National Advisory Council for Education and Training Targets (1995) *Summary Report on Progress Towards the National Targets*, London: NACETT.

NAEGA (National Association for Educational Guidance for Adults) (1994) *Affording Adult Learning: Financial Barriers to Access and Progression*, Glasgow: NAEGA.

National Board of Employment, Education and Training (1992) *Changing Patterns of Teaching and Learning: The Use and Potential of Distance Education Materials and Methods in Australian Higher Education*, Canberra: Australian Government Publishing Services.

National Curriculum Council (1990) *Core Skills 16–19, A Response to the Secretary of State*, York: NCC.

Neville, C. (1994) 'Achilles' heel: developing provision for unemployed men', *Adults Learning* 5, 8: 207–209.

New London Group (1995) *A Pedagogy of Multiliteracies: Designing Social Futures*, Sydney: NLLIA Occasional Paper No.1.

Newman, M. (1993) *The Third Contract: Theory and Practice in Trade Union Training*, Glebe: Fast Books.

—— (1995) 'Adult education and social action', in G. Foley (ed.) *Understanding Education and Training*, St Leonards: Allen and Unwin.

NIACE (National Institute of Adult and Continuing Education) (1993) *An Adult Higher Education: A Vision*, Leicester: NIACE.

Nicoll, K. and Edwards, R. (1997) 'Open learning and the demise of discipline?', *Open Learning* 12, 2.

Nordhaug, O. (1986) 'Adult education in the welfare state: institutionalization of social commitment', *International Journal of Lifelong Education* 5, 1: 45–57.

—— (1989) 'Equality and public policy: ideals, realities and paradoxes', *International Journal of Lifelong Education* 8, 4: 289–300.

Oakeshott, M. (1990) *Educational Guidance and Curriculum Change*, London: FEU/NIACE.

O'Dwyer, T. (1994) 'Education, training and the White Paper', in *Le Magazine for Education, Training and Youth in Europe* 1: 14–15.

OECD (Organisation for Economic Co-operation and Development) (1973) *Recurrent Education. A Strategy for Lifelong Learning*, Paris: OECD.

Office of Science and Technology (1995) *Technology Foresight: Progress Through Partnership 14: Lesiure and Learning*, London: HMSO.

Oglesby, L. (1991) 'Women and education and training in Europe: issues for the 90s', *Studies in the Education of Adults* 23, 2: 133–144.

O'Reilly, J. (1992) 'Where do you draw the line? Functional flexibility, training and skill in Britain and France', *Work, Employment and Society* 6, 3: 369–96.

Otter, S. (1992) *Learning Outcomes in Higher Education*, London: Crown Copyright.

Owens, C. (1985) 'The discourse of others: feminism and postmodernism', in H. Foster (ed.) *Postmodern Culture*, London: Pluto Press.

Pantzar, E. (1993) 'The principle of permanent education as the basis for educational planning in Finland', in Gam, P., Tøsse, S., Tuomisto, J., Klasson, M. and Wahlgen. B. (eds) *Social Change and Adult Education Research: Adult Education Research in Nordic Countries 1991/92*, Copenhagen: Royal Danish School of Educational Studies.

Parsons, S. (1993) 'Feminist challenges to curriculum design', in M. Thorpe, R. Edwards and A. Hanson (eds) *Culture and Processes of Adult Learning*, London: Routledge.

Pateman, C. (1989) *The Disorder of Women*, Cambridge: Polity Press.

Payne, J. (1996) 'Who really benefits from employee development schemes?', in P. Raggatt, R. Edwards and N. Small (eds) *The Learning Society: Challenges and Trends*, London: Routledge.

Payne, J. and Edwards, R. (1996) *Impartiality and the Self in Guidance: A Report on Three London Colleges*, Callander: NAEGA/CEPAM.

Pedler, M., Burgoyne, J. and Boydell, T. (1991) *The Learning Company: A Strategy for Sustainable Development*, London: McGraw-Hill.

Phillimore, A. (1990) 'Flexible specialisation, work organisation and skills: approaching the "second industrial divide"', in G. Esland (ed.) *Education, Training and Employment, Volume 1: Educated Labour – the Changing Basis of Industrial Demand*, Wokingham: Addison-Wesley.

Pilley, C. (1993) 'Adult education, community development and older people', in R. Edwards, S. Sieminski and D. Zeldin (eds) *Adult Learners, Education and Training*, London: Routledge.

Plant, S. (1992) *The Most Radical Gesture: The Situationist International in a Postmodern Age*, London: Routledge.

—— (1995) 'Crash course', *Wired*, April: 44–47.

Pocock, B. (1992) *Women in Entry Level Training: Some Overseas Experiences*, Canberra: AGPS.

Pollert, A. (1988) 'Dismantling flexibility', *Capital and Class* 42: 42–75.

Portwood, D. (1988) *Outreach and Inreach: Colleges and Unemployment Groups*, London: FEU REPLAN.

Power, M. (1994) *The Audit Explosion*, London: Demos.

Pusey, M. (1991) *Economic Rationalism in Canberra: A Nation Building State Changes its Mind*, Cambridge: Cambridge University Press.

Quigley, B. (1993) 'To shape the future: towards a framework for adult education social policy research and action', *International Journal of Lifelong Education* 12, 2: 117–127.

Raggatt, P. (1993) 'Post-fordism and distance education – a flexible strategy for change', *Open Learning* 8, 1: 21–31.

Raggatt, P., Edwards, R. and Small, N. (1996) 'Introduction: from adult education to a learning society?', in P. Raggatt, R. Edwards and N. Small (eds) *The Learning Society: Challenges and Trends*, London: Routledge.

Ranson, S. (1992) 'Towards the learning society', *Educational Management and Administration* 20, 2: 68–79.

—— (1994) *Towards the Learning Society*, London: Cassell.

Reich, R. (1993) *The Work of Nations: A Blueprint for the Future*, Hemel Hempstead: Simon and Schuster.

Rifkin, J. (1995) *The End of Work*, New York: Tarcher/Putnam.

Rinne, R. and Kivinen, O. (1993) 'Adult education, the second chance: fact and fiction', *Scandinavian Journal of Educational Research* 37, 2: 115–128.

Robertson, D. (1993a) 'Credit frameworks: an international comparison', in FEU (ed.) *Discussing Credit*, London: FEU.

—— (1993b) 'Flexibility, mobility in further and higher education: policy continuity and progress', *Journal of Further and Higher Education* 17, 1: 68–79.

—— (1996) 'Policy continuity and progress in the reform of post-compulsory and higher education', in R. Edwards, A. Hanson and P. Raggatt (eds) *Boundaries of Adult Learning*, London: Routledge.

Robins, K. and Webster, F. (1986) 'Technology and education: progress or control', *Critical Social Policy* 15: 36–61.

Rojek, C. (1993) *Ways of Escape: Modern Transformations in Leisure and Travel*, London: Macmillan.

—— (1995) *Decentring Leisure: Rethinking Lesiure Theory*, London: Sage.

Rose, N. (1991) *Governing the Soul: The Shaping of the Private Self*, London: Routledge.

Rosen, M. and Baroudi, J. (1992) 'Computer-based technology and the emergence of new forms of managerial control', in A. Sturdy, D. Knights and H. Willmott (eds)

Skill and Consent: Contemporary Studies in the Labour Process, London: Routledge.

Rubenson, K. (1993) 'Adult education policy in Sweden 1967–1991', in R. Edwards, S. Sieminski and D. Zeldin (eds) *Adult Learners, Education and Training*, London: Routledge.

Rubenson, K. and Willms, J. (1993) *Human Resources Development in British Columbia: An Analysis of the 1992 Adult Education and Training Survey*, Vancouver: Centre for Policy Studies in Education, University of British Columbia.

Russell Report (1973) *Adult Education: A Plan for Development*, London: HMSO.

Sanderson, M. (1993) 'Vocational and liberal education: a historian's view', *European Journal of Education* 28, 2: 189–196.

Sargant, N. (1990) *Londoners Learning*, Leicester: NIACE.

—— (1991) *Learning and 'Leisure': A Study of Participation in Learning and its Policy Implications*, Leicester: NIACE.

Savićević, D. (1991) 'Modern conceptions of andragogy: a European framework', *Studies in the Education of Adults* 23, 2: 179–201.

Schön, D. (1983) *The Reflective Practitioner: How Professionals Think in Action*, London: Temple Smith.

—— (1987) *Educating the Reflective Practitioner: Towards a New Design for Teaching and Learning in the Professions*, London: Jossey-Bass.

Schuller, T. (1993) 'Education, democracy and development for older adults', *International Journal of University Adult Education* 32, 3: 1–21.

Schuller, T. and Bostyn, A. (1993) 'Learners of the future: preparing a policy for the third age', *Journal of Educational Policy* 8, 5: 365–379.

Scott, G. (1992) *Making Change in Adult Vocational Education and Training: A Handbook for Managers, Trainers, and TAFE Teachers*, Sydney: University of Technology.

—— (1996) 'Continuous quality improvement and innovation in an Australian university', paper presented at the International Conference on Quality Assurance and Evaluation in Higher Education, Beijing, China, May.

Scottish Education Department (1975) *Adult Education: The Challenge of Change*, Edinburgh: HMSO.

Seidler, V. (1994) *Unreasonable Men: Masculinity and Social Theory*, London: Routledge.

Shah, S. (1994) 'Kaleidoscope people: locating the "subject" of pedagogic discourse', *Journal of Access Studies* 9: 257–270.

Shor, I. (1987) *Culture Wars: School and Society in the Conservative Restoration 1969–1984*, London: Routledge and Kegan Paul.

Simon, B. (ed.) (1992) *The Search for Enlightenment: The Working Class and Adult Education in the Twentieth Century*, Leicester: NIACE.

Sloboda, J. (1993) 'What is skill and how is it acquired?', in M. Thorpe, R. Edwards and A. Hanson (eds) *Culture and Processes of Adult Learning*, London: Routledge.

Small, N. (ed.) (1992) *The Learning Society: Political Rhetoric and Electoral Reality*, Nottingham: Association for Lifelong Learning.

Smart, B. (1992) *Modern Conditions, Postmodern Controversies*, London: Routledge.

Smithers, A. (1993) *All Our Futures: Britain's Education Revolution*, London: Channel 4 Television.

Smithers, A. and Robinson, P. (1989) *Increasing Participation in Higher Education*, London: British Petroleum Educational Services.

Soja, E. (1989) *Postmodern Geographies: The Reassertion of Space in Critical Social Theory*, London: Verso.

Squires, G. (1987) *The Curriculum Beyond School*, London: Hodder and Stoughton.

Stock, A. (1993) *Lifelong Learning: Thirty Years of Educational Change*, Nottingham: Association for Lifelong Learning.

Stronach, I. (1989) 'Education, vocationalism and economic recovery: the case against witchcraft', *British Journal of Education and Work* 2, 1: 5–31.

Sutcliffe, J. (1990) *Adults with Learning Difficulties – Education for Choice and Empowerment*, NIACE/Open University Press.

Sutton, P. (1991) 'Lifelong and continuing education', in *International Encyclopedia of Education*, Oxford: Elsevier Science Ltd.

Tennant, M. (1988) *Psychology and Adult Learning*, London: Routledge.

Tett, L. (1993) 'Education and the market place', *Scottish Educational Review* 25, 2: 123–131.

Therborn, G. (1989) 'The two-thirds, one-third society', in S. Hall and M. Jacques (eds) *New Times: The Changing Face of Politics in the 1990s*, London: Lawrence and Wishart.

Thompson, J. (ed.) (1980) *Adult Education for a Change*, London: Hutchinson.

—— (1983) *Learning Liberation*, London: Croom Helm.

Tight, M. (1993) 'Access, not access courses: maintaining a broad vision', in R. Edwards, S. Sieminski and D. Zeldin (eds) *Adult Learners, Education and Training*, London: Routledge.

Tomlinson, A. (1990) 'Introduction: consumer culture and the aura of the commodity', in A. Tomlinson (ed.) *Consumption, Identity and Style*, London: Routledge.

Tough, A. (1993) 'Self-planned learning and major personal change', in R. Edwards, S. Sieminski and D. Zeldin (eds) *Adult Learners, Education and Training*, London: Routledge.

Townley, B. (1994) *Reframing Human Resource Management: Power, Ethics and the Subject at Work*, London: Sage.

Training Agency (1989) *Training and Enterprise: Priorities for Action 1990/91*, Sheffield: Training Agency.

Tuckett, A. (1991a) 'Counting the cost: managerialism, the market and the education of adults', in S. Westwood and J. E. Thomas (eds) *Radical Agendas? The Politics of Adult Education*, Leicester: NIACE.

—— (1991b) *Towards a Learning Workforce: A Policy Discussion Paper on Adult Learners at Work*, Leicester: NIACE.

—— (1994) 'Learning for life', *The Guardian*, 10 May.

—— (1996) 'Scrambled eggs: social policy and adult learning', in P. Raggatt, R. Edwards and N. Small (eds) *The Learning Society: Challenges and Trends*, London: Routledge.

Tuckett, A. and Sargant, N. (1996) 'Headline findings on lifelong learning from the NIACE/Gallup survey 1996', *Adults Learning* 7, 9: 219–223.

Tuijnman, A. (1991) 'Adult education: overview', in *International Encyclopedia of Education*, Oxford: Elsevier Science Ltd.

Tuijnman, A. and Bengstsson, J. (1991) 'Recurrent and alternation education', in *International Encyclopedia of Education*, Oxford: Elsevier Science Ltd.

Tuijnman, A. and Van der Kamp, M. (eds) (1992) *Learning Across the Lifespan: Theories, Research Policies*, Oxford: Pergamon Press.

UDACE (Unit for the Development of Adult Continuing Education) (1986) *The Challenge of Change: Developing Educational Guidance for Adults*, Leicester: NIACE.

—— (1989) *Understanding Learning Outcomes*, Leicester: NIACE.

—— (1990) *Black Community Access: A Development Paper*, Leicester: NIACE.

Unemployment Unit and Youthaid (1991) *Working Brief*, November.

Urry, J. (1990) *The Tourist Gaze: Leisure and Travel in Contemporary Societies*, London: Sage.

—— (1995) *Consuming Places*, London: Routledge.

Usher, R. (1989) 'Locating adult education in the practical', in B. Bright (ed.) *Theory and Practice in the Study of Adult Education: The Epistemological Debate*, London: Routledge.

—— (1993a) 'Experience in adult education: a postmodern critique', *Journal of Philosophy of Education* 26, 2: 201–214.

—— (1993b) 'Re-examining the place of disciplines in adult education', *Studies in Continuing Education* 15, 1: 15–25.

Usher, R. and Bryant, I. (1989) *Adult Education as Theory, Practice and Research: The Captive Triangle*, London: Routledge.

Usher, R. and Edwards, R. (1994) *Postmodernism and Education: Different Voices, Different Worlds*, London: Routledge.

—— (1995) 'Confessing all? A "postmodern guide" to the guidance and counselling of adult learners', *Studies in the Education of Adults* 27, 1: 9–23.

Van der Zee, H. (1991) 'The learning society', *International Journal of Lifelong Education* 10, 3: 213–230.

van Gent, B. (1991) 'Origins of andragogy', in *International Encyclopedia of Education*, Oxford: Elsevier Science Ltd.

van Tilburg, L. (1993), in Open University EH266: *Learning Through Life: Education and Training Beyond School, The Europe File*, Milton Keynes: Open University.

Wain, K. (1987) *Philosophy of Lifelong Education*, London: Croom Helm.

—— (1991) 'Lifelong education: a duty to oneself?', *Journal of Philosophy of Education* 25, 2: 273–278.

Wakefield, N. (1994) 'Becoming a mature student: the social risks of identification', *Journal of Access Studies* 9: 241–256.

Walker, C. (1993) *Managing Poverty: The Limits of Social Assistance*, London: Routledge.

Ward, K. and Taylor, R. (eds) (1986) *Adult Education and the Working Class: Education for the Missing Millions*, London: Croom Helm.

Waterman, R., Waterman, J. and Collard, B. (1996) 'Towards a career-resiliant workforce', in P. Raggatt, R. Edwards and N. Small (eds) *The Learning Society: Challenges and Trends*, London: Routledge.

Watts, A. (1994) 'The changing guidance policy agenda and the role of IT', in NCET (ed.) *The Future Use of Information Technology in Guidance*, Coventry: NCET.

Webster, F. (1994) 'What information society?' *The Information Society* 10: 1–23.

Weil, S. and McGill, I. (eds) (1989) *Making Sense of Experiential Learning in Theory and Practice*, Buckingham: SRHE/Open University Press.

Weiler, K. (1991) 'Freire and a feminist pedagogy of difference', *Harvard Educational Review* 61, 4: 449–474.

Welton, M. (1987) '"Vivisecting the nightingale": reflections on adult education as an object of study', *Studies in the Education of Adults* 19: 46–68.

—— (1993a) 'Social revolutionary learning: the new social movements as learning sites', *Adult Education Quarterly* 43, 3: 152–164.

—— (1993b) 'Dangerous knowledge: Canadian workers' education in the decades of discord', in R. Edwards, S. Sieminski and D. Zeldin (eds) *Adult Learners, Education and Training*, London: Routledge.

West, C. (1994) *Keeping Faith: Philosophy and Race in America*, New York: Routledge.

Westwood, S. (1991) 'Constructing the future: a postmodern agenda for adult education', in S. Westwood and J. E. Thomas (eds) *Radical Agendas? The Politics of Adult Education*, Leicester: NIACE.

Whitson, J. (1991) 'Post-structuralist pedagogy as a counter-hegemonic praxis (can we find the baby in the bathwater?)', *Education and Society* 9, 1: 73–86.

Whyte, A. and Crombie, A. (1995) 'Policy and provision in Australian adult education and training', in G. Foley (ed.) *Understanding Adult Education and Training*, St Leonards: Allen and Unwin.

Williams, R. (1962) *The Long Revolution*, Harmondsworth: Penguin.

Willis, P. (1991) 'Education for life transition: recollections of practice', *Studies in Continuing Education* 13, 2: 104–114.

Wilson, A. (1993) 'The common concern: controlling the professionalization of adult education', *Adult Education Quarterly* 44, 1: 1–16.

Winterton, J. and Winterton, R. (1994) *Collective Bargaining and Consultation Over Continuing Vocational Training*, Sheffield: Employment Department.

Worpole, K. (1991) 'The age of leisure', in J. Corner and S. Harvey (eds) *Enterprise and Heritage: Crosscurrents of National Culture*, London: Routledge.

Wouters, M, (1992) *Adult Education in the 1990s: Needs, Perspectives and Policy Recommendations on Adult Education in Europe*, Leuven: Catholic University of Leuven.

Wurzburg, G. (1991) 'Further education and training: demand, supply, and finance', in *International Encyclopedia of Education*, Oxford: Elsevier Science Ltd.

Yates, P. (1994) 'In search of new ideas in management', *The Guardian*, 3 March.

Yeatman, A. (1994a) *Postmodern Revisionings of the Political*, New York: Routledge.

—— (1994b) 'Interpreting contemporary contractualism', Inaugural lecture, Macquarie University.

Young, M. (1993) 'A curriculum for the 21st century? Towards a new basis for overcoming the academic/vocational divisions', *British Journal of Educational Studies* 41, 3: 203–222.

Index